Contents

Preface to the Second Edition

My aims in this second edition of *Mastering Basic Management* have not changed since the work was first published. What I have done is to examine very carefully changes in the syllabuses of the professional bodies and in the types of questions set. These changes I have endeavoured to reflect in this revision and I hope the work will continue to be found useful to those seeking an introduction to the increasingly important subject of management, whether through a professional qualification, BTEC Certificate in Management or simply by personal study.

Because this work is heavily orientated to the requirements of the professional bodies I have continued to append to the appropriate chapters questions from recent past examination papers Where the book finds favour with lecturers conducting BTEC courses I hope these questions can be used as a basis for the assignments required for these courses.

In Britain industry has been concerned to raise the standard of management and to this end in 1988 the Management Charter Initiative (known as MCI) was launched. To quote from its brochure 'The Management Charter Initiative is an employer-led drive to improve the performance of U.K. managers'. Initiated by a group of major British companies it sets standards of achievement for management training. It does not, itself, provide management education and training, but by a system of networks assists member companies to achieve this effectively themselves. The training is essentially in-house and on the job.

MCI is viewed as a great step forward in management education and training and because of this BTEC has geared its Certificate in Management requirements to it.

It had been suggested that I should include some notes on the impact of the UK's membership of the EC on management practice. After careful thought I came to the conclusion that this warrants a special study much wider than can be encompassed in this current volume, particularly in view of the new-found single European market. This view is reinforced by the fact that at least one professional body has a special paper on this subject.

Acknowledgements for the use of past examination questions are given under that heading, but I must express my especial appreciation of the assistance I have received in carrying out this revision from Mr Brian Banks, Director-General of the Institute of Company Accountants, from the Institute of Administrative Management and from the Chartered Institute of Mangement Accountants, whose help has been invaluable.

I must also extend my thanks to the British Standards Institution who kindly read and corrected my text on quality assurance, to my editor, Mr John Winckler for his suggestions, patience and support, and to my wife Irene for her continued support, encouragement and forbearance.

Finally, I must repeat from the preface to the first edition that the masculine form alone is used in the text only for reasons of clarity and ease of reading: in all cases the feminine may be substituted.

1993   E. C. EYRE

Acknowledgements

The author and publishers acknowledge, with grateful thanks, permission from the following to quote copyright material:

Longman, for the quotation from the Preface from H. Johannsen and A. Robertson, *Management Glossary*, edited by E. F. L. Brech, in Chapter 1; and for the quotation from E. F. L. Brech, *Principles and Practice of Management* (1975, p.19) in Chapter 1.

McGraw-Hill, for the quotation from Harold Koontz and Heinz Weirich, *Management* (1988, p.15) in Chapter 1.

Imperial Chemical Industries, for the quotation from *The Annual Report 1979* in Chapter 2.

Scientific Methods, Inc., for Figure 16.2, the Leadership Grid, from Robert R. Blake and Anne Adams McCanse, *Leadership Dilemmas – Grid Solutions* (Gulf Publishing Co., 1991, p.29) in Chapter 16.

Pentax (UK) Ltd, for the Pentax slogan 'Simply hold a Pentax' quoted in Chapter 18.

The following professional bodies for past examination questions:

Chartered Association of Certified Accountants (ACCA); Institute of Administrative Management (IAM); Institute of Chartered Secretaries and Administrators (ICSA); Chartered Institute of Management Accountants (CIMA); Chartered Institute of Marketing (CIM); Institute of Company Accountants (IComA); Institute of Personnel Management (IPM).

The original sources of material for the theories of motivation given in Chapter 13 are also acknowledged; the interpretations of these are my own.

A. H. Maslow, *Motivation and Personality* (Harper & Row, 1987) in **13.6**.

Douglas M. McGregor, *The Human Side of Enterprise* (McGraw-Hill, 1972) in **13.7**.

F. Herzberg, *Work and the Nature of Man* (Crosby Lockwood, 1975) in **13.8**.

W. G. Ouchi, *Theory Z* (Avon Books, 1982) in **13.9**.

Ayer & Co., for the management scale quoted in Chapter 1, from E. T. Elbourne, *Fundamentals of Industrial Administration* (1980).

BSI Quality Assurance, Milton Keynes, for the extract on registration procedure and for Figure 25.2, both in Chapter 25.

1 An introduction to management

The topic of management has become the subject of increasing study and discussion over the past few decades and has, indeed, forced itself into the examination schemes of a large number of professional bodies. Equally, it has become the central theme as a study in its own right, as evidenced by such qualifications as diplomas and certificates in Management Studies, and by the increasing influence of Institutes of Management.

Unfortunately, the would-be student of the subject is beset by two potential problems: first, the vocabulary of management is by no means standardised and, second, most books recommended for reading by examining bodies use specialist language and often have lengthy reading lists.

Little can be done about the former, though a start was made by H. Johannsen and A. B. Robertson in their *Management Glossary*, the editor of which, E. F. L. Brech, had this to say: 'Discussion in plenty has accompanied the evolution [of management], but its progress has been often hampered and sometimes halted by unrecognised barriers to mutual understanding. The blockage has never been due to any lack of words. . . The barrier has fallen quietly from frequently unrecognised differences of usage.'

It is hoped, however, that the second problem will have a partial solution in this volume: unfortunately a complete solution within the confines of one book is not possible.

1.1 Management and administration

- One of the first things a writer on management tries to do is to distinguish between what is meant by 'management' and what is meant by 'administration'. The definitions given for 'management' are many and include the following:

  A social process entailing responsibility for the effective and economical planning and regulation of the operations of an enterprise, in fulfilment of a given purpose or task, such responsibility involving:
  (a) Judgement and decision in determining plans and in using data to control performance and performance against plans; and
  (b) The guidance, integration, motivation and supervision of the personnel comprising the enterprise, and carrying out its operations.

So said E. F. L. Brech in his *Principles and Practice of Management*.

- In his book *Toward a Unified Theory of Management* Harold Koontz offered a simpler definition: 'Managing is the art of getting things done through and with people in formally organised groups.'

- E. F. L. Brech's definition seems to imply that management is a skill whereas Harold Koontz specifically states that it is an art. We could, therefore, take the essence of these two statements and create the definition that 'Management is the art or skill of directing human activities and physical resources in the attainment of predetermined goals'. Inherent in these definitions is the implication that management is about making decisions, and this view is universally accepted.

- Much greater difficulty occurs when it is required to define 'administration'. There appears to be little common ground among the various authorities and writers on this activity and even Henri Fayol, one of the fathers of the study of management, did not really make clear the distinction between the two. The problem is that the word 'administration' is used both to describe the activity of implementing policy decisions and also to describe the narrower activity of regulating the day-to-day operations of a section of an organisation such as the office. In addition we have the use of the word to describe the very top functions in public service, the most notable being that of the administration of an American president.

- It can safely be said that administration is part of management and is rarely taken to be involved in policy-making decisions. It will certainly be very much concerned in the implementing of policy, but its freedom of action will be limited by the decisions of policy laid down by those charged with the laying down and planning of general objectives. Until, therefore, there is some consistency arrived at in the vocabulary used in management studies expressions such as 'management' and 'administration' will continue to be employed interchangeably, and the student must concern himself with the propositions presented rather than the actual words used to describe them.

1.2   The practice of management

- What is not in doubt is the fact that the practice of management as a skill is quite distinct from other skills that a person calling himself a member of the management team might possess. For example, the chief accountant of a business enterprise is expert in the accounting function – the treatment of financial issues and measuring in financial terms various aspects of the enterprise for control purposes and decision-making. Such activities, however, demand only technical skill and knowledge. Similarly, the production manager will be extremely knowledgeable about production processes and about the properties of the materials his department uses, but the application of this technical knowledge does not necessarily imply that he is employing management skills.

- It is when the accountant, or the production manager, or the sales manager or any other manager directs and co-ordinates the activities of his team of people to achieve the required results through the use of finance, materials, marketing expertise and the like that he is managing.
- The sales manager may be an able salesman, and be quite successful in converting a potential customer into an actual buyer: this displays his technical skills. It is when he controls a team of salesmen, organising their activities, co-ordinating their efforts, planning their work-loads and directing and controlling their operations that he is acting as a manager.
- It will be seen, therefore, that the ability to manage is an attribute quite apart from any technical skills. In fact, one school of thought states that a manager needs no specific skills and can, therefore, switch from job to job and still be a successful manager. A corollary of this is that the successful manager can take advice from technical or functional experts, consider the information given him, and come to a conclusion that results in a management decision. So in Government a man or woman can be Secretary of State for Education one minute and Home Secretary the next. The requirement for a holder of a ministerial post is not technical knowledge about the functions of the ministry or department he or she heads, but rather the ability to organise and direct the resources available and to make competent decisions based on the advice received from those with the technical knowledge and experience.
- One authoritative writer on this subject, E. T. Elbourne, suggests that as the management scale ascends the element of technical skill used reduces and that of management skill increases. He even quantifies this:

	% managing
Managing director	90
Principal officer (a senior executive such as an accountant)	50
Foreman or supervisor	35

and while these figures are not absolute they certainly are indicative of the division of managerial and technical skills at each level.

1.3 The manager and the business

- The need to develop management as a separate study probably came about as a result of the increasing size of business and other undertakings since the latter part of the nineteenth century. At first there were only two divisions, capital and labour. The owner, who provided the physical and financial resources to promote industrial or commercial activity, was also the one who managed the enterprise, decided policy and directed the human and physical resources under his control to attain his objectives. His undertaking flourished or failed according to his business acumen, in other words according to his management flair or expertise. The attribute of management ability was looked upon as a natural talent and no training was expected or available except through experience on the job.

- In the smaller enterprise the owner was usually an active member of the working team as, of course, he is today. In the larger enterprise the owner was normally present to oversee the diligence of his senior staff who might, or might not, have been called managers. What training they received was at his hands, in his example and to his pattern. The need to develop some supervisory skills was recognised, but no formal training was given, or even envisaged.

- However, the rapid development of the joint-stock company and the increasing size of the capital investment required to operate competitively in the face of ever more complex manufacturing and other techniques eventually led to the position where the true owners of an enterprise were not personally involved in its management. It has also led to the curious situation that the true owners, or shareholders, are not in a technical legal sense, in fact, the owners since a limited liability company is a corporate entity in its own right. This came about by virtue of the decision in the *Salomon* case of 1897 and subsequent Companies Acts. However, it is convenient in the context of a discussion on capital and management to consider shareholders as owners, as is generally accepted by the community at large.

- These owners – the shareholders – who invested in large undertakings did not do so because they had a personal interest in the technical activities of their companies, nor because they thought they saw a need in the market that could be filled to some advantage to themselves: these attributes are the preserve of the entrepreneur and the real merchant adventurer. The modern investor is almost entirely interested in the financial returns that his capital will bring, either by way of income or by way of capital growth. His contribution to industry and commerce, in financial terms, is just as great, or greater, than ever it was, but he is no longer in a position to exert very much influence on the actual management of the company, part of which he owns. In fact, unless the organisation is being grossly mismanaged the average shareholder has only one chance a year to influence his company's affairs, and that is at the annual general meeting (AGM). To call a shareholders' meeting at any other time, though possible, is beset with legal procedural regulations that make it worth while only in cases of suspected serious mismanagement.

1.4   The structure of management

- Thus modern owners have to rely heavily on other people to manage and direct their enterprises, and so there has evolved the present-day system of three divisions:

> **CAPITAL** (mainly absentee)
> **MANAGEMENT** (largely salaried)
> **LABOUR**

- Of course, it is true to say that members of management are often shareholders and thus also have an interest in capital: indeed, many companies have this as a requirement for a directorship. However, this in no way diminishes the basic fact that there are now three levels.
- The management structure, itself stratified, has now become that shown in Figure 1.1.

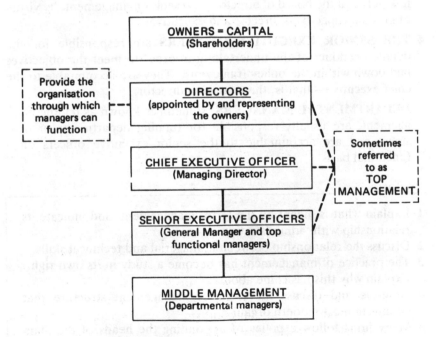

Fig. 1.1   The structure of modern management

- It must be remembered that all management personnel do not act on one level only. For example, the managing director is a member of the board of directors and also the chief executive officer.
- This division into levels is important because each level has special responsibilities, which can be quite easily seen in a large enterprise

though they may be somewhat obscured in a small one. The responsibilities of the management structure with which we are concerned are:

1 **THE SHAREHOLDERS** provide the capital to finance the enterprise. They also select the directors who represent their interests. They have little, if any, control over the objectives of the organisation or its day-to-day management. They may use argument at the annual general meeting, which may or may not be effective. Their most effective power is that of being able to discharge directors and appoint new ones more to their liking.

2 **THE DIRECTORS** are charged with the overall management of the undertaking on behalf of the owners. Acting as a board they are responsible for deciding the objectives of the enterprise and for determining its policies in pursuit of those objectives. The directors must make provision for a proper and adequate organisation, for authorising capital expenditure and for generally controlling the enterprise in the interests of the owners.

3 **THE CHIEF EXECUTIVE OFFICER**, or managing director, is the link between the board of directors and senior management, by virtue of his dual capacity as director and executive.

4 **THE SENIOR EXECUTIVE OFFICERS** are responsible for the detailed conduct of the undertaking in order to meet the objectives laid down within the policy framework. They are accountable to the chief executive – that is, the managing director.

5 **DEPARTMENTAL MANAGERS**, sometimes known as middle management, are usually responsible for running departments or divisions, and are accountable to the senior executive officers on a functional basis.

Questions

1 Explain what is meant by the term 'management' and indicate its relationship with 'administration'.
2 Discuss the relationship between managerial and technical skills.
3 The practice of management has become a study in its own right. Explain why this has come about.
4 Describe and discuss the form of management structure that obtains in most modern organisations.
5 Many firms follow a policy of appointing the heads of the main functional departments – marketing, finance, production, etc. – to the board of directors.
   (a) Why do they do this?
   (b) In what ways would the nature of the responsibilities of a marketing manager change, if he were appointed to the board?   **(CIM)**

② The purpose and nature of management

The purpose of management can be stated to be the formulation of the objectives and policies of the firm and the pursuit of all the necessary activities that will bring those objectives and policies to satisfactory fruition.

- It is commonly stated that there is one main objective to be followed, and that is to maximise profits. Certainly the entrepreneurial urge usually initiates business activity. An opportunity to fill a market need or, indeed, to create one, which will bring financial rewards frequently instigates the setting up of an organisation, or causes an existing enterprise to diversify into a field other than its own. This is undoubtedly true of the large organisation. However, smaller enterprises may not be motivated only by the acquisition of profits: often a business is formed in the first place because the original owner has a passionate interest in a certain activity from which he seeks also to derive a livelihood; or he has an idea which he feels will benefit the community and at the same time can furnish him with an income. Many large-scale businesses were originally founded on passions other than that of a desire to make money; albeit money played some part.
- Undoubtedly, however, as an enterprise grows so the emphasis on profit maximisation also grows, and it is also true that as ownership becomes divorced from management this emphasis is more pronounced. After all, shareholders invest for income or capital growth and not for reasons of philanthropy: this is particularly true of the large institutional investors – the insurance companies, the pension funds and others.
- Management, then, standing in as representatives of the owners to protect and further their interests, must take into account the financial expectations of the shareholders and the protection of their interests. On the other hand the naked pursuit of profit has become socially unacceptable in most quarters, and the effect of business activity on the community at large, on the environment, on worker relations and on consumers, has become of current concern socially, environmentally and politically. Various pressure groups have, as a consequence, been formed to protect the environment and the consumer; examples are the protestors who are opposed to the opening of any more nuclear power stations, and the various consumer protection associations. The law has been invoked through the passing of appropriate statutes in the areas of sex discrimination, consumer rights and others in an attempt to safe-

guard the interests of the public at large, or selected sections of it, against the exploitation of the public, or sections of it, in the pursuit of profit.

- Because of these factors management has a duty, willingly accepted or not, to include in its philosophy many considerations other than the financial and this is, of course, reflected in its objectives and policies.
- The formulation of objectives will come before the laying down of policies. It might be said that *objectives* are *what* the firm is aiming to achieve and that *policies* are *how* this is to be done. Both are broadly laid down by the board of directors (acting in most cases with the advice of the company's executives) and their fulfilment is the responsibility of the executives and their staffs. The nature of the objectives and policies, however, will depend upon whether management holds to the economic, or so-called classical, view of the firm or whether it leans towards the behavioural science theories.

2.1   The economic view of management objectives

The economic view of the firm is that it exists to make a profit and that all other considerations are very much subservient to this. It is in business to mix the factors of production – labour, materials and capital – in the proportions appropriate to its particular activities so as to produce an output of goods or services that it can sell at the maximum profit. The philosophy behind this view is that what benefits the entrepreneur ultimately benefits the community at large, as is enshrined in the maxim propagated by America's largest manufacturer of motor-cars, General Motors: 'what is good for General Motors is good for America.'

The revenue of the country is primarily derived from taxation, a large proportion of which comes from business enterprise, and hence if profits are maximised then so is the national revenue. Further, if customers fail to support an enterprise and consequently losses are incurred this is an indication that the resources being devoted to that particular activity need to be used in other ways and so made to produce profits.

This somewhat naïve view of management objectives is derived from the theory of perfect competition, where only the efficient survive and the inefficient are forced to use their resources in other more profitable ways; where conditions of complete freedom of action obtain coupled with a relatively compliant work-force. Further, there is the assumption that management is in the hands of the owner or very close to the owner, who is able to exert considerable influence on decisions as to objectives and policies. The fact is that nowadays this theory in its pure form must be questioned on the following grounds:

(a)   By no stretch of the imagination can it be said that business has anything like complete freedom of action. Government intervention in the operations of business is considerable and seems to be growing. Business is controlled and restricted in its activities by a host of laws relating to employment of staff, material usage, location of operations and many other areas of its activities. Such legislation increases costs without compensating opportunities for making extra profits to accommodate them, and affects small as well as large undertakings.

(b) Except in the smaller concerns businesses are no longer managed by, or close to, the owners. Indeed, for the most part the owners take no active part or interest in the actual management of the concern. The professional manager who is now in control, as a salaried employee, has his own personal interests to pursue as well as those of the owners. In consequence improved working conditions, increases in earnings, perhaps by way of bonuses, and other personal factors are likely to weigh in his deliberations as well as the prime objective of making maximum profits.

(c) Competition is very restricted in some sections of the economy by the emergence of one or two extremely large units, or by public ownership (where there can be a monopoly situation). Considerations other than competition influence the conduct of these large units, sometimes to the extent of maximising profits by reducing output rather than by increasing sales at lower profit margins. A clear example of this is the operation of the Organisation of Petroleum Exporting Countries (OPEC) where oil output is reduced to increase the price: in no sense can it be said that this policy is beneficial to the world at large.

(d) The economic maxim of the economies of scale, in which it is claimed that increases in the scale of operations bring increases in efficiency and better utilisation of resources, has proved to have severe limitations in practice. Setting objectives on the premise that maximising profits entails larger and larger enterprises, which has been the trend for very many years, has failed in many cases to yield the looked for fruits.

2.2 The behavioural science view of management objectives

The rather simplistic view of management objectives put forward by the economic theorists has been challenged by sociologists and psychologists – the behavioural scientists. They contend that because of the intervention of the salaried manager profit maximisation alone is not, and cannot be, the sole management objective. They believe that the employed manager has as much interest in his own benefits as he does in benefits for his firm, and the behavioural theory suggests that:

(a) Managers will set objectives that fulfil their own interests and which will produce profits not at the maximum, but at the level that will satisfy the owners. The behavioural scientists term this 'satisficing'.

(b) Because of the fact that each manager has his own personal objectives, which can be achieved only through his employment, and because he has at the same time to set acceptable company objectives, there is an essential element of bargaining and internal politics in the formulation of management objectives to reconcile these two elements. Since no manager is likely to be truly altruistic, some element of self-interest is bound to be present in all deliberations about setting objectives.

(c)   Bearing in mind the human element as set out in **(a)** and **(b)** objectives cannot remain static, as they would if profit maximisation were paramount. In consequence changes in the objectives must be expected because of changes in the size of the concern, changes in the technical and social environment and changes in personal aspirations.

2.3   The 'stakeholder theory'

The behavioural scientists also advance what is known as the *stakeholder theory*. This states that there are a number of interested parties to be considered in the formulation of objectives, and these extend widely to include not only shareholders and managers, but also to include other groups such as workers, consumers, suppliers and the local community. This extended concern means that management objectives must be set to include the interests of all who are likely to be touched by the business activities of the firm and so must be taken into account.

Every firm, and thus every management, has a different set of circumstances with which to contend, so its objectives will be influenced by those special circumstances. Nevertheless, in modern conditions its opinions are likely to be shaped by social as well as by economic factors and therefore, on the whole, management objectives will be seen to be socio-economic and not exclusively economic or social.

2.4   Policy-making

Policies are shaped out of a combination of objectives and the social conscience of the firm. The greater the emphasis on economic objectives the more likely it is that management policies will be materialistic and based on financial gain rather than on social considerations. If, on the other hand, objectives are formulated on the basis of social obligations as well as the need to make profits then the policies decided upon will reflect this concern. If the Stakeholder Theory is accepted by the firm then policies may even reflect a higher regard for the social effects of its policies and objectives than for the purely financial aspects of these.

●   Objectives and policies are the prerogative of top management – that is, the board of directors in a company, guided and aided by their senior executive officers. In almost all cases the board will include directors who are also executives and this liaison is thus easily accomplished and has a decisive effect upon top management's thinking on objectives and policies. Senior executives not on the board in most cases will also have their views taken into account through their close day-to-day association with their executive directors. In consequence policies can be influenced to take into consideration the points made previously about the personal objectives of managers be they on the board or not.

- Many boards of directors, however, also include non-executive directors – that is, members who do not take part in the actual operations of the company but who are included because of their knowledge and experience in certain fields and whose advice is useful to the board. Where this occurs, these non-executive directors can have a beneficial effect by curbing too great an emphasis on managers' personal aspirations: such inclusion can also influence policies so that they seek to fulfil the wider social obligations of the company in regard to its internal and its external responsibilities.

- To what extent the mix of economic and social factors is taken into account by management in setting objectives and formulating policies depends to a significant degree on the size of the undertaking. It could be argued, in fact, that in the smallest unit, the owner-manager firm, concern will be partly personal aspiration and partly economic, whereas the medium-size business will see its role more simply as that of a profit-making unit. The large organisation, on the other hand, is very likely to be very much concerned with its social obligations as well as the need to make profits. These philosophies are presented graphically in Figure 2.1.

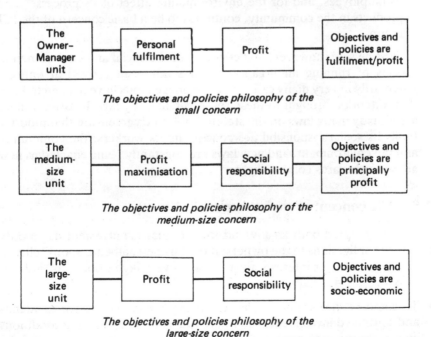

The objectives and policies philosophy of the
small concern

The objectives and policies philosophy of the
medium-size concern

The objectives and policies philosophy of the
large-size concern

Fig. 2.1 A comparison of the objectives and policies/philosophies of different-size enterprises

- Experience shows that a person setting up in business for the first time more frequently than not is motivated to a great extent by personal interest and aspirations and not principally by an urge to make money. The reasons are various and include a desire to pursue a congenial activity, a wish to be 'his own boss', or a passionate interest in a technical or artistic pursuit. As the firm grows the desire to maximise profits usually overtakes the initial personal aspirations and a sense of social obligation does not arise at this point; at least not on a voluntary basis. It can also be said to be the case that a medium-size organisation also has profit as its top priority at its inception. In the main the larger business units have, on the contrary, over the past decades taken their social responsibilities very seriously, and while profit-making is still their major goal, profit maximisation takes its place alongside social and environmental obligations.

- This is borne out, and well-illustrated, by the following extracts from one *Annual Report* from the industrial giant Imperial Chemical Industries plc. These read:

  1 **Social responsibility:** In its dealings with the various groups who make up society, ICI seeks to achieve high standards of behaviour as a socially responsible company.
  2 **Health, safety and the environment:** Care for the health and safety of its employees, and for the environmental effect of its processes and products in the community, continues to be a basic concern of the ICI group.

- It must be said, however, that concern for the social and environmental aspects of running an organisation has not been arrived at entirely voluntarily in very many cases. Some managements have needed to have their attention brought to these responsibilities by law. In Britain there are already many laws on the statute book to try to ensure that industry fulfils its social responsibilities concerning its workers, the community and the environment, and new laws are constantly being enacted as new abuses or hazards come to light.

2.5   The concept of social responsibility

It is now accepted both legally and socially that management has a duty outside its obligations to the owners of the business, albeit responsibility to the owners and their interests must remain a very high priority as, indeed, the Companies Act requires.

- To combine in one philosophy the need to make profits for dividends and continued investment, and to provide good pay, working conditions and a measure of security for employees, as well as to ensure the protection of the environment and to serve the interests of customers and of the community as a whole, is no easy task. Yet the ethical behaviour of business generally has become a matter of major public concern and in many areas of activity has become the object of various pressure groups. One instance of this is the campaign to stop the transport of nuclear materials through densely populated districts. This has, indeed, become the age of pressure groups and management must examine very carefully every major decision it makes in regard to the effect it will have on its own working environment and on the environment at large. Pressures come from employees for better pay and conditions, and for greater participation in management decisions; from consumers for more product information and product safety; from environmentalists for restrictions on pollution and other matters possibly detrimental to the environment; from conservationists for the protection of the landscape and of various forms of animal life concerned with manufacturing and agricultural operations, and not least from the Government and the European Community (EC) for changes in business practices and manufacturing standards.

- It will be seen that the nature and purpose of management are matters for various interpretations (see Figure 2.2). On the one hand it can be argued that the nature of management should be authoritarian (so far as

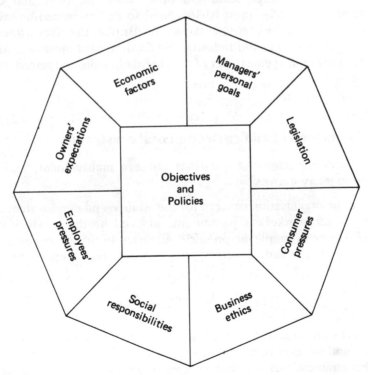

Fig. 2.2 Elements influencing management philosophy on objectives and policies

it is possible in the present climate of social and industrial relations) and that its purpose is to maximise profits to the benefit of the owners. On the other hand, it can be asserted that management should be socially conscious and that its purpose is to try to satisfy the sometimes conflicting requirements of owners' interests and the interests of the employees, have concern for the environment and respect for the consumer and for society at large, while at the same time earning enough profits to ensure the continued existence of the enterprise. In this latter context it is certain that survival of the organisation is of the essence, since all other interests depend upon it.

- However, another possibility arises where the continued survival of the enterprise is no longer possible, or possible only by severe staff reductions. Social responsibility in this situation has to be faced as the closure of a company or its very much reduced activity can result in grave repercussions for employees and the community. Such eventualities affect not only those directly involved but also those businesses, often small shops, that rely on the patronage, and therefore the continued income, of the workers concerned.

- If the redundancies are severe or total it is not unusual for the employer to set up facilities and counselling to help find jobs for ex-employees. In the event of a large scale shut-down local authority and central government agencies must be informed so that steps can be taken to attract new industry to the area. In Britain the Departments of Employment, Trade and Industry and Environment must be informed, and the continuing enactment of new legislation must be referred to and acted upon.

2.6   Management and environmental constraints

Increasingly environmental questions concern management, and these come from many sources.

- Inside the organisation concern for the welfare and employment conditions of the workers is paramount, induced by the goodwill of the employer or by employee pressure. External to the enterprise government legislation and consumer pressures put constraints on the firm's behaviour. Less forcibly concepts of morals, ethics and justice may play a part.

- The increasing numbers of and influence of pressure groups such as Greenpeace also have an effect on management action.

- Besides management's concern for staff welfare and expectations internally, and for environmental matters externally, there is also the often forgotten social responsibility between the organisation and its suppliers. A large-scale purchaser has a very great commercial advantage over its suppliers even if they are also large-scale, but this is much more evident if the supplier is a small operator. Pressure from the buyer, particularly in terms of price, can cause financial embarrassment to the supplier who may have to adopt socially unattractive practices such as lowering working conditions and/or pay for his workforce. A large buyer can, and often does, also cause financial difficulties to small suppliers by delaying payment for purchases well beyond the normal credit period.

- On the other hand, a monopoly or near monopoly supplier can also trade in an unsocial manner to deprive the purchaser of freedom of choice in his purchasing. In Britain 'tied' public houses whose managers or tenants are forced to serve only one brewer's wares are a case in point.

Questions

1 'Whatever the theorists may say, a business in fact is run primarily for the benefit of its managers; any other parties are only considered in so far as they may be able to threaten the well-being of the management.' Discuss the subject of this quotation, together with the difficulties encountered in the theoretical analysis of business. **(ACCA)**

2 In what ways may the need to exercise social responsibility shape the relationship of enterprise management to some of its internal and external stakeholders? **(ACCA)**

3 Social responsibility is expected from all types of organisations.
  (a) Discuss what, in a management context, is meant by 'social responsibility'.
  (b) State and explain the sources from which concepts of social responsibility may be derived. **(IAM)**

4 Research has identified the importance of particular external constraints related to the environment in which organisations operate.
  Discuss any THREE of the principal constraints identified. **(IAM)**

5 Organisations employ various resources (e.g., finance, raw materials, people, plant and equipment) in order to achieve objectives. Discuss the role of management in an organisation and assess the relative importance of management as a resource. **(ICSA)**

6 (a) Compare the characteristics of a sole trader, a partnership and a limited company, illustrating your answer with an example of each type of business.
  (b) Explain why, in each case, the structure is particularly suited to the nature of the firm's business. **(CIM)**

7 The responsibilities of managers include those to employees, customers or clients, shareholders, the local community and government. How may these responsibilities be discharged in the

event of a decision to close a large factory or office involving a significant number of redundancies? In responding to this question you need not refer to the detailed provisions of redundancy legislation.   **(ICSA)**

③ The directors

Before proceeding further into this study of management it will be useful to examine the role and responsibilities of the directors, who are answerable not only to their shareholders but also to the law.

3.1 The board of directors

The directors of a company are elected by the owners of the enterprise and may act only as a committee, known as a board, and not individually. In the case of a new company they are either named in the articles of association of the company or are appointed by the subscribers (that is, the first shareholders) to the memorandum of association. Thereafter, their tenure of office is as laid down in the articles, which ensure that at regular intervals a stated proportion of the board must resign and offer themselves for re-election at the next annual general meeting. This gives the shareholders the opportunity to express their confidence in the retiring directors by re-electing them, or to show their dissatisfaction with the performance of the board by electing new directors. The shareholders also have other ways of changing the composition of the board, but these belong to the study of company law. The memorandum and the articles of association, also, are the subject of company law and it is sufficient to state in the present context that they regulate the powers and the proceedings of a company.

The responsibilities of the board of directors fall into two general categories, legal and domestic.

(a) **The legal responsibilities of the directors**
   The board is responsible for ensuring that the company operates according to the law. Among the legal requirements are:
   1 to comply with all the provisions of the Companies Acts;
   2 liability to third parties on acts of the company and its servants, this being an implied responsibility;
   3 to ensure that all operations of the company are within the general law, statute and common; for example, complying with the requirements of the Town and Country Planning Acts, the Finance Acts and other statutes, and ensuring that the company carries on no illegal activities.

(b) **The domestic responsibilities of the directors**
   The duties and responsibilities of the directors are most onerous in the running of the company.

- First it must be realised that there is a trustee relationship between the directors and the shareholders. In effect the board acts as trustee for the funds subscribed by the members, and for the proper application of those funds.
- The shareholders also have a right to expect the board to act entirely in the interests of the members, and the company is entitled to the unbiased advice of each director on any matter of concern to the company. These rights are of special importance in the case of a projected takeover or merger.
- Sometimes impartiality on the part of a director is difficult because he may have a personal interest in a matter that has come up for discussion or action. For instance, he may be financially interested in another company with which a contract is being considered. In such cases it is usually required that the director concerned should declare his interest and refrain from joining in any discussion of the matter and from voting.
- As part of top management the directors are responsible for formulating the objectives of the enterprise, which was fully discussed in Chapter 2. To achieve these objectives the board has to formulate a policy which it considers will best serve to attain its goals. As both objectives and policy-making were discussed in Chapter 2 at this point it is sufficient to say simply that objectives are *what* is to be achieved and policy is *how* to go about achieving them. While flexibility must apply to both, it is self-evident that objectives must be fairly fixed in nature while policy is subject to easier modification. Agreeing objectives and formulating policy are probably the most onerous of the domestic responsibilities of directors.

3.2   The managing director

Any discussion of the board of directors would not be complete without mention of the managing director. He has a dual role, that of director on the board and that of chief executive.

- As a director he partakes in the activities of the board – the formulation of policy, decisions on capital expenditure and so on. Often in this capacity, because of his additional function as chief executive, his views at board meetings are looked upon with great respect, and he can command considerable authority.
- As the chief executive he forms a link between the board and his fellow managers, and to him falls the responsibility for seeing that management carries out the policies and decisions of the board.
- Thus he interprets and puts into effect, through his management team, the decisions taken at board level, and can follow them through down the organisation chain. He does this of course through the process of delegation and through the reporting and control systems set up to monitor company performance. He is, therefore, involved in the

day-to-day management work involved in implementing the board's wishes. Similarly, as chief executive he is made aware of the day-to-day problems and requirements of the company in all significant areas such as capital requirements, staffing, liquidity and so on. He is in a unique position to bring these problems to the attention of the board, where necessary, for their advice and possible action.

- A strong managing director is likely to dominate the board of directors and also his management team. This is the type of quality most useful in fulfilling this dual and exacting function, provided he is not overbearing or stubborn. Firmness is most essential, tempered by the ability to analyse and discuss problems with colleagues, and to change his mind where logically necessary.

3.3 The chairman

Every board of directors must have a chairman and by virtue of this office he is also chairman of the company. However, the chairman is elected not by the shareholders but by the board of directors, of which he is a member. He is usually chosen because of his knowledge and experience of the industry within which the organisation operates, though a proven record of success elsewhere may prove equally attractive to the board.

- If the enterprise is a major one the chairman will be the member of the board most in the public eye and must therefore present a suitable public image that encourages confidence both in the company and in himself.
- Unless the enterprise is fairly small the chairman usually has no executive powers and is thus free from the day-to-day problems of running the organisation. He is therefore able to devote all his energies to those problems that concern top management, such as policy-making, where his expertise and advice are most valuable. His primary technical function is to control and regulate the proceedings at board meetings, but as head of the organisation he should have the capacity to lead the management team in a positive fashion and to stimulate them to develop new approaches to management problems.
- Because of the great responsibilities carried by the managing director and because of the strength of his authority it is essential that the chairman and the managing director work in harmony. Indeed, the offices are sometimes combined, especially in the smaller concern, and one person occupies the position of chairman and managing director. Whilst this may result in the avoidance of divided opinions at the top, there are two important reasons for not combining these two offices:

(a) The task of the chairman is very onerous and requires a good deal of time devoted to it, particularly in considering matters coming up for discussion at board meetings. So far as is possible he must be detached and unbiased in his deliberations. This is difficult to achieve when a person has executive responsibilities and is thus constantly in contact with the day-to-day operations of the concern.

(b) Consultation between chairman and managing director on many matters is often helpful and fruitful because the chairman can be detached from the problem and can offer unbiased advice based on independent experience. The advantage of two opinions and two approaches is lost if the two offices are combined.

3.4   Executive and non-executive directors

Like the managing director, many directors on a board are also full-time executives of the company and have a functional managerial role in addition to their responsibilities as directors. They are, consequently, in daily contact with the progress of the business and are called upon to make decisions in relation to the policy of the board as a whole and to implement these decisions on a day-to-day basis. In his executive capacity as head of a division or function an executive director does, in fact, assume personal responsibility for running his division or function effectively within the framework of the objectives laid down at board level.

- The majority of executive directors are elected to the board on the recommendation of the managing director precisely because of their functional expertise. This has two results. First, their technical background – the word 'technical' is here used in its widest sense – may cause them to have a narrow view of the business bounded by their specialist knowledge and experience. Second, being appointed by the managing director may cause some executive directors to defer to the chief executive's views, particularly if he has a forceful personality, against their better judgement. Many companies, therefore, have non-executive directors on their boards. Such people are part-time and are appointed for a variety of reasons. Often it is to gain the experience and advice of an acknowledged expert in his field who, by virtue of his disinterest in the running of the company, can bring to bear a wider view to the deliberations of the board than can those more intimately connected with day-to-day problems. One example might be that of a highly successful and respected architect being appointed as part-time non-executive director of a property company. His extensive knowledge of architecture and his experience of the intricacies of the Town and Country Planning Acts would be of enormous benefit to the company.
- Sometimes a company is required to have a non-executive director on its board, appointed by a third party. Such a case might be where a company is being financed to a considerable degree by a merchant bank or other financial house. Such an institution might well agree to provide the finance only if a part-time director recommended by them is taken on to the board. Such a director, in an advisory capacity only, would help the company in its financial matters, and at the same time keep a

watchful eye on the progress of the enterprise in the interests of the body providing the finance.

- Perhaps the main advantage to a company of an expert non-executive director is that he is completely independent and is not, therefore, likely to be influenced by pressures put on the board by the managing director or other executive directors against his better judgement.

3.5 The board and industrial democracy

No discussion on the role and responsibilities of directors would be complete without mention of the probability of future worker participation.

- As a result of the drive towards industrial democracy, being felt in all European countries, it is increasingly possible that the board of directors as at present constituted will undergo a significant change. Already in such countries as Sweden and West Germany there is a legal requirement for there to be worker directors in companies of above a certain size (in Sweden as low as twenty-five employees). Sometimes the requirement is for the worker directors to sit on a single board with the other directors, the so-called unitary board. In such a case the worker directors have the same powers as the other directors (the owners' directors) in voting on matters of policy, company objectives and other top management decisions.
- A more favoured system is that known as the two-tier board of directors, and this idea is supported by the European Community authorities: it is, in fact, the system used in West Germany. In effect, two boards are set up, the top level being a supervisory board rather like the present boards, and the second level on which the worker directors sit, being an executive board to which the supervisory board delegates the responsibility of running the day-to-day business of the concern. The supervisory board is still responsible for decisions on policy, overall objectives of the company and other matters that concern top management, and the executive board, the second tier, is responsible for decisions needed to put those policies into action, such as organisation, market development, investment plans, management/employee affairs and so on. It is envisaged in such a system that all decisions of significance taken by the executive board will have to be ratified by the upper tier board before they can be put into effective action.
- Opinion is divided in Britain as to exactly how this two-tier system should be implemented if and when the appointment of worker directors becomes mandatory. The three major political parties are in general agreement as to its adoption and it appears that the trade unions are, in the main, also in favour. Only the Confederation of British Industry (CBI), representing the country's major employers, has come out decidedly against it.

- The main area of contention is the manner in which worker representatives should be appointed or elected. The trade unions, of course, want worker directors to be drawn from their members, whereas management contends that this would be inequitable to those members of staff who did not belong to a trade union and, indeed, might operate to the detriment of such members of staff.
- Also in contention is the proportion of directors representing shareholders and directors representing workers. The European Community published a draft directive on company law (the fifth directive) in 1983, proposing that in large companies the representation should be two-thirds shareholders' directors to one-third worker directors, and that the latter should be full-time employees.
- Another problem about which decisions will have to be made is the manner in which worker directors will be selected, and then elected or appointed. As yet there seems to be little common ground among those concerned.
- There is no doubt that the introduction of employees on to the boards of directors of companies will have a profound effect on top-management decisions, whether the unitary board system is adopted or whether the two-tier system finds favour. Certainly it seems inevitable that the shareholders' directors will experience some constraints on their freedom to make decisions. One major concern is that board meetings may become talking shops, perhaps centred chiefly around management–staff relations and other purely domestic matters, instead of being platforms for the discussion of the future objectives of the company and its prosperity.
- Whatever the course of developments in this area there will be much of interest to those having any concern about management and its problems. Already, for example, some workers are saying that being an employee director will cause such a worker to become part of management to the detriment of his role as a member of the work-force: to this extent he will, perhaps, tend to forget the interests of his employee colleagues.
- Problems will also arise, of course, concerning the legal responsibilities of worker directors, even in such mundane matters as signing the company's accounts. The Companies Acts lay heavy responsibilities on directors of companies: it remains to be seen whether these will be accepted by worker directors or whether special protection must be devised for them.
- Time alone will give the answers to the numerous questions that this particular area of industrial democracy poses.

― **Questions** ―――――――――――――――――――――――――――

1 Compare the role of non-executive directors with the role to be played by full-time employees (both management and worker) on the board of a company.   **(ACCA)**

2 Discuss what is meant by the term 'two-tier board of directors', and suggest plausible functions for each tier.   **(ACCA)**

3 In what ways would the marketing manager of a large company be able to do a more effective job, if he were appointed to the board as a marketing director? How would his responsibilities change?   **(CIM)**

4 Objectives and policy

It was stated in Chapter 2 that the setting of objectives was the prerogative of top management, and that these would be formulated according to the accepted philosophies of the firm and its management. The same remarks were also applied to the creation of policies, indicating that objectives must be formulated first because they are *what* is to be done, and policies to pursue these objectives are formulated afterwards because policies lay down *how* the objectives are to be achieved.

4.1 Defining objectives

To travel with certainty it is necessary to have a goal, otherwise effort and energy is wasted journeying along byways and side roads which do not lead directly to the final destination.

The same remarks apply to organisations: they must have specific goals in order to use all their resources in the most effective fashion. These goals are the objectives of the firm, the end-results that have to be achieved.

- Unfortunately, as with much of the terminology of management studies, the word 'objective' is open to more than one interpretation and it is even occasionally taken to be inseparable from policy. So far as this work is concerned, therefore, it is necessary to define what is meant by this term, which can be stated as follows: 'Objectives are the goals a firm seeks to attain, and which constitute the principal reasons for its existence.'
- An organisation's objectives should be set out as clearly and as precisely as possible: only in this way can a certain path for the future be laid down. However, the precision of their formulation will depend a great deal upon the time over which they are expected to be achieved. Given the imponderables of the future, it would be unrealistic to try to formulate precise long-term objectives; these must be expressed in terms of ambition rather than accurate prediction. On the other hand, short-term goals can be formulated with a high degree of expectation of achievement, and on these the longer-term objectives can be built. Suppose, for example, it is an objective to capture 20 per cent of the market in a particular product in ten years' time: this target will be achieved by shorter-term objectives of a smaller percentage expressed in yearly steps. Undoubtedly, the short-term objectives can be tackled with greater precision than the ten-year ones.

4.2 Deciding objectives

The decisions as to what objectives to pursue are influenced by three principal factors:

(a) The philosophy of top management, whether economic in outlook, socially orientated or holding to the Stakeholder Theory.
(b) The opportunities that present themselves, or are likely to present themselves in the foreseeable future.
(c) What resources are or can be made available.

- The philosophical outlook of management has a bearing on objectives and their formulation less in regard to what goals to pursue than in regard to the vigour and single-mindedness of their pursuit. It is in this area that objectives and policy become very much interrelated. An example will clarify the situation. If the objective were to be to corner the market in a particular product, in other words ultimately to achieve 100 per cent of the market, the purely economic philosophy would see no detriment in this. In fact, when this objective had been achieved the probability of profit maximisation would also have been realised. A management holding to the socio-economic viewpoint, or the views expressed in the Stakeholder Theory would be reluctant to see as an objective the capture of the total market, for the simple reason that such a monopoly could or would undoubtedly prejudice the welfare of sections of the community. A simple case would be that of an employee wanting to change his job: in the event of a monopoly there would be only one employer he could work for, so his freedom of choice would have disappeared.
- A business or an organisation of any kind exists only so long as it fills a need, either present or able to be created and at a price attractive to the market. In considering acceptable objectives, therefore, management will have to consider what goals will be viable both in the immediate and in the long-term future. The setting of objectives in consideration of present or future opportunities, in the modern world of rapid technological development and change, is a difficult and challenging exercise. All businesses succeed or fail in the market-place, and consumer tastes and expectations change rapidly under the pressures of increasing sophistication of products and marketing campaigns. Objectives must be set, therefore, in the knowledge that constant product development will be called for to maintain the momentum to make achievement possible. Similarly, organisations engaged in providing services of all kinds will also have to take account of changing consumer requirements in assessing the viability of long-term objectives.
- These factors lead to the forming of appropriate objectives for staff training, staff recruitment and other associated programmes so that the personnel needed are ready and available when required. Objectives set by opportunity possibilities must, in fact, be supported by departmental

objectives in all the relevant areas such as sales, production, purchasing, research and development, administration, and personal and industrial relations. All of these objectives are interdependent and vital to the achievement of the main, ultimate, goals.

- Management must also relate its objectives to the resources it has available or is willing and able to make available. It must, therefore, ascertain the extent of the commitment required in pursuance of its objectives in labour, plant, buildings and material resources, not forgetting the necessary supporting administrative services. It must then determine to what extent current resources match up to the requirements of the goals to be set. Short- and longer-term secondary objectives will then have to be set, if necessary, for the financing of any additional resources that will be required.

- It will be seen, then, that the main goals of an enterprise rest on the fulfilment of a number of secondary and short-term objectives being satisfactorily achieved. The fewer the principal objectives the more concentrated can be the effort to achieve them, but that is not to say that an organisation must have only one purpose to be sure of succeeding. On the contrary, provided objectives are interrelated they can work to their mutual assistance, particularly if they are socially orientated. Thus, an objective to achieve an increased market share can be helped along by a realistic programme of sales training with the objective of improving the performances of sales representatives, and by an objective to gain the best customer and supplier goodwill.

4.3 Objectives and profit

Whatever the objectives laid down for a firm, however, there is no doubt that the objective of profit must be recognised as being of prime importance because only from profit can come the financial resources to support other, more socially inclined, objectives previously discussed. It is useful, therefore, to examine the benefits that profit brings to the firm, and these may be set out as follows:

(a) Only by making adequate profits can the firm survive. If the firm fails, all objectives will fail, so profit is the foundation upon which all else is built.

(b) Profit provides a measure of how efficiently the firm's resources are being used. Comparison with other firms' profit results also gives an indication of the relative success of the firm against others in the same industry, which in turn may initiate an investigation into the use of resources if the comparison is unfavourable.

(c) The performance of the management of a firm, particularly top management, can be assessed very much by the profit earned, particularly when measured against the capital resources employed.

(d) Equally, the pursuit of profit provides an incentive to management to succeed, and a spur to greater effort.

(e) It is the source of dividends for the shareholders or owners, and also provides the revenue to pursue objectives that are considered to be of benefit to the community.

(f) When new capital is required the performance of the firm in regard to earning profits is an important item in the deliberations of potential investors. This is also true when it is necessary to borrow funds from any of the usual sources of finance.

(g) Adequate profits not only provide income for the owners and financial resources for furthering the more socially orientated objectives, they also provide internally generated capital for the expansion of the business: self-generated finance is the least expensive source of funds and should have a high priority when considering objectives.

(h) Finally, adequate profit goes a long way to ensuring job security, and thus high morale, for the work-force.

4.4 Objectives of non-industrial organisations

So far the objectives that have been examined have been those applicable principally to profit-making private industry. However, the problems of management do not concern only such organisations: banks, building societies, local authorities, industries in public ownership and many others have to be managed and have to work towards certain goals. The problems of setting objectives, therefore, also concern these various organisations, but their main goals may differ very much from the type so far discussed, and can be looked at under their particular headings:

(a) **Banks:** While the need to make profits is an important consideration, the primary objective of a bank could be said to be to ensure the safety of the funds entrusted to it by its customers. Without the confidence of its customers in this respect its scale of operations would be severely curtailed because of its consequent inability to attract adequate funds. A further objective of high priority could be seen to be the support of local industry by providing loan capital in various ways, the availability of which would depend upon the previous priority.

(b) **Building societies:** The main objective of building societies is enshrined in the reason for their invention over a century ago – that is, to provide finance at reasonable cost to enable ordinary members of the community to become owners of their own homes. This main objective has given rise to a highly important second objective, which is to provide a safe form of investment for the small investor, which in turn has established a third objective of ensuring security for investors' funds. Emphasis is on the small investor in that practically all societies put a limit on the total funds they will accept from one individual, and this can be seen as an objective to help the average member of the community rather than the wealthy. Recent legislation in Britain enables building societies to expand their activities beyond the home mortgage market, but this in no way detracts from their main objective.

(c)   **Hospitals:** The primary objective of hospitals run under the National Health Service (NHS) must surely be to maximise the number of successful treatments. This in turn gives rise to the secondary, but important, objectives of a quicker turn round of patients, an improved utilisation of resources such as beds, wards and staff, and a reduction in costs without detriment to patients.

Nursing homes or hospitals run by profit-making organisations, such as those existing in the private sector in Britain and in America, will also have profit as an objective, though patient care will still be the primary objective. The profit motive will have no place in the deliberations of hospital managements in the National Health Service, however, though the need to conserve financial resources will be important. Nevertheless, the development of hospital trusts in Britain as a result of government reforms of the National Health Service in the late 1980s has led to a market approach to hospital patient care. Because these trusts are no longer under the jurisdiction of their regional health authorities, but are entirely responsible for managing their own affairs, the cost of services to patients has greater emphasis than hitherto.

(d)   **Local authorities:** Local government's primary objective must be the provision of adequate services to the local community. The second can be seen to be the most economical use of the funds available to it. The welfare of the community in all its aspects very much influences the formulation of the objectives of local authorities, and therefore there can arise severe conflicts between the two objectives just mentioned. Hence, the objectives finally decided upon are usually very much modified from the original proposals just because of these conflicts.

Each area of activity for which local government is responsible, for example, education, roadworks, social services and so on will have its own set of objectives and thus claims on funds, and so inter-activity conflict also arises. Local authorities' objectives are also very much subject to the influence of central government, which provides a substantial proportion of the finance local government spends, and also to the influence of local political and other pressures.

(e)   **Publicly owned industries:** Industries were taken into public ownership, in theory at any rate, in order to provide a better service to the community than can be provided by private enterprise with its concern with profit, and so that the nation has some control over those activities seen as being vital to the country and its welfare. All such industries are also required by the statutes that created them to make a profit or, at least, to break even; that is, to ensure that their revenues at least meet their costs. The overriding objective is to provide a satisfactory service to the community and a second to do this as economically as possible. As with local government, central government often interferes in the management of these industries and its requirements tend to change with the political complexion of the party in power in Parliament.

Despite the differences that emerge as the principal objectives of the various types of organisation just examined, as compared with profit-making industry in the private sector, nevertheless overall secondary objectives must be seen to be common to all forms of activity. Concern for staff, for the environment and for the community figure in the objectives of all forms of enterprise.

4.5   Departmental objectives

The corporate objectives of any type of organisation cannot be decided in isolation; their achievement rests on the performances of the various sections or departments comprising the whole. Therefore it is just as important that there be departmental objectives as that there should be corporate ones.

- Departmental objectives are formulated in much the same way as corporate ones and are subject to much the same constraints. The main difference is that a division, department or other section of an organisation works within the environment of that organisation, and the philosophies and constraints on its goals are conditioned by this fact in the same way as the wider, corporate objectives are to a large extent conditioned by the world outside the organisation.
- For example, a departmental manager will be concerned with the need to run his department as economically as possible, thus contributing to the overall profitability of his firm. He will also be concerned with the welfare of his staff (a social responsibility) and with the necessity of co-operating and co-ordinating with other departments and divisions. Every worker from the managing director down is a stakeholder whose interests must be safeguarded (see Chapter 2). Thus departmental objectives must be set within this framework. In addition, the departmental manager will also be inclined to set objectives that will be appropriate to his own personal aspirations and for their furtherance, as mentioned in Section 2.2 above.
- Because of their overriding responsibility to ensure the success and continued survival of the organisation, the directors or top executives of a firm, or the governing body of other types of organisation, must approve the sectional objectives put up by the managers concerned to make sure that they are properly within the framework of the total organisational objectives, and that no conflicts are apparent or likely to arise.

4.6   Policy-making

Just as objectives are *what* the organisation seeks to achieve, so policies are *how* these objectives are to be pursued: and as with the formulation of objectives so with the formulation of policies, this is the ultimate responsibility of the board of directors. In fact, it is generally the case that overall policies are laid down solely by the board.

● Policy formulation may be considered to be the laying down of company attitudes in the achievement of objectives, and to this extent the board will set the overall attitudes to be adopted in relation to all the functions of the business. In doing this it may decide that some areas such as marketing require a conciliatory policy to be pursued with customers, whereas in regard to purchasing it might consider a very firm line with suppliers should be adopted. However, it is unlikely that the members of the board will be experts in all the functions of the enterprise. It is thus generally recognised that in the larger concerns at least policy committees should be set up for the various functions to deliberate on the policies that should be adopted relative to the objectives set. Members of these committees are expert in their fields and are usually principal executive officers and their senior staff. Their knowledge and experience enables them to deliberate expertly upon the relevant facts and trends and to advise top management, with authority, on suitable policies to be pursued. Policy committees do not, as a general rule, have executive powers but are required to report their recommendations to the board: it is the board of directors who will make the final policy decisions.

● The following are some of the policy committees that might be found in large organisations:

(a) **The finance committee,** who will discuss policies as to sources of funds, whether to borrow money or float shares, what proportion of loan capital there should be to equity capital (i.e. owners' capital), whether loans should be short- or long-term, and whether loan finance should come from a commercial bank, a merchant bank or by way of debentures.

   Such a committee might also consider policy in regard to granting customers credit, the extent of leniency in time allowed for payment, and so on. Their experience in the area of finance will enable the committee members to put forward a prudent but sensible policy for consideration by the board, who will then be able to lay down the appropriate official company policy on this matter.

(b) **The marketing committee,** who will deliberate on marketing policy, what markets to penetrate, and the extent of the possible penetration; on policies concerning customers such as company practice as to contract conditions, exchange and return facilities and after-sales service; on the proportion of the marketing budget to be spent on publicity and advertising; on the kinds of public relations exercises to be undertaken; and on the many other facets of the marketing activity.

(c) **The personnel committee,** who will give consideration to matters of human relations policy concerning recruitment and training; on promotion and whether this should be entirely internal or otherwise; on staff welfare and on pay and pensions.

(d) **The production committee,** who will consider production programme policy, output levels, quality-control tolerances, whether various components should be manufactured within the factory or whether some should be bought outside the firm, and similar matters.

- It should be noted that some aspects for consideration by these committees overlap: thus finance and marketing are both interested in expenditure on publicity, and on terms of credit for customers. Consequently there must be adequate liaison by all committees formed for policy-making purposes.
- These examples are sufficient to illustrate what can be done by committees to assist the board to formulate general policies for the organisation as a whole and, if it is a group of companies, for the whole group. In fact, even the formation of a group is a matter of policy: if the board decides to expand does it do so by natural growth or by acquiring other companies? Does it want to diversify? A policy of acquisition is particularly helpful in this case.
- Out of the policy decisions arrived at should flow the following:

(a) The structuring of the organisation so that it has the ability to carry out the activities necessary to achieve the objectives of the company as laid down by the board.

(b) The provision of a sound and workable financial structure adequate to adjust to future needs, both for investment and for working capital.

(c) Consideration for the technical aspects of the company, and for adequate research and development facilities to keep abreast of technological change and to cope with competition.

(d) Adequate provision for the training of all staff, both administrative and technical, and for retraining all types of worker where operations alter owing to technical change. Such changes are prone to lead to the deskilling of some work (computerisation of an operation for example) or may require the learning of new skills or the adaptation of old ones, such as a typist changing from a typewriter to a word-processor.

(e) Co-ordination of the efforts of marketing with production and finance.

(f) The provision of after-sales servicing and of maintenance, where necessary. The question of guarantees is an important issue, as is the question of how long to go on making spare parts for old and obsolete models of manufactured goods where this applies.

(g) There must be an awareness of the social responsibilities the firm has

to the world at large and in particular to its customers, its suppliers and its staff.
(h) Management development and training should also be of considerable concern to the policy-makers.

4.7   The flexibility of objectives and policies

The question of how flexible objectives and policies should be is an important one.

- So far as the objectives of an organisation are the reasons for its existence then they can be said to be relatively unalterable. If the objectives set are unattainable owing to lack of resources, collapse of a market or governmental intervention, then that firm ceases to be able to function as it was set up to do. A change of **objectives** could therefore be seen as a change of organisation, even though it continues with the same name and the same directors and staff. A company set up to deal in scrap metal does not remain the same company if it forsakes that activity to make electric train sets.
- That is not to say that external forces may not impinge on the organisation to make it modify its objectives, but such modification would not be substantial. In the short term temporary modification of objectives to cope with a temporary bad trading period may be justifiable but the long-term objectives should remain.
- **Policies**, on the other hand, are much more flexible. These can be adjusted to deal with problems that arise in the pursuit of the firm's objectives or according to immediate operating conditions. For example, if the firm's cash-flow position becomes difficult and a policy of allowing extended credit to be taken by customers has been pursued, this policy can readily be modified so that stricter limits on credit are imposed: this more stringent policy can then be relaxed again, if thought desirable, when the cash position improves.

4.8   Communicating objectives and policies

Objectives and policies cannot be formulated without being communicated to those who will be affected by them.

- Since, on the whole, objectives remain static then these are usually incorporated in a statement of objectives and published in the document defining the constitution of the body concerned. In the case of a limited company, for example, they will be embodied in the objects clause of the memorandum of association, one of the legal requirements for the formation of a company.
- Policies, on the other hand, being determined ultimately by the governing body of the organisation, the board of directors in the case of a company, will be written into the minutes of the meeting at which they

were decided. This, however, is usually insufficient publication and it is not unusual for there to be a statement of policy published for the organisation's staff. Other means of ensuring that policies are known to those whom they concern are by statements in staff handbooks, in written operating procedures issued to those engaged in specific routines such as credit control, sales and so on, and by information given during staff training sessions. Policies affecting customers and suppliers are normally incorporated in conditions of sale and conditions of purchase, printed on sales order acknowledgement forms, invoices and purchase orders.

4.9   Policies by consent

While it is true to say that the policies of an organisation are laid down by its governing body, using advice offered by various functional policy committees, it must be recognised that nowadays control is by consent. Consequently, policies that are at variance with the desires of those they affect will stand little chance of being fully accepted and thus of working as effectively as they should.

- For example, promotion policies that are seen by staff as being inequitable are likely to be the source of discontent at the very least, and may lead to bad management–staff relations and thus inefficient operation. The result may also be a high turnover of staff with the consequent disruption of work and the cost of recruitment and training of new staff.
- Thus, while policy formulation may be a high-level activity, in effect it is extremely important that the views of those likely to be affected by the policies laid down should be sought and given consideration. Imposed policies are unlikely to work effectively: policies formulated by consent are likely to have a very good chance of success.
- Even when the policies affect those outside the organisation they must be acceptable to be able to be implemented. A policy to tighten up credit may meet with resistance simply in the form of customers going elsewhere to satisfy their needs. It is therefore not possible to formulate policies in isolation from the environment in which they are required to work.

Questions

1 What would be the major factors you would consider if you were drawing up the objectives of **one** of the following organisations:
   (a) a hospital
   (b) a bank
   (c) a manufacturing company
   (d) a nationalised industry.   **(ICSA)**
2 (a) Review the differences between objectives and policies of organisations.

    (b) Why are both an essential part of the managing and organising process?   **(IAM)**

3 'Objectives are needed in every area where performance and results directly and vitally affect the survival and prosperity of the business' (P. Drucker). Discuss this statement and identify those key objectives you consider to be most important to a business. **(IAM)**

4 What is meant by 'the policies of an organisation', and how are policies formulated? What influence do the objectives of an organisation have on the policies decided upon?

5 Why may an organisation's goals change over time? Discuss, making reference to an example from your own experience.   **(ICSA)**

6 In the area of business planning it has been suggested that 'objectives' need to be thought of in terms of:

    (i)   a central purpose;

    (ii) responsibilities which an organisation has to its many stakeholders;

    and

    (iii) a field of activities within which the organisation intends to operate.

    (a) Illustrate the extent to which a changing environment makes an impact upon 'objectives' thought of in this way.

    (b) Give three examples, with appropriate details, of how 'happenings in the environment' might change such objectives.   **(CIMA)**

7 **(a)** Explain the meaning of the term 'policy', in a business context.

    (b) Describe **four** areas which could be expected to be covered in the marketing 'Policy' of a firm engaged in the manufacture of industrial products.   **(CIM)**

Short-range and long-range forecasting

Having decided upon what its objectives are, the firm must plan how these are to be achieved. However, plans can be made only on the basis of what is expected to happen in the future, both within the organisation and in the world outside: this means that likely events and conditions must be forecast before plans for the attainment of objectives can be laid down.

Forecasting is normally done for two periods, short-range and long-range. Both are necessary if the firm is to be successful in achieving its objectives in the long term and so can formulate plans for such achievement.

5.1 Short-range forecasts

Except for totally unforeseeable events, short-range forecasts, which are normally taken to be those of a year or less, can be reasonably accurate, and can be seen rather as a prediction than as a statement of probability. It can also be seen that the shorter the term involved the more accurate the forecast is likely to be: a forecast for a week ahead in a very high percentage of cases will be absolutely accurate; for a year ahead the chances of variance are much greater.

- The sources for information and data for short-range forecasting are partly internal and partly external, and can be enumerated as follows:

(a) **Information from internal sources**
   1 The most obvious information on which to base short-range forecasts is that of the actual achievement of the firm for the previous year (or part of year if the period is shorter) and the current year to date. This information is, or should be, readily available from the records kept by the organisation. Data should be available for the separate functions of the firm, such as sales, production and so on, and these activities should have analysed data in their records, such as the sales and trends for each product and for each market in which it is sold.
   2 The length of time the firm's present products have been on the market and the expected remaining life of each based on the projected life span when each was launched.
   3 The probability of the launch of new products during the term of the

forecast, and the development stage reached on all such new ventures.

4 The probable cash-flow requirements as suggested by management's financial policies.

5 The probability of bringing new and more efficient machinery into use as determined by management's capital investment policies.

6 The cost of labour per product unit and the trend shown by the records; the cost of administrative staff.

7 The state of industrial relations within the organisation, time lost because of disputes, and the trends in this area.

8 The way the firm has maintained its market share, or whether it has increased it or has suffered a reduction.

(b) **Information from external sources**

1 The outlook in the market or markets in which the firm is involved: is demand growing or declining?

2 The behaviour of the firm's competitors: have they been aggressive and increased their share of the market, perhaps at the expense of the firm? Have they launched up-dated competing products?

3 The behaviour of price levels: have competitors' prices fallen in comparison to the firm's own? Have competitors held their prices level while the firm's have risen?

4 The type of product offered by competitors in the immediate past: have completely new designs been introduced, perhaps utilising the most modern technology, which have made the firm's products seem out of date?

5 Has the company much loan capital, or is it likely to need it? In this case the cost of money on the market will be very significant. In times of high inflation and high-interest rates this area of forecasting is of very great importance when forward planning is being discussed.

6 The possibility of government interference in the industry, threats of nationalisation or government regulation; the possible influence of government fiscal policy: such possibilities can be of enormous significance in the exercise of formulating forecasts.

If the organisation is concerned with international trade, either as an exporter or an importer, or simply has to rely on the import of materials or components, the following further items of information will be pertinent:

7 The state of international trade: is it buoyant or depressed?

8 Is there the likelihood of political instability in the areas of the world where the firm's interests lie?

9 The state of the international currency market: are rates of exchange adverse or favourable? Are they stable?

10 The foreign competition: are overseas competitors developing new and more attractive products? What is their pricing policy?

- Much information about the external factors influencing forecasting can be obtained from various government reports and statistics, the reports of independent economic forecasting organisations, from trade organisations, trade journals, and from the more informative daily and weekly newspapers such as the *Financial Times*, who regularly include business and financial supplements.
- While short-range forecasting cannot be absolutely accurate it can often be nearly so and, naturally, the shorter the term the more accurate it is likely to be, as previously pointed out. Even so, even the shortest forecast can be made to be hopelessly wrong if a totally unforeseeable event should happen. The unprecedented steep rise in the price of oil in 1974, after decades of cheap oil, upset all forecasts, as did the prolonged drought in Britain in 1976. Accurate forecasts about the weather of more than a day or two ahead are notoriously difficult, and industries very susceptible to weather conditions, such as farming and the civil engineering industry, find even short-range forecasting far from easy. Short-range forecasts where fuel is an important ingredient can also be less than reliable due to the instability of prices, but the certainty of price rises can be assumed; the only doubt is the extent of the rises.

5.2 Long-range forecasts

Any forecasts for periods in excess of a year may be said to be long-range forecasts, and are generally accepted as such, though periods of between one and three years might more properly be called 'medium-term forecasts'. Most authorities, however, restrict their definitions to short-range and long-range, and for the latter it can be said that the type of activity will, in most cases, determine how long is 'long'.

- To make this clear an oil company will commonly forecast for twenty to thirty years ahead whereas a manufacturer of women's fashion wear would find it difficult to make any forecast exceeding two or three years hence, and even then he would stand a good chance of being very wrong. This is because of the different environments within which each operates.
- An oil company works in a relatively stable marketing environment and the life of any particular oil field can be predicted with reasonable certainty. Whatever the fluctuations in world oil prices there is a minimum level of demand that will inevitably be maintained because of the reliance on oil as a fuel by much of the industrial activity of the developed world. Only if some revolutionary new fuel were to be developed would the demand for oil change radically, and even then it would take a considerable time for industry to change over to using the new fuel because of the vast capital investment already tied up in oil-burning plant. Thus an oil company can look ahead for ten, twenty, thirty or even more years: its chief uncertainty would probably be in the

area of discovering new oil fields to replace those running out. Here again, however, it takes a decade or more to bring a new oil field to full production. In such an industry, therefore, long-range forecasting over very long periods, while not easy, can have a fair degree of certainty in it. Another factor affecting very long-range forecasting for an industry such as oil production is the unstable political state of the world. Regimes that were once stable have now become unstable politically. Where these regions are major producers of vital raw materials and fuels, such as the Middle East for oil, very long-range forecasting becomes very difficult.

- On the other hand, a manufacturer of women's wear is faced with a very volatile market in which taste changes in the very short term. Even the most highly proficient fashion house can go sadly wrong in predicting even next year's fashions, and long-term forecasting is a near-impossibility. Not only has the forecaster to contend with the unpredictability of women's tastes; he also has to cope with the inconsistent nature of the weather. Yet some forecasting for a period of about twelve months is necessary because garments must be designed and then samples made and be ready for showing at least six months before the goods are put on sale to the public.

These two examples clearly indicate that long-range forecasting is different for different business activities, both in regard to time span and to the possibility of anything approaching accuracy. In fact, generally speaking long-range forecasts are subject to considerable inaccuracies. There is very little firm information that can be used with confidence, and the data previously suggested for short-range forecasting would be dangerous to use for long-term purposes: for instance, who can tell what the cost of money will be even five years hence? However, some sort of prediction of probabilities is essential, to be applied flexibly during the course of the years, and in the main the experience of the forecasters is usually a sound guide, albeit only a guide.

5.3   The effects of forecasting on general objectives

It was seen in Chapter 4 that the main objectives of an organisation are formulated as the basis of its existence, and it follows therefore that these objectives must be seen to be reasonably attainable.

- Such a supposition, however, must be based on something more valid than guesswork or pious ambition: in fact the basis is forecasts prepared to ascertain what are likely to be the future possibilities for the organisation.
- Consequently, general objectives are very much dependent on the forecasts made, both short-range and long-range, but particularly the latter. If, for example, an increase in the sales of bicycles is predicted over a period of years then it can be confidently forecast that there will

be an increase in the demand for the many ancillary items for bicycles such as bells, locks and chains, carriers, safety helmets and the like. An opportunity in one or more of these products is thus presented and any one of many manufacturers may be tempted to set up a specialist department, or even a subsidiary company, with the main objective of satisfying the expected demand for such products. Without the forecast the special objective would not arise.

- Similarly, a forecast can lead to a change in objectives, or a modification of them, though, as pointed out in Chapter 4, a fundamental alteration in effect changes the organisation. Thus, a forecast of a severe decline in the birth-rate could persuade a baby-buggy maker to forsake his objective of being a major manufacturer of prams: instead he might change to the manufacture of trolleys for supermarkets where the forecast is of significant growth. Such a change of main objective need not, however, change the supplementary objectives such as total of turnover, required return on capital and so on, albeit the organisation is no longer a manufacturer of baby buggies but of supermarket trolleys.

5.4 The business cycle

In preparing forecasts for the long term the phenomenon of the *business cycle* must be taken into account.

- An organisation can be said to be organic, and like all organisms it begins, grows and can then decline. Unlike natural organisms, however, its decline can be retarded or can be prevented altogether; in fact a firm can continue into perpetuity. Continued existence, however, can be maintained only if management appreciates the fact of the business cycle. Normally this cycle is taken to relate to a firm's products; they are designed and developed, launched, have a period of popularity and then decline because of the entry into the market of newer, simpler, cheaper or more attractive substitutes. A similar pattern of growth and decline can be found in all aspects of a business. Methods of manufacture, from being modern and up to date become obsolescent and inefficient, causing high costs and hence high prices for the products, which result in customer resistance and a diminishing market. Personnel practices, from being enlightened and far-sighted become dated and less acceptable to workers, resulting in deteriorating industrial relations. The manner of the acquisition of capital may cease to achieve the results of the past and may lead to under-capitalisation with its attendant problems of reduced cash flow and insufficient funds to renew old equipment.

- Two problems, then, assail the preparation of long-range forecasts: the prediction of when changes are likely to be required to ensure a continuance of the existence of the organisation, and the fact that different activities in the business have different time cycles. Much of the influence on the organisation that results in the decline of any sector is external – change of customer taste, new technology, changing interest rates on money – and some of these are hard to predict, particularly as to when change is likely to happen. It is incumbent on those responsible for forecasting, therefore, to keep abreast of developments in all relevant areas through publications, conferences and similar sources of information. Much guidance on the course of the business cycle can also, however, be gained from internal records, internal statistics and so on. For example, falling sales can be seen from sales records, while the reasons for this can often be determined from the reports of the sales representatives in the field. Falling productivity can often be discovered through comparison of present and past records, and also by interfirm comparisons. A high labour turnover as indicated in the personnel records can mean unsatisfactory personnel practices, even though previously they had been accepted as very good.

5.5   Technological forecasting

Probably the most fluid circumstance that the forecaster has to deal with is the rapid changes taking place in technology and its application to manufacturing and other processes. This has led to the need for technological forecasting, which can be defined as 'forecasting the expected technological development in a given area of activity over a given time'. It differs from business forecasting (which has been the subject of discussion so far) in that it can be more certain than business forecasting. This is so because the aims of technological research and development are normally well-defined: the required outcomes have been determined and the chief problem is not 'what' but 'when'; in other words the main uncertainty is the time the development will take to reach the stage of application. Even this is controllable to some extent by simple measures such as overtime working on the project, reducing testing times and similar expediencies.

- Some examples of technological change which have occurred and which should have been taken account of in the forecasts of the appropriate organisations are:
  1 The change from mechanical to electronic office machines and cash registers (one well-known company in this field neglected this change and is no longer in business).
  2 The change from leather soles to plastic compounds in footwear.
  3 The change from paper to plastic sheeting in a wide range of products such as food bags, carrier bags and so on. Similarly, the change from glass to rigid and flexible plastic sheeting in such items as roofs for lean-to buildings, some greenhouses, agricultural cloches and other products.
- Technological changes now taking place include (among very many):
  4 The use of special plastics instead of steel or other metals where strength is required.

5 Non-silver imaging in photography, which will revolutionise photo-graphic materials and processing.

6 Total electronic automation in such activities as stock-keeping and warehousing.

5.6 Forecasting in the public sector

There is no fundamental difference in forecasting in the public sector from that in the private sector. As in private industry the circumstance obtaining, and the limits for reasonable forecasting, depend very much on the area of activity under consideration.

- In the publicly owned industries the normal trading constraints apply, as these are, indeed, trading organisations subject to consumer behaviour.
- In other areas, however, such as local government and certain departments of central government, forecasting should be a more exact science because figures for specific trends are available to the forecasters. One example is education. The authorities keep exact records of births and therefore it is no difficult matter to predict the number of five-year-olds who will be ready to start school at any time. Accurate figures are also maintained of the proportion of pupils who go on to further and higher education, and so estimates of probable demands over the long term on the resources of colleges and universities can be determined with reasonable accuracy.
- As with business forecasting, however, the unexpected may always happen to upset long-range forecasts: this is inevitable. Similarly, short-range predictions in the public sector are more likely to be right than the long-term ones. Nevertheless, in both sectors of activity all forecasts are subject to varying degrees of uncertainty.

5.7 Forecasting and error

Forecasting, as pointed out already in this chapter, is subject to the probability of error, and the longer the range of the forecast the more likelihood there is that it will prove to be incorrect to a lesser or greater degree.

- Nevertheless forecasts are essential for planning the activities of the organisation. What, then, can be done to reduce the incidence of error to the smallest possible degree? The answer lies in examining past forecasts and comparing them with what actually occurred. From these comparisons it is possible to assess the percentage error that has shown itself in each case: this can then be projected into future forecasts. This will not, by any means, make future predictions accurate, but will tend to reduce the amount of the variance between forecast and actual performance.

- There are many reasons for errors occurring in forecasts, most of them subjective. They include:

  1 Undue optimism or pessimism, which prejudice the forecaster's judgement.

  2 Unwillingness on the part of the forecaster to accept the conclusions that the data he has been using indicate.

  3 Faulty and inaccurate assumptions from the data and information the forecaster has been using. This may arise from a combination of 1 and 2 above.

  4 Unforeseen events, such as a significant change in government policy or a change of government, prolonged strikes, political or military activity abroad.

5.8   Mathematical methods of forecasting

In recent years, in order to take some of the uncertainty out of forecasting, mathematical methods of determining probability have been increasingly used. However, these are properly the tools of the practitioner in operational research, and can be misleading if used by the inexpert. The manager, therefore, may use the services of operational research to assist him in making his forecasts, but the ultimate responsibility is his and not that of the operational research specialist. The latter acts only in an advisory capacity. Further, the results coming out of the mathematical models that the operational research practitioner uses can never be more accurate than the data fed into them, which are supplied by management.

Those who are interested in the techniques of operational research are advised to consult specialist textbooks on the subject, such as T. Lucey, *Quantitative Techniques* (D.P. Publications).

Questions

1 Discuss the ways in which short-range forecasting differs from long-range forecasting, and explain the reasons for this.

2 What are the factors that forecasters normally take into account when developing short-range forecasts? How much reliance can be put on historical data in this connection?

3 Distinguish between business and technological forecasting. How does technological forecasting assist management to respond effectively to technological change?   **(ICSA)**

4 What differences, if any, are there between the bases for long-range forecasting in the public sector as compared to the private sector? Do these differences hold good over all the public sector, and if not, why is this?

5 One of the essential tasks of a marketing department is to prepare a detailed forecast of sales for a future period. What is the purpose of such a forecast
   (a) to a production department?
   (b) to an accounting department?   **(CIM)**

 Planning

A plan is the route to an objective. If an organisation is to achieve the objectives it has set itself, then clearly it must plan courses of action that will enable it to attain these goals. Without proper planning the organisation will be at the mercy of management whims and external pressures that may make it lose sight of its objectives: yet it is surprising how many businesses do not, in fact, have any significant forward plans but are content to carry on operations virtually on a day-to-day basis.

- This lack of planning does not make for the efficient use of resources and it is important that management be alive to the need for definite plans to set the enterprise on course and to keep it there. Often it is considered that as current world conditions, both economic and political, are so fluid with no clear views ahead, anything but short-term planning is a waste of time. Nothing could be further from the truth. The greater the uncertainties the more important it is to plan what can be planned.
- One of the essential features of planning is flexibility: plans must be flexible so that they can be modified in the light of events. In this way conscious deviation from the original plans can be embarked upon without losing sight of the ultimate objectives. Departures from the original plans can be, themselves, clearly planned with the aim of regaining course at the first opportunity. Without this flexibility the possibility of meeting the specified objectives of the enterprise is much reduced.

6.1 Short-range planning

- Plans that are to run for a year or less come under the heading of short-range planning. Many of them fall into the category of everyday decisions, especially if they cover only a few days or weeks, and they can be expected to run precisely as predicted. Thus, the work-rate and material requirements for decorating an office suite over the span of three weeks can be planned with the virtual certainty that no divergence will occur to the plan, or will be needed. This would be a contract where the work would be done under cover, not subject to the vagaries of the weather, and the time span is so short as almost to obviate any contingency likely to upset the plan.
- If the contract were for a complex of office blocks and the work time a

year, though the very length of time might mean contract planning would be subject to some unforeseen circumstances, nevertheless it could be assumed that the work should be able to be carried out exactly according to plan.

- So, with short-range planning there is every possibility that few adverse contingencies will arise to upset the plan, and the shorter the period of the plan the less likelihood there will be of emergencies arising. Nevertheless, flexibility is still needed in even the shortest plans. In the first example the unexpected illness of a specialist foreman might mean the work would not be able to continue. Two circumstances then arise which need attention. The first is the requirement to complete the work in the allotted time. The second is to find remunerative work for the men who are unable to carry on at that site, because of the incapacity of their foreman, until such time as they can again return to the interrupted contract. So contingency plans are required; that is, flexibility in planning, even for the shortest time span.

- A firm engaged on the three-week contract would, undoubtedly, redeploy the men on another site in order that this valuable resource should be profitably employed. Plans to finish the contract in three weeks would have undoubtedly been made on the assumption of normal working hours. Depending upon the seriousness of the foreman's illness, the management would either abandon work on the site if the indisposition were reckoned to last only a day or two and recommence on the foreman's return, or would deploy another gang either of their own or of a sub-contractor if the illness were likely to be protracted. In either case the contract time would be met by working overtime; another deviation from the original plan.

- Over longer periods even more flexibility would be needed in connection with the planning exercise, and the more vulnerable the subject of the planning to outside influences the more flexible must be the plans drawn up in pursuance of any specific objective. In the second example cited, if this were exterior and not interior decoration the weather over a year would certainly interfere with the initial planning.

- In most cases of short-range planning contingency plans can be laid to cope with commonly experienced eventualities so that alternative action can be taken quickly if circumstances so require. Where the time span is relatively short the totally unforeseen eventuality is comparatively rare.

6.2 Long-range planning

- Long-range planning takes into account periods in excess of a year and may cover periods of any number of years according to circumstances. Circumstances include the type of industry concerned and the manner in which it operates. An engineering contractor, for instance, involved in the construction of off-shore oil rigs would plan on a contract basis, the term being the length of time it would normally take to construct a rig.

His plans would be largely operational over, say, two or three years and he would have to take account of the many imponderables likely to occur during that time, such as labour disputes, material shortages, economic climate and weather conditions. Experience gained on previous contracts would guide him in formulating his plans.

- He would, of course, be concerned with other long-range planning, for instance the continued existence of his enterprise on the completion of his current work. So in such an industry long-range plans can be put into two categories. The first is where actions are severely circumscribed by contract conditions, particularly in regard to the time element, and flexibility of manœuvre in the event of necessary deviation is severely limited. The second category is that where planning is in the longer term and, simply, is concerned with the survival of the organisation. In this case maximum flexibility is required. The goal is not the completion of a specific contract, but the continuing effort required to attain the organisation's major objectives.

- An oil company, on the other hand, would enjoy greater flexibility in both its short- and long-term planning. The engineering firm is bound by contract and has a specific cut-off point: failure to comply may attract severe cash penalties in favour of the oil company for which it is working. The oil company itself is not so tightly constrained. True, failure to achieve a planned date for the installation of a new oil rig would result in loss of revenue, but the oil company is answerable only to itself. Complete flexibility in the case of delays might mean that it could increase production at another oil field while the delays on the new one were resolved.

- In consequence of the difference in the operating structure in these two industries an oil company, unlike an engineering contractor, can plan for very much longer periods ahead and, in fact, does: long-range planning really does mean just this, running over periods of ten, twenty, thirty or even more years. In both instances long-range planning is, in fact, in large measure 'strategic' planning (see **6.6** below).

- As with forecasting, therefore, the periods of time in relation to planning will depend very much upon the type of industry and activity concerned.

6.3   The relationship between forecasting and planning

Without some guidance as to what may happen in the future both short-range and long-range planning would be mere guesswork. Forecasting is, therefore, essential in order that management may carry out its planning function. Forecasting on its own is sterile. Only when its findings are utilised in the formulation of plans for the future is it fruitful. It follows, also, that the more accurate the forecasting is the higher is the possibility of producing reliable plans and the greater, therefore, is the likelihood of attaining set goals.

- Those responsible for developing plans for an organisation's future will, inevitably, rely heavily on forecasts, but the final responsibility for the results of the plans will rest with the planners. They will, therefore, combine their own experience and knowledge of their firm and its industry with the forecasts available. By this means they will produce plans, both short-range and long-range, in which they have confidence and which will set and maintain the firm's course towards the achievement of its objectives.

- In the exercise of their function the planners must try to anticipate likely problems that may arise to upset their plans. It is not enough to set a plan into action and expect it to run smoothly. Its progress must be constantly checked and controlled. Performance must be monitored and compared with the plan over the period of its life, and reasons for deviations discovered. In this connection, forecasting is again a tool that can be usefully employed, particularly in long-range planning.

- Forecasting should be looked upon as a continuing exercise, and forecasts should be available at regular intervals, monthly, quarterly, half-yearly or annually as the circumstances appertaining to a particular planning area demand. Those responsible for planning can then compare the latest forecasts with those on which they based their original plans. By doing this they are able to ascertain whether any modifications are required to their plans to meet changing circumstances; thus they may avoid problems before they arise.

6.4 Evaluating pre-planning forecasts and information

There is, however, one circumstance that must be commented upon both in regard to monitoring the progress of plans and also in regard to the original process of planning. This is the question of an over-abundance of information and data.

- Gathering the information on which to base the planning operation is rather like any other research: there is a tendency to collect too many statistics, forecasts and other material that will be likely to affect the planning. This has two effects. First the plans may be imprecise and difficult to understand clearly because they are likely to contain a great deal of detail and may even specify slightly conflicting actions where the source material has been in some way contradictory. Second, because of the abundance of information, there may be a tendency for the planners to detail too many specific courses of action to deal with possible deviations, thus depriving those managers responsible for carrying through the plans of the opportunity to use their initiative to act as they see fit in these cases.

- The remedy is for the planners to examine critically each forecast and other material, and to look carefully at their own experiences bearing on the projected plans. They must discard ruthlessly any material that does not have a very precise and definite bearing on the plans they are preparing. Contradictory information must be evaluated and decisions made as to what is really relevant and pertinent. Especially, they must differentiate between opinion and fact and discard the former in favour of the latter where there is conflict, however informed the opinion might be. In this way the source material will be reduced to manageable proportions, and will thus assist in the preparation of clear and understandable plans.

6.5   Levels of planning

As all aspects of an organisation are susceptible to planning, each individual activity should follow a plan, however short the time span.

In formal management theory it is usual to consider that there are three basic levels of planning, though in practice there will be more than three levels of management and supervision, and to an extent there will be some overlap of the planning activity. These three levels are:

(a) **Top-level planning**

This is done by top management – that is, the board of directors or other governing body – and is often termed 'strategic' planning. It encompasses the long-range objectives and policies of the organisation and is concerned with corporate results rather than sectional achievements. It also involves corporate planning, which is dealt with in Chapter 7. The chief executive, as a member of the board, will be very much involved in strategic planning and is the link between this level and the next. Top-level planning is entirely long-range and is inextricably linked with long-term goals. It might be called the 'what' of the planning activity.

(b) **Second-level planning**

This is carried out by senior executives and is formally known as 'tactical' planning. Just as strategic planning is concerned with 'what' so tactical planning is concerned with 'how'. This means that it is involved with planning the deployment of resources to the best advantage. Tactical planning is concerned principally, but not exclusively, with long-range planning, but its nature is such that the time spans are usually shorter than those of strategic planning. This is because its attentions are usually devoted to the step-by-step attainment of the organisation's main objectives: thus the very long-range plans of top management are segmented. It is, in fact, orientated to functions and departments rather than to the organisation as a whole.

(c) **Third-level planning**

Frequently termed 'operational' or 'activity' planning, third-level planning is the concern of departmental managers and supervisors. It confines itself to the very short-term, involving departmental operations and also individual assignments, and it establishes performance controls.

6.6 Strategic, tactical and operational planning

The three levels of planning, of necessity, react on each other, but the resulting effects are different in each case.

- Operational planning may impose restraints on tactical plans because of practical difficulties arising from time to time. The effect of a necessary alteration in an operational plan, because of the short term involved, is likely to be more of an inconvenience than a reason for abandoning a tactical plan. Operational plans are unlikely to have any effect on strategic planning, as they are relatively remote from each other. On the other hand, strategic planning will, although remote, have some effect on operational planning because the mode of operational activities will to some extent depend upon strategic plans.
- There is a closer relationship between operational and tactical planning because the former arises very directly out of the latter. A change of tactics may very well impose adjustments to operational plans. For example, a small change in the design of a product – a tactical decision to combat new competition – may well cause production plans at shop-floor level to be drastically revised. Unless, on the other hand, tactical planning has been very rigid, modifications in operational planning can often be absorbed at this level without difficulty.
- A similar situation exists between strategic and tactical planning. The strategic plan may remain constant despite the fact that the tactics employed to achieve it may have to be modified from time to time. In other words, tactics can change without alteration to the strategic plan becoming necessary. However, if the strategic plan alters, the tactical plans will amost certainly have to be changed to suit the new situation.
- Two other distinctions should be noted in connection with the relationship between strategic and tactical planning. First, strategic planning is concerned with the principal objectives that have been set for the organisation and with what to do to achieve these goals. Second, tactical planning accepts the objectives set by top management and concentrates on ways to bring the strategic plans to successful fruition. Strategic planning is concerned with ends: tactical planning is concerned with the means to achieve those ends.

6.7 The principles of planning

Whatever the planning period certain principles are involved, which can be set out as follows:

(a) The purpose of the plan must be determined. Planning cannot be done in a vacuum and the goals to be achieved must be clearly identified.

(b) Plans must be formulated on clearly defined data and information. Forecasts help in this direction but other sources must also be used, such as past records, performance experience and the like. The planners' own past experiences can be utilised, but in this connection it is vital to separate fact from opinion or prejudice. However, an excess of source material must be avoided if planning is not to become too complicated.

(c) Plans of the various sections of the organisation must be co-ordinated, otherwise confusion is likely to result. The effects of one department's plans on those of others must be recognised and accommodated. Co-ordination is relatively easy at operational planning level because times are short and the personnel involved are in close contact with each other. Co-ordination becomes progressively more difficult as it reaches the level of long-range tactical planning largely because the staff involved are remote from the operational level. Of course, the ultimate aim should be total co-ordination, one of the aims of corporate planning.

(d) Standards to be achieved by the plans must be set and performance monitored. Failure to attain the set standards may be caused by over-optimism by the planners or by external factors not previously foreseen.

(e) Plans must be flexible to allow for modification in the light of experience. Failure to attain standards is one of the indicators of the need for modification.

(f) Full communication of all concerned in operating the plans, at any level, is essential: consultation with them during the formulation of the plans should also take place. Involvement by all concerned is an important factor in successful planning.

(g) Plans must be seen to be achievable. Over-ambition must be avoided as this leads to discouragement and frustration in the failure to attain the goals set. On the other hand, under-ambition in planning provides no incentive and encourages inefficiency.

6.8   Special considerations for long-range plans

In addition to the foregoing general principles long-range planning has to concern itself with a number of other factors mainly impinging on management from outside the enterprise.

- These include recognised or conjectured trends in the political, social or economic climate; increasing concern for the environment, particularly where pressure groups are very active; general international and national trends in the markets in which the enterprise is engaged; changes in social habits; the availability of external investment; threats from take-over predators; and external competitive pressures.
- While the past experience of the planners will be vital here their sober

and considered judgement will also be extremely important. It has even been suggested that intuition might be helpful. By 'intuition', of course, is meant the undefinable flair and business acumen which so many successful top managers possess.

6.9 The importance of planning

Operational and short-range planning are important because they relate directly to the day-to-day activities of the organisation. No enterprise can function at all effectively if daily, weekly or monthly functioning is left just to chance. This type of planning is also mainly carried out at the lower levels of management and supervision, with the emphasis on the practical.

Long-range planning, both strategic and tactical, is also of vital importance, and is the only means of setting and keeping an organisation on course for the attainment of its principal objectives. The policies and objectives of the concern are laid down by its governing body: planning will bring out what resources will be required, will suggest the organisational structure needed to pursue these policies and objectives, and will be instrumental in promoting the controls necessary to carry out the plans formulated.

- Every aspect of the organisation should be subject to planning in order to make the utmost use of resources, to stimulate programmes for staff and management training, to promote sales and financial targets, to ensure a reasonable return on capital and investment, and generally to guide the enterprise in the attainment of its objectives.
- The development of well-considered plans enables management at all levels to take a hard look at itself and the organisation in which it operates. Management is required to examine its activities in the light of the past and the possibilities for the future, and to justify its decisions before they are implemented.

6.10 The responsibility for planning

- Operational and very short-term tactical planning is usually carried out by the manager or supervisor actually concerned with the activities involved. Thus, the office manager will formulate the plans necessary for providing office services over the short term, possibly subject to constraints such as limits on expenditure, staff recruitment and other matters under his direct control. His typing-pool supervisor, equally, will take the responsibility of planning the operations of her service over the day or the week.
- Long-range tactical planning will be carried out by the more senior executives in the areas such as marketing and production. In these cases, however, they will probably be aided by their immediate subordinates who will, in turn, have at their command reports and other information

concerning operational capability. Forecasts in the areas concerned will also be taken into account, and these may be, in a large organisation, the output of a special department staffed by experts, such as operational research. In smaller organisations senior executives and their immediate staff will have the responsibility for gathering the necessary forecasts through perusing trade journals, government reports and the like, as indicated in **5.1** and **5.2** above.

- Long-range strategic planning will be done by the governing body with the assistance and advice of its senior executives. Forecasts from internal and external sources will be utilised as well as analyses of the past performance of the enterprise, and managerial experience.

- In both tactical and strategic planning, however, the actual activity is often delegated to a planning committee or, if the concern is large enough, to a planning department. This means that more uninterrupted time can be given to the planning exercise than would be the case if the directors or senior executives tried to formulate plans while still engaged in their day-to-day activities. Effective planning needs the undivided attention of the planners. Nevertheless, whoever draws up the plans, it is the chief executive who must assume ultimate responsibility for long-term planning, either strategic or long-term tactical, as he has to do for all the other major activities of his organisation. The approval of and authority to implement plans are his responsibility; the planners normally only advise.

- The separation of the planning operation from the senior executives by the setting up of an independent department does raise some difficulties. First, the planners may take into consideration information and forecasts to which the executives have not had access. Second, the executives who have the responsibility of operating the plans may not be aware of the precise information and data on which the planning was done, and particularly what was omitted from the planners' deliberations. Third, executives of long standing, who have previously had autonomy over their activities and have formulated their own plans, may feel resentment at having plans imposed upon them by others, however expert. This may lead to disharmony, to the detriment of the successful implementation of the plans.

- Finally, as may happen with any department, the planning department may be inclined to view their activity as an end in itself rather than as a service for the benefit of the organisation and its progress.

6.11 Monitoring

The subject of monitoring the implementation of plans needs consideration. Chapter 12 deals in detail with various aspects of control, but two techniques that have a particular interest in connection with planning are the Gantt chart and network analysis.

- The Gantt chart is relevant to short time span plans and is used to set out the planned progress of a procedure and the actual achievement so that any deviation from the plan can be seen in good time, and steps taken to correct the deviation. An example of a Gantt chart is shown in Figure 12.1.
- Network analysis is more relevant to long time plans. A number of techniques fall under this heading, but they can be grouped under (i) Critical Path Network (CPN) and (ii) Program Evaluation Review Technique (PERT). Both techniques are concerned with defining a 'critical path' for an activity to follow to minimise time and resource costs in its achievement. CPN is calculated on the assumption that completion time can be forecast precisely whereas PERT assumes that an accurate prediction is not possible, as explained in **24.2(d)** below.
- The importance of planning cannot be over-estimated. In effect, in large measure the planners decide the future of the organisation. The plans they draw up set its course both in the short and the long term.
- Because of this it is essential that the final decision on the adoption of all proposed plans must lie with the chief executive. It is he who is responsible, ultimately, for the successful achievement of the objectives of his organisation, and who is responsible to the board of directors or other governing body.

Questions

1 What are the main components of long-range planning and to what extent should planning include judgement, experience and even intuition?   **(ICSA)**
2 Do you think that the effectiveness of any public or private sector organisation can be improved by long-range planning? State your reasons.   **(ICSA)**
3 Make a case for the establishment of a long-range planning unit in an organisation where the management feels that even its one-year plan is rarely on target.   **(IAM)**
4 Your managing director has attended a conference at which a speaker said that long-term strategic planning was obsolete. He is naturally concerned about this comment.

    You are required to draft a report to your managing director stressing the benefits of long-term strategic planning and examining the case for its abolition.   **(CIMA)**
5 Who has executive responsibility for long-term planning in a commercial enterprise? What may be the main obstacles to the development of long-term planning into a worth-while discipline with set procedures?   **(CIMA)**
6 It is suggested that longer-term planning is currently inappropriate because of the rapid rate of environmental change and that there is an inherent rigidity in all planning which could sap initiative.

(a) What is your view of this suggestion?

(b) What may be done to reduce planning 'rigidity'?   (CIMA)

7 Illustrate with examples, the essential differences between strategic, tactical and contingency planning.   (CIM)

Corporate planning

Chapter 6 looked at short- and long-range planning, as these are common to the majority of organisations. Strategic planning was considered to be the province of top management, tactical planning that of senior executives and operational planning that of lower management. The result of this approach is the fragmentation of the planning operation possibly resulting in conflict of interests in various parts of the enterprise. As organisations have become larger, either by natural growth or by amalgamation, this course has become less efficient, and it has been realised by very many managements that a different approach is necessary. This new procedure is corporate planning, and although not new in concept has been slow in being widely adopted.

7.1   A definition of corporate planning

Corporate planning is specifically strategic in nature: in fact it is frequently termed 'strategic' planning by some authorities though this term is also used by others to mean simply long-range planning by top management.

- Corporate planning may be defined as 'a systematic and comprehensive process of long-range planning taking account of the resources and capability of the organisation and the environment within which it has to operate, and viewing the organisation as a total, corporate, unit'.
- By its nature, corporate planning takes the long view, and its time span is normally over a minimum period of five years and frequently extends very much longer than this. As with other forms of planning, the type of activity the organisation is engaged in determines to a large extent the time period for the plan. Further, the plan must be frequently up-dated and it is usual to review performance and adherence to the corporate plan at least annually so that modifications may be made in the light of experience.

7.2   The needs of corporate planning

The obligations imposed upon those responsible for preparing the corporate plan are extremely important to the success of an enterprise, as they require a very hard and careful examination of a number of factors essential to its survival and growth. These are:

(a) The need to identify specifically all the attainable long-term objectives possible, and to decide which to pursue.

(b) The need to evaluate all the internal resources of the organisation, including finance, marketing expertise, productive capacity and the like.

(c) The need to appraise the external environment of the organisation within which it operates, including the economic environment, present and possible future government action, the legislative climate, developing technology and so on.

(d) The need to co-ordinate all activities and plans throughout the enterprise.

(e) The need to establish the internal strengths and weaknesses of the organisation, and the possible external opportunities and threats. This is known as the SWOT approach, and is dealt with more fully in **7.6** below.

(f) The need to establish a formal planning procedure with an effective feedback mechanism.

(g) The need to recognise that, though long-range, corporate planning requires constant reviewing and up-dating if it is to be effective. A corporate plan review committee can be helpful here.

7.3 Factors in corporate planning

Because corporate planning embraces the overall strategy of the organisation it is most commonly carried out by a planning committee made up of senior executives especially drafted to this work because of their knowledge and experience. If the organisation is very large a special planning department may be created. The long-range strategic objectives having been decided upon, the following actions will be taken:

(a) An appraisal of the existing internal situation of the enterprise. This involves an examination of the financial position, return on investment, the productive capacity, marketing effectiveness, the range of products or services offered, the extent of research and development, the utilisation of the labour force, training programmes and any specialised skills available.

(b) A review of the organisation's position in the market-place, whether its position is strengthening or weakening. Is the market generally expanding or contracting? Is the organisation following this trend?

(c) An evaluation of present and future competition. In the business environment, are competitors' products more advanced technically or are their services more efficient? What is the trend in these areas?

(d) An assessment of the economic factors surrounding the organisation's activities. Is there a slow-down in economic activity? Is it difficult to obtain finance or is it expensive?

(e) A review of the legal aspects of operating the organisation. What laws are likely to be enacted that may influence industrial relations, credit operations, the environmental aspects of the firm's operations such as pollution, consumer protection and so on?

(f) A review of the effect of immediate and possible future governmental action. What may be the government's position in regard to changes in various taxes such as corporation tax, VAT, various levies, licensing regulations in some areas, import restrictions and so on? In Britain, also, the impact of changes and regulations imposed by the European Commission must be taken into account.

The results emanating out of these deliberations will be the starting-point of corporate planning. The manner of obtaining the information required will differ from enterprise to enterprise. Two commonly used techniques are 'top-down' and 'bottom-up'.

7.4 Top-down planning

This method starts the planning process at the top in the planning committee or department, normally on the initiative of the chief executive.

- The long-range strategic plans are formulated by the specialist planners following the setting of the strategic objectives. The corporate plan is then broken down for use by the various divisions or departments of the organisation, each receiving its own sectional strategic plan from the top.
- Frequently the planners have the assistance of operational research personnel who produce mathematical models of forecasts and trends to aid the planners to formulate their plans.
- While this method has the advantage of the use of highly specialised skills and is widely used, it has the following drawbacks:

(a) Often there is no involvement in the planning by the operating managers, thereby causing resentment or even hostility on the part of those who have the task of putting the plans into action.

(b) Where operational research models have been used, the operating managers may not understand the mathematical techniques involved and thus may lack confidence in the plans.

7.5 Bottom-up planning

In this method the various divisions or departments are required to produce their own separate plans, and these are considered together by the central planners and used as ingredients in the corporate plan after appraisal and modification or rejection as is considered necessary.

- This method has the advantage, so it is claimed, of ensuring the involvement in the organisation's strategic planning of all those who will be required to implement their own parts of it.

- It is suggested that its disadvantage is that top management, through the planning committee or department, may pay only lip-service to the sectional offerings and may pursue strategies outside the corporate plan so evolved.

7.6   SWOT

SWOT is the acronym for **Strengths**, **Weaknesses**, **Opportunities** and **Threats**, and is in effect a distillation of all the steps and considerations that should be taken to formulate an effective corporate strategic plan.

(a) **Strengths**

In this area will be found all the advantageous aspects of the organisation. Examples would be exceptional customer goodwill and brand loyalty, highly efficient technical staff, adequate financial resources and an enthusiastic sales force. The strengths represent the foundations on which continued success can be built.

(b) **Weaknesses**

These must be honestly investigated and faced because they represent retarding influences on the success and growth of the organisation. Remedies must be sought to overcome them. Weaknesses occur in all areas of an enterprise, some examples of which could be obsolescent machinery, no provision for senior management succession, in-adequate research and development facilities resulting in lack of new products to succeed current production models. What remedies to apply would depend upon the weaknesses revealed. In the given examples the organisation should consider carefully investment in new machinery, the promotion of management training schemes and increased investment in research and development.

If finance is a strength then these remedies would not be difficult to implement: if a weakness this would have to be given attention first.

(c) **Opportunities**

Whereas strengths and weaknesses emanate chiefly (though not entirely) from inside the organisation, opportunities are usually external. They may come about fortuitously or by the application of some research. The important point is that they should be recognised and grasped firmly when they arise. Some examples of opportunities are a new market opening up that could be filled from existing resources, the opportunity to take over another company which would improve the organisation's capabilities, such as a manufacturer taking over a retailing chain, or the opportunity to take on to the management team an expert in some appropriate field who would improve the organisation's performance.

Opportunities abound if they are sought for and recognised. They are important for the organisation, and its management should be ready for them so that they are able to be taken when they occur, provided they coincide with the main objectives of the firm.

(d) **Threats**

Like opportunities, threats are most often from outside, and like opportunities must be recognised and steps taken to deal with them. Though the actual threats are mostly external, their disadvantageous repercussions on the organisation are chiefly due to weak or inept management and management planning. Some examples of threats are changing technology, thrusting competition especially from overseas, economic and political uncertainty.

Three very important threats emanating internally must be mentioned, however. The first is management complacency, the second inadequate financial management and the third low staff morale. Complacency results from the assumption that things will always remain as they are and management therefore has no plans to meet technological or other change, or the consequent strong competition. Examples of this abound in lost or reduced industries both in Europe and in America. These include radio and television equipment, photographic equipment, motor-cycles and office machinery, where technical innovation by manufacturers in Japan and elsewhere has overtaken the slow to change Western manufacturers.

Inadequate financial management results in insufficient financial resources being available for research and development, for expansion and for the seizing of opportunities as they arise. This can come about by ineffective or inadequate credit controls, faulty pricing policies or unwise internal investment decisions. Low morale in the workforce, often brought about by unpopular personnel practices, can undermine the efficiency and thus the productivity and profitability of the enterprise.

- The advantage of the SWOT approach to corporate planning is that it requires management to look very closely and analytically at every aspect of its operations so that objectives can be assessed as attainable, and a clear picture built up of the strategies that must be adopted to achieve them. Every strategy must also be examined with care so that the constraints under which operations have to be conducted will be recognised. Some of these constraints, which may cause certain strategies to be abandoned, will be external and some internal.
- Some external constraints may be outside management's control altogether: these would include raw material price rises, government legislation and the economic climate. Others may be circumvented, examples being the substitution of an alternative material for one whose supply has ceased, or finding a new outlet for products whose overseas market has ceased to exist because of import bans.
- Internal constraints include the lack of specialist labour, bad industrial relations, faulty products owing to poor quality-control and lack of

research and development support. Such constraints may require corporate strategies to be re-examined, and the planners and management will have to consider the alternatives of abandoning some strategies or of remedying the constraints.

7.7   The corporate gap

Corporate planning is planning for the long term. As previously mentioned in this chapter its strategies must be reviewed periodically and the necessary modification made to keep the organisation on course to the ultimate objectives. Flexibility is essential.

- At any point in its operations the actual results of the existing activities of the enterprise can be compared with those required at the same juncture by the corporate plan, and these can be projected into the future, when the results expected from continuing the current course can be assessed and set against the planned results. Where actual results fall short of planned results, this is termed the 'corporate gap'. The procedure which analyses this problem is known as 'gap analysis'.
- The most frequently considered failure is that of net earnings, or profit, and is termed the 'profit gap', but this technique is also applied to all other aspects of the strategic objectives, such as sales, production and so on. The extent of the gap indicates the amount of effort that is required to achieve the long-range objectives, taking into account the incidental gap failure. Strategies will, therefore, have to be adjusted on this account and all the components going into the corporate plan that bear on the problem will have to be re-examined.

A graphic illustration of gap analysis is shown in Figure 7.1.

7.8   Entrepreneurial activity and corporate planning

It is sometimes held that corporate planning can have a deadening effect on entrepreneurial activity, which is the exploitation of market opportunities as they arise or are discovered. The opportunism of the entrepreneur is seen to need complete freedom of action within the resources available to him or that he can make available through his particular entrepreneurial skills.

- To a very large extent the restrictions of a rigidly operated corporate plan could inhibit opportunism and with it the opportunities to create rapid growth or greater profits. Again, corporate strategic objectives are seen as more than maximising profits or producing quick expansion: they are also concerned with customer satisfaction, social responsibilities and staff welfare among other things
- However, corporate planning should not be restrictive or inflexible otherwise it will fail in its objectives of the survival and growth of the

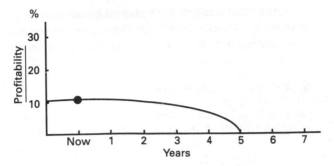

Forecast of profitability if current plans pursued

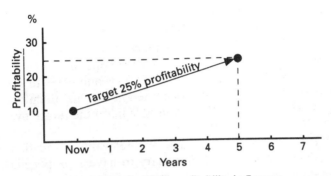

Target of 25% profitability in 5 years

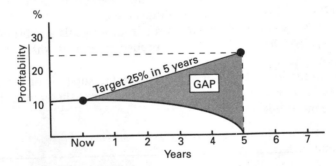

Target curve superimposed on current plan curve produces gap

Fig. 7.1   Illustrating gap analysis

organisation. Change is vital to continued existence and to progress. Hence, there should be little conflict between entrepreneurial pursuits and the strategic plan. The corporate plan is not an end in itself: it should be the means to pursue the ultimate objectives of the organisation, and should thus provide opportunities for entrepreneurial initiative.

- Provided, therefore, that there is sufficient flexibility in the strategic planning and top management is alive to the need for innovative activity, entrepreneurial opportunism should be able to add dynamism to the organisation. Equally, such activities of the enterprise must be kept within reasonable bounds and within the resources available.

7.9 The advantages of corporate planning

The advantages and benefits that an organisation can reap from efficient strategic planning and its careful implementation may be summed up as follows:

(a) It requires management to make a close, analytical examination of the organisation for which it is responsible.

(b) Provided the planning is carefully carried out and properly implemented, it ensures the continued progress of the organisation.

(c) Provided full consultation takes place, it ensures that all levels of management are involved in the planning operation and procedures. This helps the implementation of the plans and helps to generate the personal interest of all those concerned in carrying them out.

(d) It requires that adequate attention be paid to the future over the long period.

(e) Because of the need for adequate and relevant information in regard to all activities, it becomes necessary to have a proper management information system (MIS). An adequate information flow is essential for effective management whatever the range of the plan. Short-term planning also benefits from this requirement.

(f) It helps to concentrate attention on corporate goals and broadens the horizons of those whose main preoccupation is that of tactical planning.

(g) Those at the lower levels of management and supervision are enabled to appreciate how their operational plans fit into the grand scheme of the organisation.

Questions

1 Define strategic planning. Explain the steps which should be taken in the development of a corporate plan. **(IComA)**

2 Define the term 'profit gap' in the context of corporate planning, and discuss its relevance to the planning process. **(ACCA)**

3 Describe the different components of strategic planning at its corporate, tactical and operational levels, and show the relationship between these components. **(ACCA)**

4 It is felt by the many opponents of strategic planning that in instigating strategy, one is putting an organisation into a straitjacket, and that there is a resulting loss of flexibility which renders impossible the exploiting of opportunities on a more free-wheeling basis. Evaluate this statement. **(CIMA)**

5 Define and explain the principal elements of a Corporate Plan. State the contributions to the plan to be expected from
   (a) a senior functional manager;
   (b) a Chief Executive.
   (Answers should include examples from an organisation with which you are familiar.)   **(ICSA)**

6 Discuss the criteria, financial and non-financial, which a business should use for the purpose of evaluating possible strategies. **(CIMA)**

7 (a) Indicate what an organisational SWOT analysis entails.
  (b) Why should social responsibilities be taken into account when considering organisational objectives?   **(IAM)**

8 Organisation (1)

Organisation can be defined as 'the framework of responsibilities, authority and duties through which all the resources of an enterprise are brought together and co-ordinated for the achievement of management objectives'.

It is a pattern of relationships formally established which has as its purpose the creation of a structure through which the activities of personnel at all levels can be utilised in an orderly and controlled manner to the benefit of the enterprise as a whole.

8.1 Responsibility, authority and duty

The terms 'responsibility', 'authority' and 'duty' are basic to discussions of organisation and it would be useful at this point to give definitions of these terms used in the present context.

(a) **Responsibility**

In the context of organisation this term can be considered to be the same as accountability. It is the obligation to make sure that authority is properly used and that duties are properly carried out. It carries with it the prerogative to delegate authority and duties, but does not carry the right to avoid accountability. In this sense responsibility flows from the bottom of the organisational structure to the top since each supervisor or manager is accountable to his immediate superior for the proper use of his authority and the proper performance of those duties, whether done personally or not, for which he is responsible. In this way the chief executive carries the full and ultimate responsibility for the effective functioning of the organisation.

(b) **Authority**

This is the power to assign duties to subordinates and to ensure that they are carried out, and involves the acceptance of accountability for the proper exercise of this authority. The precise extent of the authority must be clearly defined to the holder and he must act only within those limits. Authority, unlike responsibility, can be delegated, and flows downwards through the organisation structure. At all times authority must be commensurate with the accountability imposed, and all subordinate staff subject to the authority must be made aware of it and of its extent.

(c) Duty

This is the obligation to comply with orders and instructions given by those in authority, within the limits enjoyed by that authority, and within the sphere of activity designated to the staff member who is required to accept those instructions. Orders do not have to be explicit: there is also a duty to act on implicit instructions; that is, to carry out tasks necessitated by instructions given, though those tasks are not actually specified. For example, if a manager gives one of his staff instructions to take a car to another depot it is implicit in those instructions that the staff member will ensure that there is sufficient fuel in the vehicle to accomplish the journey: a specific instruction on this point should not be necessary as it is within the duty of the member of staff to perform this task effectively.

8.2   Setting up an organisation

In a very large number of enterprises the organisation pattern has simply grown to accommodate changing requirements and circumstances rather than having been planned. Where a concern has developed from small beginnings, or where a department has expanded to take care of greater volumes of work, this is understandable. However, this practice does not lead to the most efficient form of organisation. An effective organisation structure must be properly planned, and the following rules have been arrived at in order to set up an effective organisation:

(a) The various activities necessary to pursue and achieve the objectives of the enterprise must be determined. The most logical division is by function, e.g. marketing, production, finance and so on, and most small- and medium-size concerns are organised in this fashion.

Larger enterprises, however, may be divided up by customer, by product, by location, or in any other fashion that is appropriate for efficient working.

(b) These activities must be divided into logical sectional activities. Thus the marketing division may be split into home sales and overseas sales. These sections may then be subdivided into geographical areas, product types or any other suitable categories.

(c) Leaders must be appointed for each whole division and for each section of each division. The marketing division, therefore, will have a marketing manager, probably a senior executive, and there will be a home sales manager and also an overseas sales manager, both invested with the necessary authority to do what is necessary to pursue the marketing objectives of the undertaking, and both accountable to the marketing manager.

(d) Each section must now be staffed. The number of operating members of staff will be determined on the basis of the forecasts of the volume of work to be expected. Middle and junior managers and supervisors will then be provided for, ideally on the basis of the principles of delegation and span of control discussed in **9.4** and **9.5** below.

(e) The necessary equipment for the efficient operation of each division and section must be determined and proper provision made.

(f) Effective procedures and communication systems must be designed and installed to ensure the proper co-ordination of all parts of the organisation.

(g) The extent and limits of responsibility, authority and duty of every member of the organisation must be clearly defined and made known to all concerned.

(h) The power to delegate authority must be given to all those who have managerial or supervisory responsibilities.

(i) Ideally, written procedures should be prepared for all aspects of the organisation. For managers at various levels there should be management job descriptions (MJDs) which set out managerial responsibilities, authority and duties. For other members of the work-force there should be operational procedure manuals giving written expression as to how the various work-routines are to be carried out.

From **8.2 (d)** it will be seen that organisation should be planned on the basis of the expected work-load. This will determine the number of operating staff required to cope with the work effectively. From this the number and levels of supervisors and managers can be determined. Unfortunately, this planning is not often practicable. By the time the need for a formal organisation structure has been realised there is already a form of organisation pattern in existence, one which has grown without deliberate consideration but purely through expediency. However, the rules set out above should be taken into account when a major reorganisation does become necessary.

8.3 Forms of organisation

In considering the forms of organisation it is usual to think in terms of four distinct and traditional types. However, in actual practice it is rare to find any one type in its pure form, and most organisations operate with varying degrees of combination. Further, modern thinking has produced some organisation patterns outside the traditional ones. The four traditional patterns are as follows:

(a) **Line organisation**
This is the simplest form of organisation. The enterprise is divided into departments, usually by function such as accounting, marketing and so on, and a controlling head is appointed. In a primary function such as accounting the head is usually a senior executive: in subsidiary functions the rank of the departmental manager will depend upon the status of the department. For instance, the personnel manager in many concerns occupies the status of middle manager.

- The important aspect of line organisations is that there is a clear line of responsibility and authority right through the management structure from the governing body, say the board of directors if a company, to the lowest level of supervision, and below. Authority is derived by any level of supervision from the one immediately above. The chief executive derives his authority from the governing body and the departmental heads derive theirs from him. The assistant chief accountant, for example, draws his authority from the chief accountant. So authority can be seen to flow downwards.
- In a similar fashion each level of supervision is accountable to the one above. So in the example just given, the assistant chief accountant is accountable to the chief accountant, who is in turn responsible to the chief executive, not only for his own actions but also for the actions of his subordinates to whom he has given authority.
- In this way responsibility can be seen to flow upwards and, in theory at any rate, the chief executive, and through him the governing body, is responsible for the proper conduct of the organisation throughout. In a limited company it would be the board of directors accountable to their shareholders and in a public body such as a local authority it would be the council members acting as a body accountable to their electorate.
- The pattern of line organisation can be seen in the organisation chart shown in Figure 8.1.
- It must be emphasised that the various departmental management posts do not necessarily have the same status in the management structure though they are drawn at the same level in the chart. It is a convention to draw charts in this way to make them easy to read: to try to indicate relative status would make such charts difficult to draw and confusing to read.
- Line organisation is also called military organisation (this is how armed forces are organised), scalar organisation and, occasionally, vertical organisation.
- It has the following advantages and disadvantages:

Advantages
1 It is simple and direct and is not difficult to understand.
2 There is a direct chain of command and thus decisions are rapidly made and implemented.
3 Co-ordination of the activities of members of a department is simplified because of this directness of control.
4 For the same reason effective delegation of authority and duties is straightforward, and it is relatively easy to inspect and control the work of delegates.
5 The position and status of the various members of a department are readily understood and appreciated.
6 Because of its simple structure, line organisation promotes staff discipline more easily than other forms.

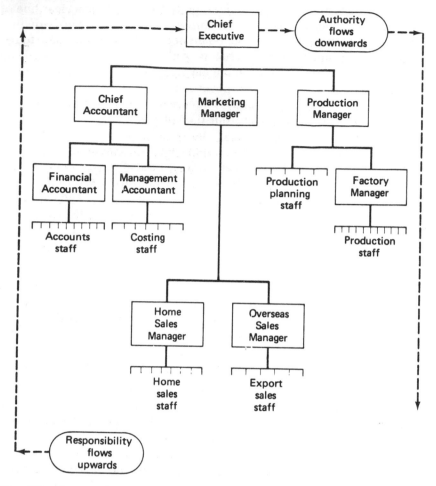

Fig. 8.1   Specimen of a line organisation chart

7 The extent and limits of responsibilities, authority and duties of all members of a department can be clearly defined and so readily recognised and understood by those concerned.

Disadvantages

1 To all intents and purposes each department is autonomous within its own sphere of activity. This leads to limited opportunities for its members to acquire experience of the other functions of the enterprise.

2 The head of each department is afforded total control of his workforce and to this extent the effectiveness of his department depends upon his capabilities. If he is active and enterprising then the department may be able to play a stimulating role in the total

organisation. So often, however, a departmental manager can be cautious and conservative, leading to a stagnating department.

3 Where this happens there is inflexibility, and the departments concerned find difficulty in coping with changing circumstances and with expansion, with a consequent deleterious effect on the organisation as a whole.

4 Where a manager has been head of a department for some considerable time there is the danger that he will become autocratic and that he will view the organisation solely from the standpoint of his own department. This gives rise to difficulties in co-operation and co-ordination between the various departments of the undertaking: often, even, to hostility and bad feeling between them.

- Despite the inherent drawbacks in line organisation, in practice it can be very efficient, particularly in small- and medium-size concerns. Larger undertakings also sometimes find it beneficial to decentralise certain aspects of their activities and to organise them on the line pattern.

(b) Functional organisation

In this type of organisation it is the function itself that determines the flow of authority and responsibility without reference to actual operating divisions. Each function of the undertaking is determined and an expert put in charge who will have direct control of that function wheresoever it occurs. His authority will, therefore, override that of the line manager within whose department the function is being carried out and who is responsible for the discipline and other matters concerning his staff.

- An example will make this position clear. If a production expert is appointed to act as functional executive responsible for the manufacture of a firm's products then he will have the authority to give instructions to anyone in any department where his function touches, without reference to the line manager concerned. Thus he can direct sales staff to promote certain items because they suit his production schedules without consulting the sales manager. Equally, he can insist that purchases of materials are made from specific suppliers despite the fact that the accountant is unhappy about the financial aspect of such purchases. This is because the production function is concerned both with the articles sold and the materials purchased, and because the sales manager and the accountant are line managers whose authority can be overridden by the functional executive. It will be obvious, however, that if the accountant and the sales manager were also functional executives then there would be a conflict of authority. In any event, in this situation line managers find their authority reduced, not only in relation to functional activity but also in relation to discipline and staff relationships. The workers themselves are left in doubt as to whose authority they should accept.

- In some measure the problems inherent in functional organisation can be alleviated by curtailing the authority of the functional experts and requiring them to consult line managers on significant matters concerning the latters' departments while at the same time keeping the final responsibility and authority in the hands of the functional specialists. The latter would, in fact, retain their executive powers.

- The fact that this type of organisation pattern results in workers being subject to the authority of more than one superior means that it is at variance with the concept of the unity of command, as explained in **10.3** below. It is not commonly found in practice in its pure form, but nevertheless its advantages and disadvantages must be examined.
- Figure 8.2 illustrates functional organisation and indicates the possibility of confusion inherent in this pattern for the work-force.

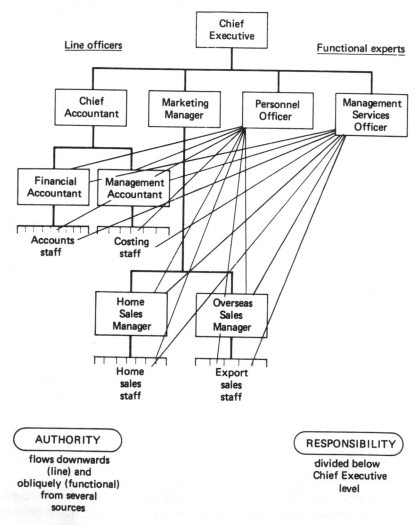

Fig. 8.2   Specimen of a functional organisation chart

Advantages

1 The undertaking benefits from the expertise of the functional specialists, who have direct authority in all aspects of their speciality wherever it occurs.
2 The functional experts are not involved in the day-to-day running of the organisation; this is done by line management. They are consequently free to concentrate exclusively on their function and its application.
3 The organisational structure is flexible and is able to respond to external or internal changes quickly, one of the functions of the specialist executives being to monitor what is happening in their spheres of interest outside and inside the enterprise.
4 Because the activities of the functional executives penetrate all sectors of the organisation they are excellently placed to assist in the effective co-ordination of the efforts of the various departments, to the benefit of the undertaking as a whole.

Disadvantages

1 There are no clear lines of authority in this form of organisation, which can make systematic control difficult, because the executive powers of the specialists cut right across departmental boundaries.
2 This, in turn, leads to difficulty in establishing responsibility when failure occurs, and also makes remedies to put things right more difficult to apply.
3 Functional experts command high salaries, and a large number are needed to operate the functional type of organisation satisfactorily. This can mean that this form of organisation can prove extremely expensive, sometimes too expensive to be economically practicable.
4 Workers can become confused by the many superiors who have direct authority over them.

(c) **Line and staff organisation**

Despite its drawbacks, functional organisation gives many benefits, as already explained in **8.3 (b)** above. In consequence it has been married to line organisation to produce a form that seeks to provide the best of both types, namely line and staff organisation.

- The availability of the services of functional experts is maintained in this form of organisation, but the specialists are required to act in an advisory capacity only and have no executive powers. These are the staff officers. The line organisation structure is maintained and line officers (line managers and line supervisors) retain responsibility for the day-to-day running of their departments: authority over departmental staffs is theirs alone. In this way the functional expertise is provided, but only as advice to line officers who then implement it if they see fit: the staff officers have no power to enforce compliance with their decisions. Line and staff organisation is illustrated in Figure 8.3.

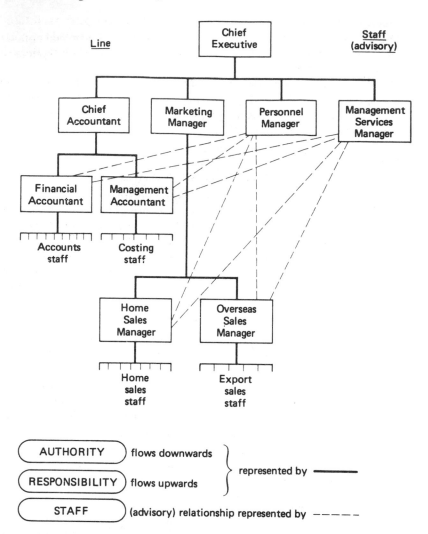

Fig. 8.3   Specimen of a line and staff organisation chart

- In practice, line and staff organisation is the pattern most commonly employed and the one that seems to be the most successful. Its advantages and disadvantages can be set out as follows:

Advantages
1 As in line organisation, the lines of responsibility and authority are clearly defined, and obvious to those they concern.
2 The departmental line officers retain total control of their departments.
3 Nevertheless, functional expertise and experience is available, thus bringing some of the benefits that accrue to pure functional organisation.

4 Similarly, co-ordination throughout the undertaking is facilitated because of the fact that the interests of the functional experts permeate throughout the various sections of the organisation, though on an advisory basis only.
5 Provided that the line officers maintain their own initiative within their own spheres of action, and do not lean too heavily upon the functional experts, decisions should be arrived at as quickly as they can be in purely line organisation.

Disadvantages
1 Inasmuch as the functional officers act only in an advisory capacity and have no executive authority, line officers are free to accept or reject their advice. In the latter case this means that the expensive expertise of the staff officers is being wasted, possibly to the detriment of the efficiency of the undertaking as a whole. A line officer is primarily concerned with his own department and may not be able to appreciate fully the effects of his decisions on the total organisation: the functional (or staff) officer on the other hand has an overall view of the enterprise.
2 There is a danger that staff officers may try to usurp the authority of line officers. This can come about through frustration at advice being rejected, particularly if this happens frequently, or because the staff officer has an overbearing personality. Whatever the reason, when this happens an unco-operative attitude is generated between the two types of officer. Further, where the line officer does not exert his proper authority this may be seen to be a weakness by his staff and his effectiveness and general discipline may suffer as a result.
3 Where clashes of opinion occur frequently between the staff and line officers this will be reflected in a lowering of the efficiency of the organisation.
4 As in pure functional organisation, line and staff organisation can be confusing to the workers, though this can be avoided if they are properly informed of the differing roles of the types of officer.
- In practice it will usually be found that line executives are those who control the primary functions such as marketing and production, and whose efforts are directly concerned with pursuing the main objectives of the organisation. In industry, therefore, they will be those charged with ensuring profitability and the survival and growth of the enterprise, while in local government, for instance, they will be those concerned with providing the services demanded by the local population, such as refuse collection (the public health officer) well-maintained roads and pavements (the highways engineer) and so on. Staff officers, on the other hand, are normally concerned with subsidiary functions which assist line personnel to carry out their activities in the most efficient manner. Examples are the industrial relations manager whose function is to deal with worker–management problems, the organisation and

methods (O&M) officer whose function is to improve office procedures and systems and the personnel manager who provides an expert service to all line executives in regard to recruitment of staff, welfare and other staff–management matters of a similar nature.

- To be able to pursue his function effectively a staff officer needs a thorough training and substantial experience. This he acquires through dedication to his chosen activity, to the exclusion of the wider aspects of management. His value to his organisation is that he is able to take an objective view of the undertaking he serves so far as the operation of his function throughout is concerned. His training ensures his objectivity and his position in the organisation ensures freedom from involvement in the day-to-day operations of the concern.

- The running of a line department does not give a line executive the same opportunity to stand back and observe the operation of the organisation as a whole: hence the value of the complementary roles of line and *advisory* staff.

(d) Committee organisation

The previous three types of organisational pattern are often referred to as the traditional or classical forms. To these formal types must be added committee organisation which has become increasingly used in recent years.

- Committee organisation has always been that employed in non-profit-making undertakings such as charities and in central and local government. The increasing complexity of modern industry and the greater participation of workers in certain areas of management decisions (pay and welfare conditions, for example) have led to greater use of committee organisation both in private enterprise and in the industrial sector of public enterprise.

- Management by committee requires that committees be set up to deal with specific areas of activity. In industry a large number of committees are concerned with problems concerning staff and industrial relations. These will be serviced by members both from management and from workers. Other committees operating might be design committees, safety committees and so on. Local government has committees for all the areas for which it is responsible, for example, the highways committee, the housing committee and the finance committee.

- Members of a committee may be either appointed or elected, depending upon the circumstances of the case. In some committees both methods may be adopted. For instance, a wage-negotiating committee may consist of members from management who have been appointed because of their position in the concern and workers' representatives who have been elected by the work-force.

- The authority a committee has must be clearly defined and differs from committee to committee. Some do have executive power, particularly in local government, although generally this is not so. Most committees'

authority is limited to giving advice and recommendations to management, which may or may not be heeded.
- The advantages and disadvantages of this type of organisation pattern may be said to be:

Advantages
1 Problems are considered from more than one point of view with the result that better-balanced decisions are more likely to be taken than if they are the province of one individual.
2 Expert advice is available to committees, either because members are experts in their fields or through an expert being co-opted. Most committees have the power to co-opt outside advice.
3 Where committee members come from different sectors of the organisation a greater understanding of each other's difficulties in day-to-day administration is likely.
4 Because of 3 better co-ordination in the implementation of decisions is likely to result.

Disadvantages
1 By their very nature committees are prone to slowness in reaching decisions. Discussion has to take place and the larger the committee the more time is taken up in discussion. A strong chairman is required to keep members from being too talkative.
2 Committee decisions are collective decisions. Hence no individual responsibility can be fixed in relation to the decisions arrived at. No member has power to act on his own.
3 Decisions are often the result of compromise between the various viewpoints, rather than the result of persuasion to a single point of view. This can lead to imprecise recommendations and actions. (It is said that a camel is a horse designed by a committee, which vividly illustrates this point.)
4 The slowness with which committees are prone to act may have an adverse effect on the day-to-day operations of the organisation.
5 A dominant member of the committee, often the chairman, can push through his views by force of personality.

- No undertaking could operate successfully by means of the committee pattern of organisation alone, even if each committee had executive powers. It is too slow and too unwieldly. Consequently, committee organisation must operate within the context of a line or a line-and-staff organisation. Even in a trade union, where it is normal to have an executive committee to make operational decisions, such decisions require a line organisation for their implementation.
- A further problem encountered with the committee structure is that of communication. The passing on of decisions and instructions verbally, though sometimes the method used in various undertakings, is not without risk. Even where a proposal, after discussion, has been formally put and voted upon it is still possible that individual committee members will leave the meeting with a less than clear idea of the exact decision

agreed. In these circumstances erroneous actions may be put into operation, albeit in good faith.

- It is essential, therefore, that the business transacted at committee meetings be properly recorded in formal minutes, and that these minutes be circulated to all those affected before the actions arising out of the decisions taken are put into effect (see **15.7–15.11** below). Not only does this practice ensure that decisions are correctly interpreted, but also it helps to prevent the circulation of false rumours, or to quash them if they have arisen. Where possible, it is also advantageous if the individuals responsible for acting on the decisions taken, or for implementing them, are named in the minutes.

- It is sometimes not realised that in business the most powerful committee is the board of directors and it is, of course, one with executive authority. Furthermore it is one that is required by law and is governed by legal and internal regulations. Minutes are required to be kept of the decisions taken at the meetings which are at once a record and a communication of the business transacted.

8.4 Informal organisation

The traditional forms of organisation pattern just described are based upon the work to be done and how it fits into a formal organisation structure. Workers are placed in situations according to the tasks to be carried out without regard to the personal needs of the people concerned. This provides a neat hierarchical pattern easy to identify. The primary concern is the achievement of management objectives.

- The development over the past few decades of a less rigid social structure in the world at large has had its impact on workers' attitudes, and this change has been reflected in attitudes to the organisational structure of all forms of undertaking. This phenomenon has been made the subject of study by social scientists who have introduced the concept of informal, or organic, organisation. They maintain that a worker's main interest lies in achieving a satisfying life and that in consequence he is not interested in the attainment of his employer's economic goals, but rather in his own aspirations: to this extent the aims of the undertaking and those of the individual worker sometimes conflict. These social scientists also suggest that, despite the existence of a formal organisational structure, workers will tend to form themselves into organic groups by skills or other interests, and that the undertaking as a whole should be looked at not as an economic organism, but rather as an association of many working groups.

- Where this theory is applied on a practical basis it takes the form of group working. In these cases workers are formed into integrated working groups so that each group consists of the various skills required to make a complete component. This is in contrast to the normal work pattern where each worker is on a production line doing only one task and not seeing any end-product. These 'organic' groupings provide some work satisfaction to those involved and prove preferable to the usual, more sterile, type of work situation. Initially employers found this workstation method of working economically unsatisfactory. However experience gained over recent years has shown that this type of organisation can be very profitable and is beneficial to human relations.

- Nevertheless, it is now recognised by many employers that though a formal organisation pattern is required to ensure adherence to management planning, some form of informal organisation needs to be married to this to take care of the social needs of the work-people, and thus to ensure a happy and efficient work-force.

8.5 Matrix organisation

At first sight matrix organisation seems to have all the characteristics of functional organisation, in that functions are isolated and carried out by specialists. However, in point of fact this system is a hybrid formed from a combination of line and functional organisation.

- Each function to be employed is made the subject of a specific grouping of specialists under a functional manager. At the same time each specialist is a member of the line staff of an operating department under a line manager. In effect each member of staff is subject to two sources of authority, that of his specialist manager and that of his operational manager. The former is responsible for his team's technical performance, while the latter is responsible for all other aspects of staff matters such as discipline, welfare and so on. The specialist teams service all operating departments wherever and whenever their special expertise is required.
- This type of organisation is very common in colleges of further and higher education where, for instance, there may be a department for professional studies devoted to preparing students for the examinations of the various professional bodies. The head of this department will be a line manager with a staff of people with various qualifications teaching various subjects such as accounting, economics, management and so on. Other departments will also be staffed by specialists under a line head, and some of these staff may also teach accounting or economics. Such might be the case in a department of management studies for example.
- In matrix organisation the specialist accountants, economists and others will also be grouped in divisions according to their speciality, under the control of a head of division. Thus, each accounting lecturer will be responsible to two managers, the head of department and the head of division. All subject-servicing will be done by the divisions for the departments, and although staff are attached to a particular department

the head of that department will have to request the use of such staff from the division head for his department's courses.

- The benefits claimed to flow from matrix organisation are that there is a concentration of functional expertise which gives rise to cross-fertilisation of ideas within the functional division, that there is a consistency of application wherever a particular function is employed, that it maximises the use of manpower and that it is administratively convenient. Further, the fact that interdisciplinary teams are created by the coming together of specialists within the authority of the line managers stimulates competition and innovation while encouraging co-ordination and co-operation, to the benefit of the organisation generally.

- Against these advantages must be set the fact that there is no unity of command which gives rise to the possibility of divided loyalties on the part of the staff concerned. Further, there is evidence that it can lead to the development of a narrow outlook by the division and particularly on the part of the head of division, despite the possibility of enhanced co-operation as stated above.

- Experience also shows that divisional heads can try to usurp the authority of the departmental heads, which can lead to conflict and so have a detrimental effect on the smooth running of the organisation as a whole. Finally, matrix organisation can be administratively costly to operate.

8.6   Organisational styles

Three concepts or styles of organisation which can be found as part of the main organisation structure should be mentioned:

(a) **Bureaucratic organisation.** This occurs where formal procedures are rigidly adhered to and there is little or no provision for exceptions. It is found particularly in local government and in organisations where work people are allowed little discretion.

Its virtue is that it provides what might be termed 'programmed decisions', and the hierarchical structure is well defined.

Its disadvantages are that response to change is slow, the rigid adherence to rules discourages initiative and communication is usually slow.

(b) **Contingency organisation.** This concept is akin to the law of the situation as expressed in **10.2** below. The organisation structure is fluid and is determined by the current factors of the environment, developing technology, the changing size of the enterprise and its personnel. It could be said to be the opposite of bureaucratic organisation, particularly in its response to change.

(c) **Just-in-Time organisation.** Generally known as JIT, this system of organisation is mainly applicable to production in manufacturing industries and to retailers. Fundamentally it seeks to minimise stock-holding (in one case no stock at all was held and purchases were made locally as and when required to be used). Obviously such a system requires tight liaison with suppliers, who must be of proven reliability as regards delivery times. A high standard of product quality must also be assured in purchases so that there is no disruption to production flow through faulty goods. JIT also calls for a high degree of responsibility in the affected work people so that the undoubtedly tight supply and demand schedules are met. In fact, the reliability of staff is vital in this respect.

The advantages of JIT are the minimising of stock levels so freeing cash that would otherwise be locked up in stock and the reduction of the risk attendant in holding large stocks. Another advantage is the reduction in possibly expensive floor space otherwise required to store stock.

Its disadvantages are the necessary reliance on third parties for continuous supplies and the need for very highly motivated staff.

Questions

1 Line and staff relationships are often thought to be a source of conflict. Taking account of the roles and responsibilities of line and staff positions, what factors may lead to conflict? How may such conflict be handled? **(ICSA)**

2 A company owns and operates 50 small hotels in its home country, 30 more in five other countries of the EEC, and six in Africa. The hotels are purpose-built to the company's design. Each one has about 25 rooms, a lounge area, and a restaurant in which simple standard food is served. The hotel manager has about ten staff.

You are required to draw an organisation chart (or charts) suitable for this company with notes as appropriate, showing clearly at which levels the important functions of the business are managed. **(CIMA)**

3 You are required
  (a) to describe **four** advantages and **four** disadvantages of committees;
  (b) to give **two** reasons for their increased use. **(CIMA)**

4 **(a)** Differentiate between the 'formal' and the 'informal' organisation structure of an enterprise.
  (b) Discuss the advantages and disadvantages of an 'informal' organisational structure. **(IAM)**

5 Explain, with particular reference to the words underlined, the statement 'a manager who arranges or organises a <u>formal structure</u> determines how <u>authority</u> will be distributed in the total organisation'. **(IAM)**

6 Discuss the advantages and disadvantages of matrix organisation

structures. How may we handle conflicts between the demands of a project, and the demands of the discipline or department within that structure?   **(ICSA)**

7 Distinguish between 'bureaucratic' and 'contingency' concepts of organisation structure.   **(IAM)**

8 Describe Just-In-Time systems, and their effect on organisation and management.   **(CIMA)**

9 Organisation (2)

When an organisation is small it will be centralised: that is, it will consist of one unit and responsibility and authority for all activities will rest with the chief executive (by whatever name he is called). With growth and enlargement, however, it is necessary to consider very carefully how the organisation is to develop: whether an ever larger unit should be planned or whether the unit should be split into parts each with a measure of autonomy. The first is centralisation and the second is decentralisation.

9.1 Centralisation

- This is the practice of having all responsibility and authority concentrated in one place, so that major decisions are made by the central controlling body and little initiative is in the hands of those lower down the management ladder. At its very worst it leads to a situation where all management decisions have to be approved by the chief executive before they can be put into operation: at best it means that line and staff officers can be inhibited from embarking on non-routine courses of action without prior approval from the top. In many cases over-centralisation results in a bureaucratic organisation stilted in outlook and subject to over-administration.
- The increasing complexity of modern organisations, in industry and commerce, and in the public sector, has led to the twin problems of achieving effective control of widespread activities so that policies are properly adhered to, and the necessity to adjust operations at local level to take into account the differing needs of those activities at the point where they take place. An example will make the position clear.
- A chain of retail shops may be centrally controlled and specific policies laid down as to the range and variety of goods to be stocked at each shop. This provides the organisation with the benefits of a restricted stockholding range (with the minimum amount of capital tied up in stock) and the ability to obtain very favourable terms from suppliers because of bulk purchasing. Managers of individual shops will, in these circumstances, be unable to satisfy special local needs outside the stocking policy of head office – the centralised control: in such cases simple customer requests must be denied. A common occurrence, for instance, is the refusal of shops to split prepackaged goods so that a customer must buy, say, twenty-five screws in a packet when he needs only five. It is not only in small domestic items, however, that this

happens. A similar attitude prevails in centrally controlled retail outlets selling expensive goods.

- What are the advantages and disadvantages of centralisation? They may be listed as follows:

Advantages

1 It provides absolute control over the organisation and ensures adherence to laid-down policies.
2 It is administratively convenient: the focal point for each function is readily discernible.
3 It is possible to have common standards throughout the organisation. For instance, salary and wage scales can be standardised; policies on customer relations, granting of credit and similar matters can be the same throughout. In the public sector common procedures for the implementation of regulations can be put into effect; application procedures for building planning permissions is a case in point.
4 It is possible to engage very highly qualified functional experts whose high salaries can be justified only because centralisation enables them to engage exclusively in their specialism because of the heavy work-load.
5 The volumes of administrative work generated by centralisation justify the employment of expensive machinery, which reduces costs in such areas as payroll processing, accounting and stock-control methods.

Disadvantages

1 Control can be become autocratic and inflexible.
2 It can lead to frustration where members of staff, particularly managers and supervisors, are unable to use their discretion but are forced to operate according to inflexible rules.
3 Bureaucratic control methods may be imposed, resulting in a proliferation of forms and rigid procedures, slowing down the operations of the organisation.
4 Managers may see themselves not as independent decision-makers, but rather as order-taking subordinates. This becomes particularly frustrating when they feel that those giving the orders are not sufficiently aware of what is needed at operating level.

- Centralisation to be effective and efficient needs to have unified controls throughout. These include common documentation for all routines and operations, common codes and terminology for the same things throughout, a system of regular reporting from each unit with specific dates and times for the production of these reports, and the appointment of a specific senior officer to ensure compliance with these controls.

9.2   Decentralisation

- Decentralisation (or departmentalisation as it is sometimes called) is, of course, the opposite of centralisation. It occurs where responsibility for various functions and operations is devolved from the centre and rests at the point where operations occur. If the example of the chain of retail stores is again referred to, decentralisation would mean that each shop would be responsible, under its manager, for all the operating functions required to carry on business, such as purchasing, the range of goods stocked and customer service. In this way each decentralised part of the enterprise can be geared to accommodate the specific needs of its operating environment, and can adapt itself to meet those needs without reference to central administration. Decentralisation, of course, does require the services of high-calibre managers who are able to anticipate and provide for local needs. It also poses considerable problems in overall control from top management, and in the integration of the activities of all the decentralised units into the overall strategies of the undertaking.

- The advantages and disadvantages of decentralisation can be set out as follows:

Advantages
1 It provides flexibility to meet changing needs at local level because that is where control resides.
2 It is rewarding to managers and staff because it enables them to exercise their own judgements and initiative and so promotes job satisfaction.
3 It provides good management experience to managers and supervisors. This promotes their personal development and thus their services become of greater value to the organisation.
4 Administrative paperwork may be reduced to a minimum at operating level, though more reporting to central control may be necessary.

Disadvantages
1 Central control is difficult because each section may not be following the same pattern of procedures.
2 In consequence more reporting and inspection may be needed than if control were centralised (as suggested in 4 of advantages above).
3 Because the organisation is, in fact, operating as a series of small units, the benefits of bulk buying, centralised accounting and similar benefits of centralisation are not available. This leads to more costly operation.
4 It is possible that some decentralised sections may develop a narrow-minded, parochial view of the organisation, leading to difficulties in relationships with other sections.

- As in the case of organisation patterns, completely centralised and completely decentralised organisations are very uncommon. The most effective and convenient practice is for there to be a combination of the two, the degree to which an organisation leans towards one or the other depending very largely upon the kinds of activity it pursues. In banking, for instance, though there is a large measure of centralisation, the branches also enjoy a high degree of autonomy. This is partly from tradition and partly because each customer is a problem peculiar to himself and no rigidly applied central rules could cope with the varying requirements at branch level. On the other hand, the grocery supermarkets are highly centralised, all buying and pricing, for instance, being done by headquarters. This is so that they can take advantage of their huge buying power to affect manufacturers' prices and so as to be able to make strategic and tactical decisions over their whole operations to meet competition from rivals.

9.3　Divisionalisation

- 'Decentralisation' is the term used to describe the dividing up of activities of an organisation while still retaining a central controlling function within the framework of that organisation. This is so, for example, when a retail chain gives autonomy to its branches for purchasing, accounting and so on, but retains overall control within the organisation for major planning and general management authority.
- When an enterprise becomes very large, or when it grows by taking over other organisations, particularly if they operate in different spheres, then the need to divisionalise arises. This usually comes about because the undertaking has become too large to administer from one central control owing to a variety of reasons which include:

(a) Difficulties in establishing and maintaining effective lines of communication because of sheer size.

(b) Similar difficulties because the various activities of the enterprise are spread over a geographically wide area (this is especially relevant to multi-national corporations).

(c) Widely diverse activities with little or no relation to each other, an example being a company engaged in the manufacture of farm chemicals, pharmaceuticals and paint.

- Simply stated, divisionalisation involves carrying on diverse activities by means of subsidiary or associated independent organisations, central control being vested in a separate organisation. In industrial and commercial practice this is best exemplified by a holding company and its subsidiaries. Each subsidiary company has its own board of directors and managing director and has, virtually, a free hand in pursuing its objectives. It is, however, subject to the overriding authority of the holding company and its board, from whence the overall strategic planning of the group will derive.
- Co-ordination of the activities of the various divisions is achieved by the simple expedient of having the managing director, and maybe other directors, from each subsidiary company on the board of the controlling company. Further, it is also usual for there to be set up executive

committees drawn from the boards of the group companies which will meet more frequently than the central board of directors and are thus able to resolve inter-group problems and difficulties without the necessity to call a meeting of the full board.

- The advantages and disadvantages of divisionalisation are very similar to those obtaining in decentralisation. However, it has further merit in that it provides opportunities to take advantage of large-scale working, and the member companies have the benefit of the backing of a powerful central management team.

9.4 Delegation

Since it is patently impossible for one chief executive, one local government official, or even one executive committee to carry out all the functions and duties necessary for an organisation to operate effectively, it is necessary to pass on authority to subordinates to pursue certain activities. This process is known as 'delegation': without it no undertaking larger than that manageable by one person doing every duty can exist. In fact, it is one of the major functions of effective management.

- The process of delegation relieves a manager from involvement in the day-to-day detail of running his particular function, but at the same time does not absolve him from the responsibility of ensuring that the duties he has delegated are correctly and efficiently performed. It does mean, however, that he can spend more time in the pursuit of his primary function of managing – pursuing objectives, making decisions and dealing with problems of policy.
- Just as a manager finds it necessary to delegate, so at every level of management and supervision delegation has to take place, either because of the need for specialist knowledge which the delegator does not possess or because of the amount of work he has to perform and which becomes physically impossible by virtue of its volume. In the first case, for example, the managing director may not have specialist production knowledge; thus he delegates the management of the production function to a production manager. Equally, the production manager's work-load may make it impossible for him to supervise personally each production shop so he will appoint a shop foreman for each process – that is, he delegates his power to the foreman to supervise the workers at operational level. Authority is thus passed on to the delegate and he has power to act on behalf of the delegator. Nevertheless, though authority is delegated, responsibility is not; it passes right back to the top, i.e. to the managing director, because the foremen are accountable to the production manager and he, in turn, is accountable to the managing director.
- Many people in positions of authority find it difficult to delegate; sometimes because they feel that their subordinates are not adequate;

sometimes because they, themselves, feel insecure and they are reluctant to relinquish any power; and sometimes because they think they may become out of touch with the day-to-day events in their sphere of activity. Nevertheless, effective management relies on proper delegation and a competent manager or supervisor recognises this. It is not enough, however, for a manager or supervisor to delegate aspects of his work and then to sit back and await results. Delegation must be planned properly and adequate monitoring must be put into effect. A delegator must therefore:

(a) Determine what tasks are most suitable for delegation, both from the point of view of his own overall work responsibilities and from the point of view of the organisational benefit.

(b) Select very carefully the subordinate to whom authority is to be delegated, from the aspect of the delegate's competence and in respect of his personal qualities.

(c) Specify very carefully the duties to be taken over, and the limits of the authority invested in the delegate.

(d) Ensure that the delegate is properly acquainted with (c) and provide guidance and training if and when necessary.

(e) Ensure that the authority delegated is fully commensurate with the responsibilities the delegate has to assume. It is not only useless but also patently unjust to require duties to be properly performed without at the same time giving sufficient authority to accomplish them.

(f) Allow the delegate to carry out his duties with as little interference as possible, after having ascertained that he is competent to perform the tasks delegated to him. After all, the purpose of delegation is to free the delegator of the burden he has delegated. Further, the responsibility undertaken should increase the competence, self-confidence and potential of the delegate.

(g) Despite (f), ensure that some form of checking is instituted to ascertain that the delegate is performing effectively. As has been pointed out, delegation does not absolve the delegator from responsibility for the work delegated. It has been said, with truth, that inspection is the corollary of delegation. What form the checking will take depends upon the status of the delegate. At the lower levels of supervision physical inspection is not only simplest, it is expected. However, nearer the top of the management ladder inspection must be more covert, and may take the form of reports and the like.

- It cannot be emphasised too strongly that the ability to delegate effectively is an essential attribute in a successful manager. Failure to do so results in a work overload, less than accurate decisions, and leads to stress. Failure to delegate also gives staff the impression that the manager does not trust them to work efficiently, which can result in resentment and a lowering of morale.

9.5 Span of control

Sometimes known as 'span of management' or 'span of responsibility', span of control refers to the number of subordinates who can be effectively supervised directly by one manager, supervisor or other person in authority.

- Sometimes the number six is given as the effective span, but this is too simplistic to fit all but a few cases. The number, in fact, depends on several circumstances and it is not possible to use a rule-of-thumb guide. It has been shown that as the number of subordinates supervised increases so the number of relationships between them and their supervisor also increases but disproportionately, which is itself a limiting factor.
- As a point of interest mention may be made of V. A. Graicunas, a management consultant who in 1933 published a paper in which he formulated a theory on the span of control, showing mathematically by formula how the number of relationships increases disproportionately as the number of subordinates under control increases. Graicunas's reasoning and formula, both theoretical, are complex and do not concern us here, but the difficulties experienced as the number of subordinates grows must be recognised and remembered.
- Besides the complexity of relationships other circumstances affect the span of control and are, perhaps, less subject to theoretical argument. They certainly must be taken into account when determining the amount of supervision an organisation needs and the number of supervisory levels that will have to be arranged. These may be stated as:

(a) **The abilities of those being supervised.** If they are competent and well trained they will need less supervision than if the reverse is the case.

(b) **The complexity of the work being done.** If the work is complicated more queries arise and closer supervision is needed. If the work is simple less supervision is required and more workers can be directly controlled by one supervisor.

(c) **The consistency of operations.** If the work varies a good deal of supervision will have to be given, and it will have to be constant. Thus fewer workers will be able to be supervised than if the operations are, and will remain, the same over a long period.

(d) **How effective communications are.** The supervisor must be able to make his instructions clear and understandable to his work-people otherwise queries will result and more time will be needed for supervision per worker. Equally, workers must also make themselves easily understood by their supervisor otherwise the same result will obtain. More time spent with each worker means that fewer people can be controlled.

(e) **The ability and personality of the supervisor.** If he is technically competent and fully conversant with the work of his subordinates his workers will be inclined to respect him and need less supervision. If he appears incompetent he will find it more difficult to be accepted and supervision will suffer. Equally, if he has human feeling, is understanding and patient he will generate loyalty and supervision will be easier than if he is abrasive so making his workers reluctant to co-operate.

(f) **Labour turnover.** Where there is a constantly changing work-force the need to keep training newcomers and supervising them closely until they become fully competent means that fewer can be controlled than if they are all fully trained and experienced.

- It is of the nature of things that the span of management is narrowest at the top and widest at the bottom. The managing director may have accountable to him just four or five departmental or functional senior executives: a foreman on the shop floor, making a simple component, may be responsible for the supervision of 20 or more workers.

9.6   Organisational relationships

Every pattern of organisation gives rise to relationships between the people who comprise it, and these can be classified into four categories as follows:

(a) **Direct**

This type of relationship exists between the manager and the managed. It is the relationship that flows down the chain of command, as exists in line organisation. Referring to Figure 8.1 (p. 68) it will be seen that the marketing manager has a direct relationship with his home sales manager, and similarly the latter has a direct relationship with his sales representatives and, of course, the reverse is the situation in both cases. Direct authority and accountability exists in this form of relationship, which is also known as the line or executive relationship.

(b) **Indirect**

This is a functional relationship and exists where advisory (or staff) officers are present in an organisation and where their expertise is available for use by the line officers. It is shown clearly in the line-and-staff organisation chart at Figure 8.3 (p. 72). Here it will be seen that the management services manager (a staff appointment) has an indirect relationship with the financial accountant (a line officer). He can guide and advise the accountant but cannot instruct him in the operation of his accounting system.

(c) **Representative (or staff)**

This relationship must not be confused with the advisory function of a staff officer in a line-and-staff organisation. It is unfortunate that the same term, 'staff', is so frequently employed when reference is made to the representative relationship. This form of relationship exists between an executive and his personal assistant. It is an especially difficult one for the assistant concerned because he has no delegated authority to make decisions for his executive, yet because of his close association with his chief other members of staff are inclined to assume that he has this power. It is a frequent source of misunderstanding and possible resentment. A refusal to act or make a decision is often seen as an unco-operative attitude, despite the fact that the personal assistant has no authority. Being the assistant to the managing director is not the same as being the assistant managing director, though to third parties the two positions are often confused.

(d) **Lateral**

Often called 'horizontal relationships', lateral relationships exist between executives, supervisors and staff at the same level of responsibility and authority in different departments. They exist for purposes of co-operation and co-ordination and no organisation could function effectively without them. There is no direct authority flowing along the lines of lateral relationships and activities are agreed and co-ordinated by consent. Examples of this type of relationship are that between the sales manager and the production manager, perhaps about matters of product delivery, and between the accounts credit controller and the sales office manager about a customer's credit rating.

9.7   Simplifying management levels

- As organisations grow there is a tendency to increase the number of levels of management to ensure adequate supervision of staff. Slavish adherence to the rules of delegation and span of control given previously in this chapter may give rise to this condition.
- Recently, however, many large businesses have started to question the need for such a proliferation and have begun to reduce the number of levels of middle and senior management. This process shortens the lines of vertical communication and so improves its speed and its accuracy. As a consequence decisions and action are speeded up.
- Long lines of communication slow down communication and can lead to distortion. A saving in overhead costs also results when the number of management levels is reduced.
- This process, however, has its disadvantage. It means that the span of control of the remaining managers is widened. Unless the managers concerned and the staff they supervise are highly competent and highly motivated there is likely to be a diminution in the efficiency of the organisation.

___ **Questions** ___

1 'Effective delegation is often preached but rarely practised.' Outline the essential actions a manager should take if delegation is to be effective.   **(ICSA)**

2 In what ways will the extent of decentralisation in an organisation create impetus for greater accountability of individual departmental managers to the top management team?   **(ICSA)**

3 Henry has for some time been in charge of a department which was producing satisfactory results before he took over. However, recently, several of his staff have asked whether jobs in other similar departments are available. There have also been a number of unexpected mistakes, and information has not been transmitted properly.

   You are Henry's manager. As a result of your concern you have been keeping an eye on the situation. You have found that Henry comes in early every day, stays late, takes large amounts of work home with him, and is showing definite signs of strain.

   In the meantime his staff appear bored and uninterested. You are required to describe

   (a)   possible causes of this situation;

   (b)   what you would do to determine the true cause;

   (c)   with reasons, the changes you propose.   **(CIMA)**

4 'Responsibility' and 'Accountability' are terms often misused in relation to delegation. Define each and clarify your answer with examples.   **(IAM)**

5 Some business organisations are highly centralised with power concentrated in head office. Discuss the possible advantages and drawbacks of this type of organisation structure.   **(IComA)**

6 In recent years many organisations have adopted 'flatter' organisation structures reducing the number of levels of management. Discuss the possible benefits and dangers of this policy.
   (IComA)

7 Some administrative activities lend themselves to centralisation whereas others are less easily organised in that way. Select an activity with which you are familiar, and state the problems associated with making it central to a large organisation.   **(IAM)**

8 Line and staff relationships are found in many organisations. Briefly differentiate between these two relationships, and discuss how, in a large manufacturing organisation, they could create inter-personal problems, and suggest how such problems might be overcome.   **(IM)**

⬡10 **Direction or command**

In all human enterprise, in whatever sphere it exists, wherever a group of people are concerned with achieving specified objectives there arises the need to have someone with ultimate responsibility; in other words a leader or commander to whom authority is given to direct the group's activities and to assume command of the resources devoted to the requirements of the enterprise.

The word 'command' suggests a rather military arrangement that demands unquestioning adherence to orders or instructions from the top, and while this may have been the case in the past, this is not so in the modern industrial society. Most instructions nowadays are, in fact, presented in the form of requests rather than in the form of orders, albeit they may have the same ultimate effect. People at all levels, from departmental managers to shop-floor workers, are sensitive of their personal value and are inclined to resent any tacit suggestion, which may be implied in an order, that they are unable to think for themselves or have no opinions. It is suggested, in fact, that less than a third of the orders given to subordinates take the form of firm instructions.

10.1   Chain of command

However command is carried out, in effect it starts at the top and, through the process of delegation, travels down the management structure to find the level at which action is required. Each level of command, therefore, has a narrower sphere of influence than the one above it and a narrower field of accountability. It is also a fact that the span of authority also narrows in the same way. On a line organisation chart this is shown very clearly, as illustrated in Figure 8.1 (p. 68).

The level at which direction is given also affects the type of instruction that results. Instructions from the upper levels of management, from the chief executive or the senior executives for example, may be subject to judgement by higher and middle managers on the various aspects of the content of the instructions. At the lower levels of supervision instructions will, for the most part, be laid down according to specific rules and a minimum of individual judgement will be required.

10.2   'The law of the situation'

- In a small organisation the chain of command is obvious with or without an organisation chart. As organisations have become more complex, and particularly where there is decentralisation, the chain of command becomes much less obvious and direct commands are less easy to give and have accepted. Departments have become specialised and top management's command is not so much related to its own exclusive views as to the furtherance of plans that have been formulated in consultation with the specialists and on their advice. In fact it is often asserted that plans and objectives are now very much influenced from below and that command is thus as much by consent as by direction.

- In turn this leads to the setting up of a code of standard practices that are required to meet the requirements of the plans, and workers no longer obey orders as much as adhere to standard practices. These standard practices are developed out of the needs establishing themselves to meet circumstances as they arise in pursuit of the plans laid down, and workers expect to be relied upon to take the steps necessary to deal with the situation. Direct instructions, in these circumstances, can be resented by workers unless their precise relevance is demonstrated. If such direct orders are considered necessary the workers expect to have this necessity explained. In other words a worker needs to be satisfied that direct instructions result only because of the facts of the situation, and are not given as an expression of authority only. Mary Parker Follett, an accepted authority on the use of power and authority in industry, expressed this concept as 'the law of the situation'. Nowadays it is suggested that the exercise of authority or power should be replaced by the personal influence of the manager in the relationship between the manager and the managed, at whatever level it occurs.

10.3   Unity of command

As was shown when functional organisation was discussed in **8.3 (b)** above, people are apt to become confused if they are answerable to more than one authority. In the direction of an enterprise this is also very true and hence it is considered essential that there should be what is termed 'unity of command', that is there should be only one source giving directions.

This is usually taken to mean that one manager only should be in the position of commander, this person normally being the chief executive. It is true that he is the ultimate authority, but it is unrealistic to suppose that he can act entirely on his own. It is probably truer to say that unity of command entails top management speaking with one voice: in other words that differences at board level or among senior executives are resolved before instructions are issued, and that no dissension is observable by those being managed.

Lower down the management ladder the same observations apply. No worker should be required to accept orders from more than one supervisor, neither should any department or division be the subject of the command of more than one manager.

10.4   Difficulties in achieving effective command

The difficulties in achieving effective command are primarily those of failures in communication, which will be discussed in Chapter 14, and failure to achieve positive unity in authority; in other words failure to ensure unity of command.

- Unity of command must be seen to obtain. Jealousies or other personal disagreements must be kept within the confines of the boardroom and not allowed to become the subject of common knowledge, as this can destroy confidence down the line. The authority of the chief executive must be maintained at all times, and be seen to have the backing of the board or other governing body.
- Another difficulty leading to a reduction in effective command is the failure to ensure that the duties and scope of each department or division are very clearly defined, and there is no overlap. A simple example is where both the sales department and the production department have direct access to customers. This results in a dilution of the authority of the sales department in customer relations and the inevitable reduction in effective overall command, because each of these departments will try to assume control of a common aspect of the product with a probable divergence from laid-down procedures. It is very necessary, therefore, that clear lines of demarcation are laid down for each sector of the enterprise to ensure that command is effective.
- However, it must be accepted that unity of command may not be absolutely possible in some circumstances, and that exceptions must be accepted which will not necessarily create difficulties in practice. Citing the example just mentioned, it is common practice in highly technical industries for a member of the production staff to have to follow up the contact of a sales representative to clarify certain technical aspects of a customer's order which the salesman is not competent to resolve. In such circumstances, of course, the utmost co-operation must obtain between the two departments. Similarly, the credit control department may call on the assistance of the sales people to help in resolving a customer's financial difficulties on the basis that the sales representative is likely to know the customer and his business better than does the credit control clerk.
- There are many more such circumstances that could be mentioned. If effective command is to be maintained in these conditions it is essential that trust and confidence is built up between the participants and full co-operation is developed.

10.5   Decision-making

Inherent in the activity of command is the need to make decisions and it can be said with truth that, fundamentally, all management is concerned with decision-making. Also inherent in the activity of command is the need to delegate authority and functions, and so the power to make certain decisions has also to be delegated. It is necessary, therefore, to examine the process of decision-making from the point of view of the levels at which it operates.

There is no consensus of opinion among writers on management as to the categories into which decision-making should be divided, but a useful classification as shown by practical experience could be as follows:

1 **Long-range decisions** that will affect the prospects of the organisation for a very long time. These are almost certainly the province of top management, who are charged with the responsibility of the continued survival and prosperity of the enterprise. Such decisions include major capital investment, determining the sources of finance for such investment, product and market choice, and similar long-term problems. Such decisions embrace a considerable amount of uncertainty and take a long time for the results of their implementation to be known. They are essentially strategic.

2 **Medium-term decisions** that are less far-reaching, involving problems such as minor capital investment, product modification, tactical market planning and similar decisions that are needed to keep the enterprise on course in the implementation of top-level planning and objectives.

3 **Operational decisions** that have immediate results and are, or should be, taken at the lower levels of supervision. Such decisions include, for example, replenishment of stocks, routes for deliveries, credit control in normal circumstances and so on. All decisions can be reduced to a sequence of activities as shown in Figure 10.1. It will be seen that inherent in the implementation of a decision is the need to have feedback as to its effectiveness so that modifications to the instructions

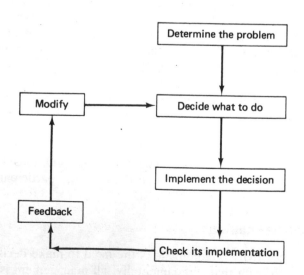

Fig. 10.1 Basic steps in decision-making

can be issued where necessary to ensure the ultimate success of the decision.

10.6 Steps to effective decision-making

Many managers and their subordinate supervisors shirk the responsibility of making decisions, and give many reasons such as not having sufficient knowledge of all the facts, difficulty in finding competent operating staff, lack of time for proper consideration and so on. Very often the real reason is lack of courage or lack of self-confidence: but even not making a decision is a decision to refrain from action. Other managers and supervisors rush into decisions without due regard for circumstances or resultant effects, sometimes with disastrous results, and sometimes with unexpected success.

Neither of these attitudes, of course, is the right one, and decision-making can be made easier and more effective by taking the following, considered, steps:

1 Define as accurately as possible the problem to be solved. This entails going into detail about every aspect of the problem and making sure no relevant facts are omitted, however remote they may appear to be at first sight.
2 Ascertain the relevance of this problem to other areas that might be affected by any decision taken.
3 Analyse the problem into its component parts so that each can be considered fully.
4 Review the resources available to solve the problem, or those that can be provided if necessary.
5 Determine as many possible solutions as can be reasonably considered given the circumstances as stated.
6 Test the most attractive solutions on the basis of their probable success and their impact on the rest of the organisation.
7 Determine the solution that promises to be the most effective.
8 Implement the decision and monitor its effectiveness.

It is obvious that not all these steps will be necessary at operational level, but they may be thought essential for long-term and medium-term decision-making.

10.7 Programmed and non-programmed decision-making

It is also common to divide decision-making into programmed and non-programmed, and it is considered good management practice to have as many decisions as possible in the first category.

• Programmed decisions are simply those that are taken automatically in any given set of circumstances. They are thus those normally taken at the lower levels of supervision. An example is that of stock replenishment. If it is a rule that the stock of a certain product should not fall below one hundred units, then the decision by the storekeeper to replenish the stock when this level is being reached is a programmed one. The amount to be ordered will also be programmed by the setting of a maximum stockholding figure, the reorder amount being the difference between maximum and existing stock. This decision is now commonly made by computer, where an automatic reorder request is produced: a perfect example of programmed decision-making.

- Non-programmed decisions require the exercise of managerial judgement, and the higher up the management hierarchy the decisions are required to be made the greater the exercise of judgement that is required. A decision to invest large sums of money in new buildings and plant requires judgement of a very high order and is done at the level of top management.

- However, judgement at all levels is required where the decision is not automatic. Taking the case of stock replenishment again as an example, should the firm be offered a quantity of the product at a very attractive price, but this would mean departing from the laid-down stockholding level, a judgement would have to be made as to the wisdom of departing from the normal holding. This requires a decision of a non-programmed kind even though it may be taken at a low level of management. It involves assessing the risks of having stock left on hand, of tying up working capital which, perhaps, could be better used in other ways, of taking up storage space and other associated problems.

10.8   Where decisions are made

Every level of management and supervision is responsible for making decisions within its own environment.

- The extent to which such decisions are matters of judgement and experience depends upon the level at which they are taken and the extent of initiative allowed at each level by top management. However, it is often said that all decisions are really made on the shop floor. This is because the implementation of decisions, at whatever level they are taken, depends ultimately upon their acceptability by the general work-force. Even the installation of the most modern equipment, decided upon by top management, will not be effective in production if the workers refuse to operate it. Without their agreement the decision is a sterile one, so their consent must be assured before implementation.

- Similarly, many of the factors upon which decisions are made emanate from the shop-floor. Such items as production levels, machine utilisation, job sharing and the like are shop-floor-level factors which management must take into account.

- Many organisations, cognisant of this fact, now have regular consultations with employees before taking significant decisions that will affect working conditions, pay and job security. This is approved by many as a step towards industrial democracy and certainly entails the involvement of the labour-force in the making of important decisions. In turn, this should lead to the co-operation of the work-force in the implementation of the decisions. On the other hand, it is undeniable that the viewpoint of the workers will be limited to seeing their own advantage and disadvantage and they will probably be unable to appreciate the long-term significance of decisions suggested to them. In this case it might mean a slowing up of modernisation, and probably a measure of overmanning, which would appeal to the employees more readily than possible redundancies however well-managed the redundancy scheme, and so possibly to the ultimate detriment of the enterprise.

10.9   Aids to top-level decision-making

Long-term decisions are fraught with the problems of uncertainty, and errors can have the most far-reaching repercussions. Yet decisions have to be made for the future of the organisation if it is to survive.

- To try to take some of the risk out of these decisions management now makes use of many sophisticated techniques, mostly mathematical or statistical, some of which are touched on in Chapter 24. It must be remembered, however, that these are only tools to aid managers and do not usurp their responsibility to exercise their own judgement born of their own knowledge and experience. Unfortunately it is a fact that many of the specialists in these mathematical and statistical techniques do sometimes give the impression that their contributions are the complete answer to managerial decision-making.
- The findings of these specialists are only part of the range of factors that management has to consider in its deliberations: management decisions must remain within the judgement of the managers, whatever tools they use.

10.10   Rationality of decisions

So far decision-making has been examined on the basis that the decisions are arrived at rationally given the factors known and recognised, even though there may be elements of uncertainty. Unfortunately this may not always be the case. Some decisions are arrived at through the influence of personal prejudice by the decision-maker (for instance a bias for a particular make of machine), political manoeuvring between the parties involved in the decision-making, nepotism, and the degree of risk acceptable to the decision-makers.

10.11 Decisions by committee

The question of committee organisation has been dealt with in **8.3 (d)** above. The main function of a committee is to make decisions, and because such bodies are made up of people with diverse views and experiences, including prejudices, the decision-making process can be both very difficult and prolonged.

- However, some rules can be formulated to expedite the process and to make decisions easier to achieve:
  1 There should be a properly appointed chairman of the committee and he should be, and be seen to be, fair and without bias. He should have the ability to lead a discussion and should be able to draw all members into participation. He must be objective.

  Where the rules permit the chairman to have a casting vote in the event of a tie in members' voting he should cast it to maintain the status quo. Unfortunately nowadays this tradition is not always followed, and sometimes causes anger among some committee members.

  2 There should be formal procedures for the conduct of discussions leading to decisions and the chairman should ensure that these are adhered to. A formal method of agreeing a decision or a consensus should be part of the rules, the most usual method being by voting.

  3 In the composition of the committee there should be a sufficient number of members of wide enough knowledge and experience to be able to make reasoned judgements.

  4 Care should be taken that no decisions are arrived at through the influence of a *clique*. Neither should a decision be arrived at during the temporary absence of a participant. It has been known, for example, for a vote to be taken on a closely fought issue while a dissenter has been temporarily out of the committee room visiting the cloakroom. This type of action leads to resentment and can bring the committee or its chairman, whose duty it is to maintain fairness, into disrepute.

  5 Everything should be done to ensure that the committee or group meeting is not used as a means of delaying a firm decision unless this is the deliberate intention. It is not unknown for a committee, a sub-committee or a working party to be set up for the precise purpose of delaying action.

- What has been outlined for committees also applies to other decision-making groups. In these circumstances, though, procedures may be less formal and a more relaxed attitude prevail. Nevertheless it aids efficiency if a group leader is chosen to exercise general control over the discussions.

Questions

1 The process of management may be defined as comprising planning, organising, directing and controlling. Describe each of these activities, illustrating your answer using examples with which you are familiar.   **(ACCA)**

2 What are the essential differences between the approach to decision-making at the strategic level and at the operations level? Demonstrate these differences by reference to a typical example of a decision at each level.   **(CIMA)**

3 The term 'unity of command' means that each subordinate should be accountable to only one superior. Describe **two** situations where this principle might reasonably be violated by a company.   **(CIM)**

4 'In business, from the factory floor to the boardroom, decision-making by consent is replacing traditional autocracy.' Discuss.   **(CIM)**

5 Can decision-making be an entirely rational process? In what ways is decision-making limited by inadequate information and by the style of management in an organisation?   **(ICSA)**

6 How could group decision-making be made more effective?   **(IAM)**

⑪ Co-ordination

Co-ordination is the integration and synchronisation of the various activities of an organisation in order that all its functions can work harmoniously towards its common objectives. In effect it can be described as 'organisation in time' because timing is of the essence if co-ordination is to be effectively achieved. An example will make this clear.

- If a manufacturer decides to launch a new product it will entail the provision of finance to provide materials and equipment for its manufacture and marketing, it will have to be put into production and it will need a marketing and selling campaign to bring it to the attention of potential consumers. Each of these activities will have to be co-ordinated – that is, timed – so that funds are available to finance the initiation of the project or it will not be able to start, the marketing effort must be put in hand early enough to create consumer interest ready for the sale of the products directly they start coming off the production line, and manufacture must be timed so that units of production are available to meet orders as soon as they come in. A failure in the timing of any one of these activities will mean a failure to achieve maximum results from the product.
- Lack of finance at the right time may delay the start of production or of the marketing campaign: failure to time the marketing effort correctly will result either in stocks of manufactured goods awaiting customers' orders, so locking up working capital and storage space, or in lack of goods available for delivery to customers so that goodwill suffers. Failure to harmonise productive effort with selling effort will lead to goods being in stock unnecessarily, or to disappointed customers.
- Co-ordination of the activities of all the functions of an enterprise, therefore, is clearly of the utmost importance to the success of that enterprise because all functions are interdependent: the failure of one section of the organisation to meet its required objectives can jeopardise the success of the other functions that rely upon it, as the example indicates. Further, co-ordination is a continuing requirement which needs constant attention if it is not to fail at some point with detrimental consequences for the organisation. Failure to purchase materials at the right time may delay production; delayed production may result in non-delivery to customers on the promised or contract dates; non-delivery according to customer requirements may mean loss of goodwill and actual loss of customers which, in turn, may mean loss of revenue.

11.1 Planning for co-ordination

Co-ordination does not happen by itself: it has to be planned and the very act of planning emphasises the need for it to function properly.

- Co-ordination is much easier to achieve if the means to do so are recognised and worked out at the beginning of a project rather than after it has been progressing for some time. This is true whether the project is the establishment of a whole organisation or if it relates only to a small procedure involving only two or three functions. In a major project such as the installation of a computer or the building of a large factory a plan of action must be formulated at the very beginning which sets out details of all the necessary operations, with the dates and working times required, so that the various activities can be scheduled to fit in with each other. This schedule shows the completion date towards which all the activities are geared and is, in fact, a schedule of co-ordination.
- On a very much smaller scale the posting of an urgent parcel to a customer also requires the co-ordination of the efforts of the sales clerk, warehouse and post room, and this must be planned with no less care than the large project, otherwise the post will be missed.
- In order to achieve the goal set it is usually necessary to plan backwards from the completion time. In the example of the parcel, for instance, if the mail is collected at 5 p.m. then all activities must be planned and co-ordinated from that time backwards, so indicating how much time can be allocated to each of the required operations. Similarly, in a major project with a fixed completion date this date is the starting-point from which to plan so that the time allowance for each activity can be determined.
- Where certain activities have rigid time requirements other more flexible activities must be adjusted to suit the total time limitation. Critical path analysis is very useful in these circumstances to provide a clear picture of the situation (see **24.2 (d)** below) to determine those activity periods that are critical and those where times can be adjusted by one means or another to ensure effective maintenance of the schedule to meet the completion date.
- In a continuous activity there must be review points set so that it can be seen whether co-ordination has been effective or whether there has been some slipping away from the required plan. Without such review points for examination of progress co-ordination can break down completely with one or more sections of the organisation becoming entirely out of step with the remainder. An example might be the loss of co-ordination between manufacture and sales resulting in over-production and stocks accumulating. Monthly reviews of the situation would do much to bring both into line. It could even be held that the annual profit and loss account and balance sheet of a company are means of monitoring the

proper co-ordination of all of its functions, with over-stocking, poor cash flow and other indicators bringing evidence of the effectiveness or otherwise of the co-ordinating effort.

11.2   Ways to assist co-ordination

Co-ordination depends to a very large extent on the existence of goodwill between the various sectors of the organisation, so it is important that management takes steps to promote good relations between departmental managers and staff.

- It is not unknown for some managements to foster a competitive spirit between one section and another with the idea of generating an aggressive enthusiasm for their department's activities and showing themselves to be superior to the other departments. While this may be successful initially, it usually very soon results in bad feeling between the various sections, a disregard for the needs of other departments and, ultimately, to an imbalance in the organisation's activities and a breakdown in co-ordination. If the sales department is set to sell more than production can make the enterprise as a whole must ultimately suffer.
- The objectives and plans of the organisation must be clearly set out and understood by both managers and their staffs, and each sector's role must be fully appreciated. In this way the need to co-ordinate one with another will be made obvious and the risks of failure in this respect reduced.
- The responsibilities, authority and duties of all must be clearly defined, particularly in relation to the lines of demarcation. Effective co-ordination relies heavily on everyone's being aware of precisely what is required and expected of him or her. Haziness on this point results in overlap and consequent personal irritation, or in indeterminate areas of responsibility neglected by all. In either case co-ordination will suffer.
- Specific procedures should be laid down where possible to deal with routine and non-routine activities. With routine matters set procedures result in automatic co-ordination. Non-routine matters and emergencies may or may not be able to be dealt with in this way. However, if policies are formulated and well-known in regard to such eventualities co-ordination will be assured without specific executive intervention. While senior executives may be ultimately responsible for co-ordinating the organisation's activities – some would even argue that the chief executive has this responsibility – their intervention should be called for only in matters of the utmost importance.
- It is contended, with some justification, that management and staff training programmes can assist in promoting effective co-ordination. This is because such programmes tend to bring about a common approach to problems and a standardised reaction to them. Thus, in any

situation one manager can be reasonably sure what another manager will do. This common approach is a decided help in promoting co-ordination, particularly in unexpected circumstances.

11.3 Practical steps in co-ordination

Effective co-ordination is one of the most difficult goals to achieve, and while suggestions as set out in **11.1** and **11.2** above point the way, they need to be turned into practical terms if they are to be of use to management. The principal steps that need to be taken account of to ensure satisfactory co-ordination can be stated as follows:

(a) Management's objectives and policies for the organisation as a whole must be clearly defined and known throughout the concern. Communication is best done by writing, either in specific policy documents or through the staff handbook, or, where changes occur, in the house magazine if one exists.

(b) The objectives and policies of each department or division must be dealt with in the same way.

(c) The scope and duties of each job must be properly defined, and job descriptions should be written for each. Hitherto these may have been kept in a loose-leaf binder (this facilitated the problem of bringing job descriptions up to date) as a job manual, in charge of a senior departmental member. Nowadays these records are more usually kept on microfiche or on computer file.

(d) There must be a clearly defined procedure for each activity, and some form of monitoring devised to check adherence to this, particularly timing. Co-ordination is likely to fail without some form of control mechanism. An example of this is the activity of progress chasing in the factory, where the progress of work is checked at various points during its journey through the various shops in the works.

(e) All workers should be made aware of how their activities fit into the whole effort of the organisation. This can best be achieved by some form of induction when workers are engaged. Subsequently formal or informal meetings of workers or their representatives can be arranged from time to time to keep them up to date.

(f) Communication, both vertical and lateral, must be effective, which entails proper planning. Lines of formal communication must be laid down, but it must not be forgotten that informal communication has an important role to play as well.

(g) Meetings, one of the forms of communication, play a large part in ensuring good co-ordination. These range from regular meetings of senior staff to *ad hoc* meetings called for specific purposes as and when required. At all such meetings discussions on any matter affecting the organisation must include a cognisance of what effect decisions may have on co-ordination. Meetings specifically for the purpose of ensuring the co-ordination of the various activities of the organisation are recommended: such co-ordination meetings can be held at any level as the need arises.

(h) Committees are also useful in promoting effective co-ordination. Committees act at committee meetings, and the chief difference between an ordinary meeting and a committee meeting is that the latter is established to deal with one particular aspect of the organisation and is composed mainly of experts, normally specially appointed, whereas the former is more general in outlook. Further, a committee often has no executive powers, but its authority is restricted to making recommendations. Co-ordination, where formalised, is normally dealt with by a co-ordinating committee and hence the co-ordination meetings referred to in **(g)** above are usually co-ordinating committee meetings. The recommendations of other specialist committees will, of course, influence the deliberations of the co-ordinating committee.

The co-ordination of the efforts of a group of companies is normally the province of an executive committee, composed of senior executive officers from member companies. Usually such a committee does have executive powers.

(i) As much direct contact as possible must be encouraged between various sectors and people whose activities must be subject to immediate co-ordination. This may be by face-to-face communication or by internal telephone. Interdepartmental memoranda tend to make contact impersonal, are slower than direct communication, and are expensive.

Person-to-person verbal contact tends to create greater personal involvement and promotes quicker action – both highly desirable when problems of co-ordination arise. Great care must be taken, though, that there is precise understanding between the parties as to what has been decided. Verbal communication can be unreliable unless this is ensured.

(j) Where an organisation is large enough, or where circumstances otherwise make it advisable, there should be appointed one executive who has overall responsibility for co-ordination. This executive should be a senior officer who has the authority to make unilateral decisions when necessary, and who will be directly accountable to the chief executive. All necessary support services must be made available to this executive, such as an adequate information network. At section or departmental level the senior manager concerned will be responsible for co-ordination, and his authority can be delegated to supervisors and project managers under his control.

Given a properly constituted organisation and competent managers and staff, these ten steps provide a useful guide to effective co-ordination of both departmental and corporate activities.

11.4 Co-ordination and co-operation

Whatever principles and rules are laid down for co-ordination they will not be effective unless co-operation exists between members of the organisation.

- The steps set out in **11.3** above can be only guidelines to co-ordination: they are the result of a deliberate attempt to produce a pattern of activities to achieve the desired result. They do very little or nothing to stimulate a sense of co-operation in the minds of those concerned.
- Co-operation is a personal attitude and cannot be the subject of formal rules and procedures. Rather it comes about through the evolution of good management–staff relations, a feeling of personal involvement and the generation of an atmosphere of management respect and job security. It is not something that can be the subject of direct management planning: rather does it have to be earned by satisfactory personnel practices and overt fair dealings between management and managed.
- It is probably true to say that co-ordination can very well be satisfactory without specific plans and regulations on the subject if there exists a sense of whole-hearted co-operation throughout the organisation. It is also probably true to say without such co-operation the most carefully laid plans for co-ordination will be less than successful.

Questions

1 What practical steps may be taken to ensure that the activities of the various functional departments within an organisation are effectively co-ordinated?   **(ICSA)**

2 Discuss the relationship between co-ordination and co-operation, and show how the latter affects the former.

3 Discuss the possible consequences of using inter-group competition as a means of increasing performance.   **(IAM)**

4 How might co-ordination within an organisation be improved in a practical manner?   **(IAM)**

5 Define co-ordination. Describe the various ways in which co-ordination may be achieved within a business.   **(IComA)**

6 Outline the need for the marketing department to co-ordinate its activities with other management functions.   **(CIM)**

7 Explain how the necessary co-ordination between the marketing and production functions can be achieved, using an organisation of your choice as an illustration.   **(CIM)**

⟨12⟩ *Control*

Planning, both at management level and at operational level, looks to the future and lays down what has to be achieved: control checks whether the plans are being realised and puts into effect corrective measures where deviation or shortfall is occurring. Without effective controls an enterprise will be at the mercy of all the internal and external forces that can disrupt its efficiency and will be unaware of, and therefore unable to combat, such forces.

In the past it was common to review the position of an enterprise only once a year, at the time of the annual accounts. Between one year's end and another there was little information prepared to indicate the performance of the concern, and little specific control was able to be applied simply because of this lack of information. The only real controls were those imposed at shop-floor level and at staff level, particularly in regard to sales representatives, and then only because operation would have been difficult without them.

Nowadays, however, control is exercised over every aspect of an organisation's functions, from management performance to the activities carried on at every stage right down to the shop-floor. Effective control ensures that efforts produced at all levels are commensurate with those required to achieve the goals and objectives of management and of the sectional functions throughout.

12.1 Setting standards

A prerequisite of control is a standard with which actual performance can be compared. If there is no standard then there is no effective measure of attainment. At all levels of management and supervision standards must be set that reflect the required performance for each activity.

Standards fall into two broad categories, quantity standards and quality standards.

(a) Standards for quantity

The first are those which can be quantified, and thus specific standards can be set and should be met within tolerable limits. Such standards include those for sales, production, machine utilisation, output per worker and many, many others. Included in these standards may be, also, figures for the growth of the enterprise, required savings on expenditure and so on. It must not be forgotten in this connection that when standards are set the need to co-ordinate all relevant activities is an important one. Thus, for example, a standard can be set for each month's sales, but these must be commensurate with the possible level of production which will also have its monthly standards.

Standards for quantity are set on data derived from past performances and on forecasts of future possibilities where they are subject to a fair measure of external influences. Where performance is under the direct control of managers and supervisors, as is the case on the factory floor, then standards are set by reference to actual work measurement.

The time scales for standards of quantity vary according to the activity being controlled. In the actual manufacturing process standards for hourly or weekly output per worker are easy to apply and to measure. Standards for sales are frequently applied on a monthly basis as are those for the required matching production. Many other standards, particularly those relating to expenditure, are established for yearly periods but are divided into monthly rates for ease of monitoring, so that interim adjustments can be made in the light of continuing circumstances.

(b) Standards for quality

'Quality control' (QC) is a term used to cover control of all aspects of a concern's activities that cannot be quantified with any degree of certainty. This is a difficult area of control and only in a minority of cases can specific standards be set. For example, accuracy comes under the heading of quality, and it is customary to set limits to the number of errors, say, in key stroking, in the various stages of the manufacturing process, in accounting records and so on. The errors and faults can be counted and taken as a percentage of the total produced, which can be compared with an acceptable error level. However, the error level may fluctuate very considerably and a wide tolerance is usually necessary. So the standards set in these types of activity will be elastic to a certain extent. In other areas, though standards must be expected, they are difficult to specify with any precision. In what terms can management state its requirements in regard to customer goodwill, industrial relations, staff welfare and a host of other such activities? More difficult still, how can the performance of managers themselves be controlled and standards set? Yet in all these areas there must be standards to aim for and some means of monitoring performance.

12.2 Monitoring performance

When standards have been set some mechanism must be devised and installed for each activity whereby to check performance and compare it with the standard. Monitoring performance is a vital part of control because it is not realistic to expect to be able to control an activity if it is not constantly monitored. It is, for example, not possible to control the output of an assembly shop on the factory floor if the number of units completed are not counted. Similarly, inspection of the completed units is necessary to control the maintenance of quality standards.

- How the monitoring will be done depends almost entirely on the activity to be controlled. On the factory floor checking can be completely overt: workers and supervisors expect their work to be closely inspected and for controls to be instantly activated. If, in the example above, the output of the assembly shop falls short of the required standard then immediate steps will be taken to correct the situation. This will be done, in all probability, at supervisor or lower management level, and it is only if the problem persists that higher-level managers will be brought into the problem. Similarly, if quality control, or inspection as it is usually termed, sees cause to reject a greater number of units than the tolerance allowed for in the relevant standard, corrective measures will be taken without delay and often at a fairly low level of management.

- Of course, quality is not concerned only with physical factors. Such areas as customer complaints, lack of courtesy by telephone operators, slowness in replying to letters (or not replying at all) and similar quality of performance matters should also be of concern to management, as they have a profound effect on goodwill and, especially, on customer relations. The numbers of complaints received and their seriousness should be the subject of monitoring with a view to taking corrective action.

- The more difficult area of staff relations, that is the state of staff morale, can be gauged by the number of complaints from staff and the percentage of worker absences occurring. In extreme cases of staff dissatisfaction this will be indicated by a larger than average number of workers leaving. In periods when jobs are hard to find it may be that extremely aggrieved workers will express their dissatisfaction in ways other than leaving, for example, by working strictly to the rules or just being unco-operative. This is a problem that should be brought to light by monitoring and is a matter for a very diplomatic exercise in human relations.

- As the management ladder is ascended control, while still necessary, becomes less open and methods of monitoring and the application of adjusting mechanisms take longer. At the highest level of management, where the results of actions take some time to become apparent monitoring is done by means of reports, statements and the like, and modifications are put into effect where necessary only after considerable deliberation. At the very top the performance of the chief executive is gauged principally by the results shown by the annual accounts and reports, and corrective action is often a matter for the whole governing body.

12.3 Regulating mechanisms

Given that standards must be set and monitoring must take place to ensure that the standards are adhered to and deviations corrected as soon as possible, then forms of regulating mechanisms must be established. As suggested in **12.2** above these will depend upon the type and level of activity that has to be checked. Some examples are as follows:

(a) **Policies and plans**

To ensure these are adhered to there should be written policy manuals and regular reporting should be instituted to monitor the progress of the enterprise in respect of policy implementation and the satisfactory working of plans. Reports should emanate from the operating departments or divisions to top management, and regular meetings with senior executives should be scheduled to examine and deliberate on the contents of the reports. Action can then be taken urgently to regulate any serious deviations, or trends towards deviation. Similarly, departmental or divisional reporting to heads of departments or divisions by middle and junior managers can be dealt with in the same way.

Other monitoring methods that can be employed include budgetary control, management by objectives (MBO, see **16.5** below), management by exception (see **12.9** below) and even the calling in of outside consultants if matters appear to be beyond the capacity of existing managers.

(b) **Effectiveness of delegation**

The extent and limits of delegated authority and the duties of managers and supervisors at all levels should be set out clearly in organisation and procedure manuals. Internal management and procedure audits should take place in the same fashion as internal accounting audits and audit reports prepared for consideration by senior executives who are responsible for their subordinates' activities.

(c) **Operational effectiveness**

Much monitoring and regulation of the performance of workers can be carried out on the spot by supervisors and foremen. This personal control is most immediate and most effective where small groups of workers are involved. Large groups usually require such methods as job cards, progress slips, time cards and other forms of documentation. In most factories a system of progress chasing has to be established to monitor and regulate the movement of work through the various shops. This entails both the regular production of progress documents to the production planning office and personal inspection by progress chasers. In large organisations where the work is repetitive much of the checking is done automatically nowadays by computer or other means.

(d) Quality and quantity controls

Personal inspection by supervisors or quality control inspectors is necessary to control quality standards, be they applicable to work in the office or work on the production line. Quantity control is carried out by actually measuring the amount of work done, by count, weight or any other appropriate method, and comparing the results with the standards set. Visual presentation of what is expected and what is achieved is very often provided by charts or graphs. A commonly used chart is the Gantt chart (see Figure 12.1). Sales and similar activities are more easily illustrated by graphs.

The chart in Figure 12.1 reveals the performance of the assembly workers and, in particular, draws attention to exceptional circumstances. In week 3 the low output of all three workers simultaneously indicates some common problem in the shop.

(e) Expenditure control

Both capital and revenue expenditure can be regulated by budgetary control, which sets limits to permissible expenditure on all aspects of the organisation's activities. At departmental level there will be

Assembly Shop Output Control					
Four weeks commencing 18 May 1983					
Operator		Week 1	Week 2	Week 3	Week 4
E. ALING	Standard	400	400	400	400
	Actual	320	400	200	420
	%	80%	100%	50%	105%
R. EADING	Standard	450	450	450	450
	Actual	450	450	338	450
	%	100%	100%	75%	100%
S. TOKE	Standard	300	300	300	300
	Actual	285	300	210	300
	%	95%	100%	70%	100%
Key: ——— Standard output to be achieved					
———— Actual output produced					
% Percentage of actual to standard					

Fig. 12.1   Specimen Gantt chart

budgets covering sales expenditure, expenditure on production, administration and so on, and these budgets will be incorporated in a master budget which is the province of top management or, at least, of the most senior executives. Budgetary control is dealt with in more detail in **12.5** below.

(f) Reporting

Most monitoring of activities is done by reporting in one form or another. To be effective and to ensure remedial action is taken with the minimum of delay reports must be presented at the proper time, and must be in a form acceptable to those who have to use them. Thus, a specific day every week may be laid down for a cash flow report whereas a production report may be required only once a month. Sales reports, similarly, are usually presented once every month. In this connection it might be as well to remember that four-weekly reports allow more realistic comparisons one month with another than do those covering calendar months, where the number of working days varies from month to month.

12.4 Problems of measurement

It has been established that proper control cannot be instituted and maintained unless standards have been set, as unless this is done there is no basis for comparison against which controls can be installed. However, though the bases for some standards are easy to measure, others can prove very difficult. Two examples will illustrate this.

- If the output of a typing pool is to be the subject of control with output standards specified, it is not particularly difficult to measure the work-rate of the copy-typists and the audio-typists. Their work can be inspected over a period of three or four weeks, or even longer, and sensible work-levels established with the staff which can be used as a basis for the standards to be achieved. If it is desired to have a more precise measurement than this, then work-study techniques can be employed but these would hardly be necessary in this example.
- On the other hand, the setting of a standard for sales order clerks presents a very much more difficult problem simply because their work is much more varied than that of the typists. Every customer's requirements are special to that customer and there is no way of forecasting the number or length of the telephone conversations the proper fulfilment of their function is likely to demand of the sales clerks. One day may see a sales clerk constantly on the telephone and on another day the number of telephone calls may be almost nil.
- Similarly, efforts to set measures of performance for managers at all levels is fraught with imponderables which virtually defy the setting of reasonable standards. Particularly is this so where the managers are dealing with long-range plans that provide no performance indicators in

the short term. In fact it can be said that there is a direct connection between the problems of long-range planning and the control of the activities necessitated by such planning. Because the results of short-range plans become evident in a limited time their control can be exercised relatively easily. The activities required for a plan to increase sales by 10 per cent in six months can be monitored and regulated without great difficulty through the setting of targets and the comparison of weekly or monthly sales reports with such targets. A plan to make the same increase over ten years would present a much more difficult problem of monitoring and regulating performance simply because forecasting over such a period cannot be precise.

- Various methods of controlling the activities of organisations have been devised and put into practice, both in areas where control is easy and also where it is more problematic. One of the most important and most commonly applied is budgetary control.

12.5   Budgetary control

An effective way to control any of an organisation's activities is to set limits to expenditure because the managers responsible for the various departments are thereby required to examine closely any costs that they wish to incur. Such control is, however, really negative in effect because it tends to prevent action rather than to encourage it.

- The most common form of financial regulation is budgetary control and this is now very widely applied both in private industry and in the public sector.
- In practice, each department is required to forecast its future expenditure, usually for a period of a year, divided into the various elements that make up its costs. The actual period will depend upon what type of industry or activity the organisation operates within; where there are violent fluctuations in work-load, perhaps seasonally as in jobbing building, then the overall budget period may be shorter and set to cover the various periods of differing activity levels. Budgets will be prepared for production, distribution, purchasing, personnel, administration and capital expenditure, which cover the principal spending aspects of the enterprise; sales, which represent the main source of working capital; and cash flow, which represents the estimated income and payments for the period. Except for the capital expenditure budget it is safe to say that all the expenditure budgets are tied to the sales budget, which represents the target of sales and therefore the spendable income for the period set. Even the capital expenditure budget will be influenced by predicted sales because expenditure on plant, new buildings and the like will be determined to a large extent by expected sales volume even if the actual capital finance will be generated by means other than sales revenue.

- In organisations in the public service sectors such as local government, government departments and so on budgeting plays a very large part in the control activity, the chief difference from the private industrial sector being that instead of a sales budget there is a budget for local tax income, for grants, donations or taxes. Further, it appears to be the case that expenditure is planned before income is forecast and income (local tax, for example) is geared to planned expenditure. This is possible because in many cases these bodies have statutory powers to be able to raise the income they need. Even so, certain restrictions are put on such organisations that curtail freedom in this respect. For instance, central government may reduce the grants made to local authorities, and public resistance can make itself felt both in regard to high rates of income tax and to high local taxes.
- An administration budget is shown in Figure 12.2.

Administration Budget for the year *1988*			
Prepared by E. Dean		Date *1.1.88*	
Expense	Annual	Per Month of Four Weeks	Remarks
	£	£	
Salaries	26,500	2,038	
Motor car expenses	4,330	333	
Light and heat	1,500	115	
Rent	7,800	600	
		120	
General insurance	1,300	100	
Stationery	650	50	
Sundries	260	20	
Audit fee			
Totals	£ 71,500	£ 5,500	

Fig. 12.2   Specimen of a fixed budget

This is a simple statement of the budget allocation.

- The individual budgets having been prepared and agreed between departments and management, a master budget is prepared which incorporates all the separate budgets and which represents a budget for the total organisation.
- The preparation of a budget is, however, only the first step in controlling

expenditure. It is necessary to introduce some controlling mechanism to ensure compliance with the budgets prepared. This is done by requiring regular budget review statements, usually on a monthly basis. As stated previously, four-week months are to be preferred in this connection to the normal calendar month. These statements will set out the proportion of the annual budget appertaining to the month under review for each budgeted item and alongside each item the actual expenditure and the variance from budget either up or down. It is thus easy to see whether the department concerned is over-spending or under-spending, and exactly where the variances occur. These variances, especially where increased expenditure is indicated, must then be examined to discover why they have occurred so that corrective action can be taken without delay, where necessary, to bring the activity back into line (see Figure 12.3).

- It is usually considered advisable for there to be a budget committee, composed of senior people including heads of departments or their

Monthly Budget Review Statement				
Dept: *Administration*		Month		
Budgeted activity %		Actual achieved %		

Expense	Month		Variance		Remarks
	Budget	Actual	This month	Year to date	
Totals					
Signed			Date		

Fig. 12.3   Specimen budget review statement form

representatives, where budget statements can be deliberated upon and remedies discussed to ensure compliance with planned expenditure, or to examine any failure in revenue generation. Many organisations, in fact, have a budgeting officer heading a small staff whose sole responsibility is to assist in the preparation of budgets, to recommend management approval and to ensure the proper operation of a budgetary control mechanism.

- The chief problem affecting budgetary control is that sales forecasts, on which the sales budget is prepared, cannot be accurate because of the many unpredictable factors such as changing consumer tastes, unforeseen new developments in competitors' products and a change in the economic climate. If sales figures fluctuate it is obvious that budgets based on fixed figures cannot operate effectively. The solution to this problem is the flexible budget.

12.6 The flexible budget

A flexible budget is one where the various elements making up the budget are shown not only at 100 per cent for total budgeted sales, but also at varying levels of activity other than 100 per cent. Thus, a flexible budget might show permitted expenditure at 70 per cent, 80 per cent, 90 per cent and 110 per cent of budget activity. However, it is not sufficient simply to apply these proportions to all the items in the budget statement because certain expenditures do not vary in direct relation to sales volume.

- This gives rise to the concept of fixed and variable costs. **Fixed** costs are those that obtain whatever the level of activity, and include such items as rent, local tax and administration salaries. **Variable** costs are those that vary in direct proportion to the level of activity, such as materials, power consumption and, in some industries, labour costs. In between these costs are **semi-variable** costs that do not alter in direct proportion to activity but either have both a fixed element and a variable one in them (the telephone is a case in point, where rent is fixed and call charges are proportional to use) or have a time-lag before change takes place, such as canteen costs and selling expenses.
- The technique of flexible budgetary control therefore involves planning the sales target, stating this as 100 per cent activity and then preparing individual budgets and a master budget at this level and at the other levels as percentages of the target. In working out the proportionate levels account will be taken of fixed costs, which will be common to each activity level; variable costs, which will be precisely proportionate; and semi-variable costs, which will be the subject of assessment for each level (see Figure 12.4).
- A favourite device for illustrating the effects of various levels of activity in a flexible budget is the break-even chart (see Figure 12.5), which emphasises the point at which the operation becomes profitable. In this

Type		Activity below normal			Normal		Activity above normal	
	Monthly Administration Budget						Financial Year 1ЯЯЯ	
		70%	80%	90%	Month	%	110%	120%
	Sales volume	£ 28,532	£ 32,608	£ 36,684	£ 40,760	100%	£ 44,836	£ 48,912
F	Salaries	2,038	2,038	2,038	2,038	5.00%	2,038	2,038
V	Car expenses	234	267	301	333	0.82%	368	401
F	Light and heat	115	115	115	115	1.47%	115	115
V	Stationery	71	82	92	100	0.25%	112	122
V	Sundries	36	41	46	50	0.12%	56	61
F	Audit fee	20	20	20	20	0.05%	20	20
	Totals	4,240	4,543	4,852	5,096	12.5%	5,189	5,377

Prepared by   *R. Bourne*   Date *31.12.1ЯЯЯ*

F = a fixed expense   V = a variable expense

Fig. 12.4   Specimen of a flexible budget

chart the semi-variable cost is often not shown as such but is incorporated in the other two categories for simplicity of presentation.

12.7   Advantages of budgetary control

While budgetary control, contrary to some expectations, does not provide total regulation of expenditure, it does have many advantages:

(a)   The expenditure limits set do impose a brake on extravagance and unthinking financial commitments: they ensure that serious consideration is given before expenditure is indulged in instead of afterwards. Attention is drawn to undue expenditure needs at an early stage and reasons sought for them.

(b)   The preparation of budgets requires all concerned to examine very closely the working of their departments. Forecasts have to be made and targets set. These actions tend to impose restraints on unrealistic ambitions and emphasise the need for practical and attainable goals.

(c)   As all budgets are interdependent, budgetary control has a positive effect on co-ordination. Related departments must work together in order that their budgets may be compatible and correlate with each other.

(d) The requirement to prepare periodical budget review statements, and the holding of regular budgetary control review meetings ensure constant monitoring of budget performances.

(e) Such monitoring has two effects. The first is that managers and others

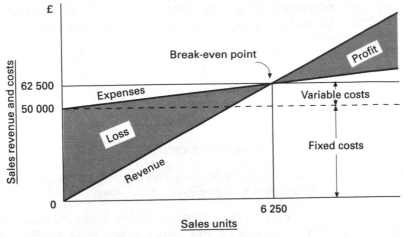

Fig. 12.5 Specimen of a sales break-even chart

Formula for break-even point:

$$B/E = F\left(\frac{S}{S-V}\right),$$

where B/E = break-even point
F = Fixed costs
S = Selling price per unit
V = Variable costs per unit

In the chart illustrated above

F = £50 000
S = £10
V = £2

Thus

$$B/E = £50\,000\left(\frac{10}{10-2}\right)$$

$$= £62\,500 = 6\,250 \text{ Sales units.}$$

Thus

Variable costs at break-even point
$= 6\,250 \times £2 = £12\,500.$

responsible for budgets are disposed to try to ensure that the budget figures are adhered to as far as possible: the second is that non-compliance with budgeted performance is brought to management's attention at an early stage so that any necessary remedial action can be taken with the minimum of delay.

(f)   Similarly, this monitoring may also reveal that the original budgets have been unrealistic and that the figures may have to be adjusted in the light of internal or external conditions coming about subsequent to budget formulation.

(g)   Because managers are responsible for their own budget figures they have an incentive to keep within the limits set, and to ensure that their staff comply with the constraints put upon the department.

12.8   Disadvantages of budgetary control

Despite the undoubted advantages of budgetary control it does have some disadvantages, which will now be examined:

(a)   A budget is a monitoring aid, it is not a regulator. Some managers are inclined to treat it as the latter and abrogate their responsibilities as managers. If expenditure is necessary outside the scope of the budget to ensure efficient operation in a specific instance, this additional cost must be argued for, not accepted as barred.

(b)   In many cases budgets are looked upon as indicators of expenditure that should be incurred. Where the budgeted figures will not be attained it is not unknown for unnecessary expenditure to be incurred because a budget surplus is available and 'must be used up'. This occurs most frequently where annual budgets are based on previous years' budget figures instead of realistic new forecasts being formulated. The oft-repeated comment is that 'our budget will be cut next year if we do not spend all of this year's'.

(c)   Where budgetary control is so fine that separate budgets are prepared for sectionalised needs it is often the case that any surplus from one budget will not be passed over to a budget likely to be in deficit, even though for practical reasons this may be highly desirable. This does not benefit the organisation as a whole. An example would be where a secretarial department has a budget for typing materials and another for photocopying materials. Nothing is gained in practical terms if a surplus on the typing materials budget cannot be transferred to make good a deficit in the budget for photocopying materials, though this attitude does often obtain. Experience shows it to be particularly prevalent in connection with small items of capital expenditure.

(d)   In times of fluctuating prices budgeting presents especial difficulties, and when high rates of inflation occur budgets become out of date very quickly. The remedies are frequent reviews of the bases for the budgeted figures and the installation of flexible budgets which can, within limits, accommodate price changes.

(e) The calculation and implementation of budgets and budgetary control does, of necessity, impose an extra burden on departmental and functional managers over and above their routine responsibilities, even where there is a budget officer or department.

(f) As there is inevitably a finite financial resource to be shared throughout the organisation, friction at its lowest and antagonism at its worst can be generated between departments seeking a proportion of this resource.

So far only financial budgets have been mentioned. However, it must be remembered that budgets can also be prepared in units other than monetary ones; for example, in units of production, volume of sales, man-hours of workers employed and so on. The type of unit used will depend entirely upon the circumstances, but the principles discussed in regard to monetary budgets remain the same.

12.9 Management by exception

Control is an important and onerous part of the mangement function and can impose an unduly heavy burden unless steps are taken to ease the situation.

- An important technique, first suggested by F. W. Taylor, is the 'exception principle' or 'management by exception' as it is commonly called. When matters are proceeding according to plan there is no virtue in actively involving the attention of the managers concerned, and the higher up the management ladder control is centred the less justification there is for taking up executive time unnecessarily. Management by exception provides that only exceptional circumstances require the attention of management, and where normal procedures are running uneventfully there is no need for the intervention of management.

- Management by exception relies for its efficient operation on regular reporting and well-defined operational limits. While activities proceed within the specified limits then no reports are required to be passed to the managers concerned: only where limits are exceeded or fail to be achieved are exception reports made. An example will clarify the matter. If the acceptable numbers of rejects of a product are laid down as between one and five in a thousand units, then within these limits the reject level will not be the subject of a report. However, should the level suddenly increase to seven per thousand then an exception report would go to production control for an investigation to be instigated.

12.10 Control decisions

As far as possible control decisions should be made automatically. The ideal situation is where the necessary control is carried out without human intervention at all. This exists, for instance, in a central-heating system where the boiler is switched on and off automatically by a thermostat which senses the ambient temperature. This self-activation is to some extent employed in some credit control systems in which the computer automatically prints payment demands when it senses that accounts are overdue.

However, in many situations it is not possible to design such automatic controls. Nevertheless to some extent the frailty of human judgement can be taken out of the control procedure in a large number of cases by the use of programmed decisions. This was fully discussed in **10.7** above and need not be repeated here.

Where judgement is needed in the control process it will depend to a very large extent on feedback in order that appropriate steps may be taken to correct a situation that is not proceeding to plan. It is essential, therefore, that a proper system of communication for management information be established so that the necessary reports can flow to the manager or supervisor responsible for the activity concerned with the minimum of delay. Such a system of control is illustrated in Figure 12.6.

It is, as a general rule, unsatisfactory to rely on *ad hoc* control

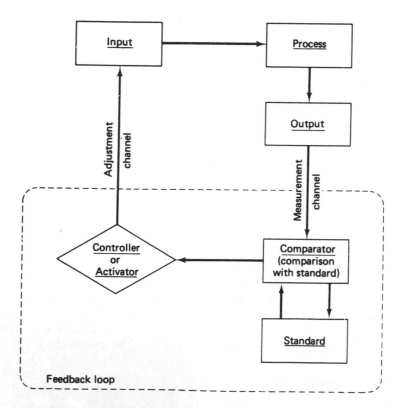

Fig. 12.6   Control system with feedback

arrangements, and the more automatic they can be made the more effective the controls will be.

12.11 Some principles of control

For control to be truly effective it must be governed by firm principles:

(a) The method of control must be suitable for the activity it seeks to regulate and should be the minimum required to achieve the desired results. Over-elaborate controls often lead to the system being ignored or distorted. Accuracy, also, should be commensurate with control requirements and no more. Absolute accuracy is often quite unnecessary and can result in unwarranted lengthening of processing time.

(b) The controls installed should not cost more than they will save. For example, a 100 per cent quality control on a mass-produced product may cost more than the replacement of defective items returned by customers.

(c) The type of industry or activity concerned must determine what types of control are needed. The controls that suit a shipbuilder will not be satisfactory for a local authority.

(d) Feedback information must be available to the controller in time for corrective action to be taken before matters have gone too far wrong.

(e) It is essential that corrective action be taken promptly and consistently, when required, and such action must be seen to be taken. It is most unwise to give subordinates the impression that they can ignore standards with impunity.

(f) The exception principle should be applied wherever possible. Nevertheless full back-up information should be available in case it is required, even though this is not normally passed on to management. This information should be filed only for limited periods.

(g) Areas of accountability and authority should be clearly defined so that there is no doubt where responsibility lies for the various control activities.

Questions

1 'The management function of control is the measurement and correction of the activities of subordinates in order to make sure that the objectives of the organisation are achieved. Control is a necessary management function at all levels in the management hierarchy' (Henri Fayol).
   Discuss. **(ICSA)**

2 Why should 'Control' be one of the key factors in the management of organisations? **(IAM)**

3 Why is quality control important in manufacturing industry? Discuss the methods by means of which quality can be monitored. **(IComA)**

4 Draw a diagram of a control system, clearly indicating the major component parts. What impact does the human factor have on the effective operation of such a control system?   **(IAM)**

5 Budgeting is a major task of all organisations.
   (a) Summarise the main features of a budget.
   (b) Identify the typical problems faced in budgeting.   **(IAM)**

6 Explain the essential contribution of budgets as a key component of the annual marketing plan.   **(CIM)**

7 Budgets are sometimes seen as plans for co-operation, and sometimes seen as restrictions to be defeated. What factors would you expect to lead to one view rather than the other?   **(ACCA)**

⟨13⟩ **Motivation**

The question of motivating the personnel of an organisation to make maximum effort towards the attainment of its objectives has always occupied the minds of managers, from the chief executive to the lowest ranking supervisor. Despite much research, study and hypotheses, however, no foolproof rules have been formulated that can safely be said to solve the many problems of motivation in all cases. In fact, no rules satisfactory for every situation can be offered simply because the behaviour of human beings cannot be predicted with any certainty except in the most rigid and military style organisation where behaviour patterns are laid down and imposed, and strict and positive sanctions are known and are applied rigorously. Nevertheless, it is the duty of managers to endeavour to attain the organisation's objectives and this can be done only through people. To achieve this goal it is absolutely essential that staff at all levels be motivated to co-operate in the organisation's plans and to work as effectively as possible. This applies as much to managers and supervisors as it does to those managed.

13.1 Motivation and incentives

It used to be thought that enhanced financial reward was sufficient to motivate a worker to maximum effort. However, this is to confuse the two terms 'motivation' and 'incentive'.

- Intrinsically they are not the same in as much as motivation springs from within – it is, essentially, an attitude of mind that may be encouraged by external factors but is fundamentally firmly related to self-discipline. Further, it can remain even when the external influences that engendered it have ceased to exist. Often it is entirely self-generated because it arises through innate character attributes and remains unaltered by external factors.
- Incentive, on the other hand, belongs to those forces that are applied from the outside and is a positive external influence to encourage improved performance. This being so, the effects of incentives cease as soon as those particular influences are withdrawn. An example would be that of sales representatives. Normally the majority of these are paid on the basis of a basic salary and commission on sales. The commission is an incentive and in very many cases if the rate of commission is reduced then the sales representatives' efforts are likewise reduced. Only if there

were personal financial commitments to be met which required greater selling effort because of the reduced commission would a particular sales representative work as hard or harder than before in order to maintain his income level. This, in itself, however, is an incentive. When the financial commitment had been satisfied (perhaps a hire-purchase agreement discharged) then it would be very likely that the selling effort would be reduced.

- However, continuing this example, very many people who take up the career of selling are motivated by the challenge it presents and a reduction in the rate of commission will not permanently affect their selling effort though it may do so initially because of a sense of pique or resentment. These sales representatives are urged on by an inner drive – that is, motivation – and not by an external factor – that is, incentive. It follows, therefore, that people at work, even managers, may be encouraged to greater effort by an increase in financial reward, be it earned by effort in the case of commission or bonus payments or by a straight increase in the contents of the pay packet. However, this will usually have an effect only while the incentive is applied (where extra earnings are added by way of commission or bonus) and in the case of a rise in pay only in the initial period after the increase is awarded. In fact, in the latter case there is some experience to indicate that after a given point an increase in pay without the stimulus of additional work or responsibility may even result in a diminution of effort.

13.2   The social sciences and motivation

If additional financial rewards are incentives and not truly motivational there must be other means of motivating staff to perform at their best. There are many theories advanced by industrial psychologists and sociologists, some of which will be examined briefly later in this chapter, but it must not be forgotten that these two sciences, now often joined under the terms 'social science' or 'behavioural science' when not purely medical, are not sufficiently advanced to give firm answers to all problems. Furthermore, the results of research projects carried out by different practitioners have not always agreed, and universal conclusions should not be drawn from the work of one or other of these researchers: often the samples are too small, or the time too short, for generalisations to be made. Further, the precise conditions from one research project to another are not truly comparable in most cases. These observations must not be taken to denigrate the work in this field that has been done and is being done: rather they are made to sound a caution against accepting such findings uncritically. Without doubt in due course a better understanding of what can be done to motivate staff to greater effort will emerge.

13.3 Non-financial motivation

If extra money does not motivate, what does? As mentioned in **13.2** above, no hard-and-fast rules can be laid down about this, but there are some general ways that are practised with success by some organisations, and these are based on experience as well as formal research. They centre round the following aspects of work and to some extent also indicate why people work. Managers should be aware of the fact that people do not work for money only: once a satisfactory income has been achieved pay becomes a secondary consideration even though it may be given emphasis in the yearly pay negotiations. Reasons for working are different for different individuals, as are the factors that motivate them.

(a) Security

A job spells security and is a common positive reason for working. Further, working within a particular organisation may spell even greater security than working within an alternative enterprise, which may motivate a person to accept one post in preference to another. Central and local government services have a great attraction in this respect.

(b) Status

To be employed gives status in the worker's own social environment, and if the work has an element of skill or social approbation so much the better. Both socially and at work some jobs are looked upon as having greater status than others and many workers are motivated to achieve such status. A skilled tool-maker, for example, has a higher status than a cleaner.

(c) Use of skill or intelligence

Many workers are proud of their skills and work to employ them to the best advantage. A dull, repetitive job is not calculated to motivate a worker to give the best possible performance. One that demands imagination or the use of initiative is more likely to do this. However, it must be appreciated that there are some workers who are content with routine work requiring no thought beyond carrying out strictly programmed actions: giving such people the chance to use their initiative will in all probability demotivate them.

(d) Goals and aspirations

Many of the more intelligent workers are motivated by the desire to achieve positions of responsibility and authority. They see themselves as being in command of a section, a department, a division or even, for the most ambitious, of the whole organisation, and so their motivation is to show their employers how well they can handle their jobs so that they will be promoted higher and higher up the management ladder. Such staff must be able to see their way to the top if they are not to be lost to the enterprise since otherwise their ambition will urge them to seek opportunities elsewhere. Hence they are better motivated if a positive promotional policy is evident.

(e) **External aspirations**

A large number of workers are not motivated by promotion prospects because of an urge to take on responsibility but rather because of the fruits available consequent upon better earnings. Such material acquisitions as a better house, a faster car or long, exotic holidays may motivate some to better work-effort so that income is earned commensurate with the cost of these external aspirations. Equally, social aspirations such as a private school education for the children or membership of an élite club may be the basis of the motivation. It would be true to say, however, that those in line for management are most likely to be influenced by social aspirations.

(f) **A congenial work environment**

Many, but by no means all, workers are positively motivated by a pleasant congenial environment in which to work. Unfortunately this stimulus has only a limited life and its effects disappear when the workers have become thoroughly accustomed to it. Equally, favourable working hours are a temporary stimulus to positive motivation.

(g) **Type of industry**

There are many so-called glamour industries which attract people, particularly the younger ones, and motivation to work in these industries can be very strong. They include advertising, fashion and the various branches of the entertainments industry. Probably a worker feels some superior status when admitting to working with, say, a newspaper even when the position is only one of clerk or storekeeper.

The reasons for people working at all are, therefore, many and various, and each worker will have a different combination of attitudes and motivations some of which may not even be conscious ones. A recognition that these reasons do exist, however, should assist management to motivate the workers at all levels to give of their best efforts.

13.4   Practical motivation

If financial incentives are not effective as true motivators what steps can managers take to create positive motivation in their work-people? It has been pointed out that different workers respond differently to any particular stimulus and it is certainly true that some motivating factors have only a temporary effect. Nevertheless there are a number of factors that are generally accepted as being of value in achieving some measure of success in encouraging positive attitudes. These include:

(a) **Atmosphere**

An atmosphere of co-operation and trust must be generated between management and staff. Perhaps it would be better described as mutual respect. The old autocratic style of management is now resented by most workers, and a manager is no longer respected just because he is a manager. Such a management style is indicative of a lack of respect for their subordinates by those in authority, and such a situation does not generate respect by the workers for their managers or supervisors.

Without relinquishing his overt authority a manager must be seen to have concern about his staff and their needs, and must nowadays actively seek their co-operation in making decisions which affect them as individuals. In other words, there must be generated an atmosphere of participation, co-operation and mutual respect. One certain sign as to whether this has been achieved is when the workers, when discussing their employers, refer to 'we' rather than 'they'.

(b) Recognition

Human beings have a need to be esteemed and the manager who realises this and actively recognises his subordinates as people rather than working units is likely to be successful in motivating them positively. Some senior executives, particularly, are aware of this as evidenced by the chairman of a substantial company who invariably made it his business to ask after the families of his staff, at all levels, whenever he made a visit to the works or branch offices, remembering personal details from the previous visit.

Recognition of the efforts of workers is also necessary. All employees like to feel that their efforts are appreciated, particularly if some improvement in performance or some contribution outside the work requirements of the job has been achieved. Words of praise or encouragement raise the morale of staff, but they must be justified: mere flattery without a sound basis will have the opposite effect to that intended.

(c) Status

Really linked with recognition, to many workers status within their organisation is important to them. To some it must be overt but to others tacit recognition of status is enough. Status must, however, carry with it commensurate responsibility and authority. Just naming a worker '*X* supervisor' or '*Y* manager' without commensurate responsibility or authority, in other words bestowing an empty title, very soon turns sour. Not only does the worker personally become dissatisfied, the respect of other workers may be lost and this mutual respect between members of a work-force is of extreme importance.

On the other hand, where someone has been carrying out the duties of a supervisor or manager without the formal title, to bestow the title is not an empty gesture, but is an acknowledgement of status.

(d) Involvement

Much has been written concerning worker participation, and it means different things to different people. In almost all cases, however, it is taken to involve formal recognition of what is stated to be the workers' right to participate in making decisions that affect their working conditions, even to the extent of making such participation a legal requirement.

Whether management accepts the view that there is this right or not, there is certainly a strong case for involving work-people in the decision-making process and even, where appropriate, encouraging them to show initiative in matters affecting the organisation.

Full participation would imply formal acceptance of workers in management business either through consultative committees or some other form of structured involvement, even to the extent of worker-directors as discussed in **3.5** above. However, such responsibility is not necessary in order to draw the work-people into contributing to management plans and decisions, and may even be unwelcome. What most motivates workers is to feel that they are thought of as human beings and not just names on a payroll. Informal discussions between managers and subordinates on matters concerning work practices, welfare and the host of other problems affecting the work-force are much appreciated, and build morale and trust. Such practices, particularly when done on a person-to-person basis, create an atmosphere of involvement: the workers feel they are respected as individuals and that their views do count for something in the organisation. Care must be taken, however, that managers are seen to treat such involvement seriously. If they appear to pay only lip-service to this practice then mistrust will very soon occur with disastrous results to any hope of positive staff motivation.

(e)   Rewards

Any form of financial reward, whether actual cash by way of an increase in pay or bonus, or by way of, say, a special holiday award (often given to sales representatives), is an incentive and not a motivator as has been pointed out previously. However, such rewards can be the basis for positive motivation in the way that they are bestowed. Thus, when such a reward is given it should, where possible, be publicised throughout the organisation by the most appropriate means. Promotions and bonus earnings are often published in the staff journal, with reasons for the award. Prizes for best performance should be announced at meetings called for the purpose. In this way all workers are made aware that management appreciates the efforts of those successful enough to be rewarded and are motivated to try to do the same as the award winners. The successful ones are also motivated to continue to perform as well as possible, beyond the thought of pure incentive.

(f)   Job satisfaction

Much work is monotonous and boring and this militates against a positive attitude by workers to their jobs. In other words, the workers derive little satisfaction from their work. Job satisfaction can however be improved, and with it motivation, by the simple expedient of making the work more interesting and requiring a greater application of thought and skill. This can be done by increasing the job content while retaining the same type of work, for instance allowing assembly workers not only to assemble one component of a unit, but to assemble all the component parts and perhaps test the completed units. This is often termed 'job enlargement'. Another method is to extend the range of tasks that have to be performed by individual workers. For example, in an invoicing department clerks could be required to price items, calculate them, total invoices and produce batch pre-lists rather than just perform one of these tasks. This is generally referred to as 'job enrichment'. Both have been used by some major employers with a marked improvement in motivation and morale.

13.5 Group motivation

The problems of group motivation are largely the same as those relating to the motivation of individual workers. There are, however, additional factors that must be taken into account:

(a) The group must consist of compatible individuals. Even one unco-operative worker can cause disaffection and thus have a deleterious effect on the group's motivation.

(b) The group must be of an optimum size. This will depend upon the kind of work being done and the abilities of the members of the group.

(c) Work must be allocated fairly between the members of the group, and must be seen to be so allocated.

(d) The group's manager or supervisor must set targets that are reasonable and achievable.

(e) The achievements of the group as a whole must be recognised by management and appreciation for these achievements made known to the group.

(f) No individual in the group should be consistently singled out for special treatment as this causes resentment and a diminution of motivation. That is not to say that an occasional word of praise for an individual worker should not be given for an outstanding contribution to the group effort.

By paying attention to these factors the manager or supervisor of a working group can do much to promote positive motivation in his group and earn the respect of his work-people.

None of these practical suggestions for motivating staff will work effectively unless they are applied honestly and sincerely, and without bias or prejudice. Any hint of insincerity or deception by management will quickly disillusion staff at any level and any hope of positive motivation will vanish.

So far this chapter has been devoted to the more practical aspects of motivation. There have been many studies made on the theory of motivation, however, and the contributions of some of the most quoted authorities on this subject will now be briefly examined.

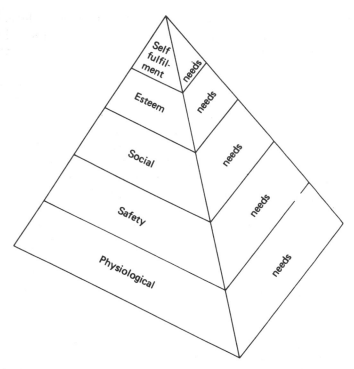

Fig. 13.1 Maslow's hierarchy of basic needs

13.6 A. H. Maslow

Maslow propounded the theory that people are motivated by five basic needs, which he called 'the hierarchy of basic needs'. The primary need is that of physical survival and at the highest level it is that of self-fulfilment. These needs can be likened to a pyramid which has the primary needs as a base and which are universal, rising in steps to the highest need, which is the least well felt. This progression is represented in Figure 13.1.

(a) **Physiological needs**, as Maslow called them, are those that are basic to continued existence. These include the necessity to satisfy hunger, to be clothed and to have basic shelter from the elements. These are primary needs and predominate in motivating an urge to work. Not until these needs are satisfied to an acceptable level, so argue Maslow and his adherents, will a person aspire to the next step in the pyramid, which he called 'safety needs'.

(b) **Safety needs** are those connected with protection. Being assured of adequate sustenance and shelter, an individual will then look for a measure of security, of protection against lowering of living standards, of his job and of the fundamental physiological elements of life. Anything that threatens the orderly organisation of life, either in the world at large or in the work-place, will be looked upon also as a threat to the individual's safety. When such threats are removed then the individual will feel safe, and will be motivated by the next needs in the pyramid, social needs.

(c) **Social needs** are those which motivate a person to enter actively into the social environment in which he or she is placed, both at work and in society at large. Such needs, at the primary level, are encompassed in love and affection, family circle and social groupings such as the club, the religious group and so on. At work they are concerned with work-groupings, social and welfare activities and, perhaps, trade union activities. The average individual has a deep-rooted need to belong to social groupings and to be accepted by his or her peers. Freed from the necessity to pursue the satisfaction of physiological and safety needs, the individual is now motivated to pursue those social needs, the gratification of which leads to the pursuit of what Maslow called the esteem needs.

(d) **Esteem needs** are those which follow from self-satisfaction arising out of achievement and the respect of others. Sometimes referred to as 'ego needs', they involve self-respect, self-discipline and a feeling of adequacy and confidence. The status flowing from the esteem of others is an important factor here. Almost everyone needs and seeks the approbation of others and gains stature from it. Only the strength of the motivation in this direction limits this need. Failure to achieve esteem within the social- or work-group often leads to a sense of inferiority and a lowering of morale.

(e) **Self-fulfilment needs**, which Maslow called 'self-actualisation', are at the top of the pyramid of needs and become active when the previous four have been satisfied. This area of need is the one that motivates a person to seek and find the activity which satisfies a deep, often previously unconscious, urge and is very frequently associated with creativity or with the drive to exercise ultimate power. So artists, writers, actors, chief executives and politicians can all be said to be attempting to satisfy this need for self-fulfilment.

It will be apparent from general observation that this hierarchy of needs is not immutable. In fact Maslow himself called attention to the fact that in some people the stages are reversed, or some are ignored. The most common examples are those of the struggling artist, composer or actor, each of whom will forgo the satisfaction of many needs in pursuit of self-fulfilment or public acclaim. Many a successful industrialist has given up the esteem of society and the satisfaction of basic social needs to pursue the goal of industrial power. Most workers, however, are not driven by such high passions and are able to feel satisfied with less than total achievement. In some ambition is almost non-existent to the extent that an income, reasonable security and shelter are all they ask.

13.7   D. M. McGregor

D. M. McGregor is probably most quoted in connection with his propositions (or theories) X and Y. These can be stated as follows:

(a)   **Theory X** asserts that the average human being:
  1 is inherently lazy and works as little as possible;
  2 has no ambition and prefers to be led rather than take responsibility;
  3 is self-centred, dislikes change and is unconcerned with the needs of the organisation;
  4 is gullible and not particularly intelligent or discriminating.

Because of these traits managers have to persuade, coerce, reward or punish workers in order to achieve organisational goals: people cannot be trusted to work effectively without active and constant supervision.

Traditional management subscribes to theory X in the main and many traditional management practices can be attributed to this belief. McGregor, however, accepted Maslow's concept of the five basic needs, which led him to formulate his theory Y.

(b)   **Theory Y** states, among other things, that people are not the selfish, indolent creatures that theory X suggests but, in fact, that:
  1 they are naturally inclined to expend effort in working and playing – they are not passive nor are they unconcerned or resistant to organisational needs: this attitude is engendered by their experience of working in organisations that do not recognise their potential;
  2 they are not without the urge to assume responsibility and have the capacity for self-discipline and self-direction provided they are properly motivated by management. Such motivation will not, however, be based only on the principles of punishment and reward: management must recognise the human need for self-satisfaction and the other needs propounded by Maslow;
  3 management, therefore, has the task and duty to harness these innate attributes to enable the work-force to contribute willingly to the achievement of organisational objectives.

Neither of these propositions, of course, can be relied on exclusively to motivate workers positively. The traditional approach is likely to be difficult to sustain given the attitudes now prevailing in most industrial relations: this approach has to be softened by a more conciliatory and persuasive attitude on the part of management, and there must be a recognition of the basic needs which must be fulfilled if co-operation is to be achieved. As many workers now earn enough to provide themselves adequately with sustenance and shelter Maslow's higher needs must be reckoned with.

On the other hand, it would appear that the majority of work-people are not yet ready for a total change to the theory in proposition Y. It could be said with McGregor that the fundamental difference between the two propositions is that theory X relies entirely on imposed and external control of people, whereas theory Y puts the emphasis on self-motivation and self-direction.

13.8   F. Herzberg

F. Herzberg's chief contribution to motivation theory was to suggest two distinct categories of factors relating to people's attitude to work, which he named the hygiene or maintenance factors and the motivating factors.

(a) **Hygiene or maintenance factors**, Hertzberg found, do little to promote job satisfaction, but their absence or presence at any unacceptable level leads to dissatisfaction, which caused him to term them 'dissatisfiers'. He likened them to hygiene in medical matters or maintenance in mechanical areas, which prevent unwanted results arising but do not promote good results of themselves: for example, good hygiene can prevent illness but cannot, unaided, cure a patient.

He suggested that these hygiene factors are:

1 organisational policies and practices; organisational rules and related factors;

2 style of supervision and management controls;

3 scale of pay and related benefits such as sick pay, retirement pensions and security;

4 interpersonal and social relationships within the working environment: status within the organisation;

5 working conditions, working environment, equipment and general work arrangements.

These factors, it will be seen, relate to the conditions under which the worker operates rather than to the actual work itself. Because of this, any improvement in a hygiene factor will have only a temporary effect. Experience indicates that, for example, improved lighting may remove dissatisfaction in this area for a short time after the improvement takes place, but familiarity soon causes the improvement to be forgotten and in consequence its positive effect also declines. In fact, further demands may be made subsequently for even better lighting.

This phenomenon of temporary effect is common to all the hygiene factors. Improvements will stop complaints for a short time, but are unlikely to have a permanent effect.

(b) **Motivating factors**, unlike the hygiene factors, have a positive and longer-lasting effect on worker performance and also, unlike the hygiene factors, they relate directly to the work itself. These motivating factors include:

1 **achievement:** this is the satisfaction derived from work well done;

2 **recognition of achievement:** the worker needs to have his efforts recognised by his superiors, which adds to his self-esteem;

3 **the work itself:** this needs to be challenging and rewarding; it is in

this area that much industrial organisation falls down in motivating the work-force, since much work is repetitive and monotonous;

4 **responsibility:** increased responsibility should motivate a worker to greater efforts, especially where it is associated with intrinsically rewarding work;

5 **self-satisfaction:** actual or promised promotion is a very positive motivator and staff development plays an important role in ensuring satisfaction.

These satisfiers, as Herzberg calls them, motivate staff in a positive fashion to produce better work, greater co-operation in aiming for organisational goals and higher morale. Though longer-lasting in their effects than the hygiene factors, nevertheless it is a fact that, generally speaking, familiarity also plays a part in these factors to make them less effective as time goes on.

13.9 W. G. Ouchi

W. G. Ouchi's contribution to management thinking is known as theory Z. In this theory management places very great importance on the participation of the workforce in operational decision-making, involving them in the operation of the affairs of the organisation, and ensuring that their commitment to the organisation is encouraged and rewarded. Management needs, therefore, to encourage a high level of consensus and trust among its workforce throughout the enterprise. To embrace this theory management requires to change its thinking in terms of the theories previously discussed and to concentrate on achieving a consensus of values throughout the organisation.

Successful management under theory Z requires:

(a) a high degree of co-operation between members of working groups, departments and other sections of the organisation; this is because a consensus for decision-making depends upon good interpersonal relationships between associated workers;

(b) minimising status differences so that informal relationships between managers and those managed can be built up;

(c) the creation of trust between workers themselves and between workers and their supervisors and managers; this assumes the integrity of each individual concerned and his commitment to the goals of the organisation; it also assumes the worker's ability to work with the very minimum of supervision – this trust is essential if decision-making by consensus is to be achieved and be successful;

(d) that there will be free communication throughout the organisation of information on operational factors, on environmental issues and on all the other matters of concern to the workforce to enable it to make informed and intelligent judgements when contributing to the group decisions;

(e) that despite the involvement of employees in the decision-making process individual managers are still responsible for these decisions in the final analysis;

(f) that a policy of long-term employment coupled with a clearly defined career structure will be pursued, to retain the services of valued staff, to reinforce and to reward commitment to the enterprise.

Unlike theories X and Y, theory Z is based on the premise of total staff involvement, together with management, in the running of an enterprise.

It will be observed that many of these factors, particularly the motivating factors, have been found to be common in all the researches discussed. It should also be mentioned that the research that Herzberg undertook was concerned principally with accountants and engineers, not with workers on the shop floor or in clerical occupations. His specific findings in certain areas should, therefore, be applied with caution to those below supervisory or management level.

A discussion of motivation would not be complete without mentioning some early work carried out in Chicago, which has come to be known as the Hawthorne Experiment.

13.10   The Hawthorne experiment

This was an early series of experiments carried out by Elton Mayo, a psychologist and Professor of Industrial Research at the Harvard Graduate School of Business, at the Hawthorne Works of the Western Electric Company, between the years 1924 and 1932. Its main findings, which broke new ground at the time, led to an entirely new outlook on motivation psychology and resulted in a changed approach both in research and in practice. A research that took place over so many years cannot be summarised effectively in a work of this nature, but the main findings can be given:

(a) social factors are of great importance at work; both the behaviour and motivation of individual workers are affected by group relationships;

(b) it was discovered that an informal organisation of work-groups exists alongside the formal organisation and that these informal group patterns contribute as much to work satisfaction and worker motivation as does the physical environment, more so in some cases;

(c) job satisfaction and social satisfaction are important to the worker;

(d) work-groups are inclined to set their own standards of behaviour and their own levels of output, often in disregard of organisational requirements; any member of a work-group who fails to conform is subject to sanctions applied by the group;

(e) the need for adequate communication between workers and management was established, as was the need for satisfactory social relations.

Perhaps the greatest contribution that the Hawthorne experiment made to industrial psychology and the study of motivation was the realisation of the need for full understanding of the human factor in industrial relations and work, and the significant impact work-group behaviour has on individual worker performance.

13.11   General observations on motivation

The problem of motivation is a strictly human problem. It is very complex and the results of positive attempts to motivate are rarely predictable. What motivates one worker may have no effect at all on another, or may even cause antagonism. Workers in a group will react differently from the individual worker to any particular stimulus. Further, the group is less likely to be reasonable and may be more intransigent than the individual. It is also true that what motivates positively on one occasion may fail entirely on another, even with the same worker or group of workers.

In consequence, the theories propounded in this chapter must be viewed with caution and applied only in conjunction with previous experience of the worker or workers concerned. It must also be remembered that most of the research studies into motivation have been carried out on workers at shop-floor level and so some of the findings cannot be transferred uncritically to the problems involved in motivating managers and supervisors. The problems associated with the development and motivation of managerial staff are dealt with as a separate study in Chapter 15.

Finally, for any scheme to improve motivation to be successful it must be continually monitored. Consequently some form of appraisal must be put in place otherwise it will gradually become ineffective.

Questions

1 Compare and contrast two recent theories of motivation in terms of their utility to management.   **(IPM)**
2 By reference to **three** motivation theories, explain the role of social factors in motivation.   **(CIMA)**
3 (i)   What do you understand by 'employee commitment'?
   (ii)   How can the fundamental human needs for power, achievement and affiliation be harnessed to develop employee commitment to an enterprise and its goals?   **(IAM)**
4 Explain the role of the system of remuneration in the motivation of the work-force. What other motivating factors should be considered by management?   **(IComA)**
5 How can supervisors effectively motivate:
   (a)   an individual at work?
   (b)   their own working group?   **(CIMA)**
6 How can senior managers set out to encourage innovation and entrepreneurial attitudes in their own organisations?   **(ICSA)**
7 (a)   Briefly discuss the principles of job enrichment.
   (b)   How could job enrichment be practically applied to administrative staff?   **(IAM)**

⑭ Communication in the organisation

Effective communication is a vital tool of management because without it all attempts to carry on the activities of an organisation must fail. Without communication nothing can happen: no instructions can be given, no orders taken, no contact made with superiors or subordinates and no information provided or received. Only by communicating effectively can any activity of any kind be planned, organised and carried through. The only exception to this is the individual working entirely alone with no contact at all with any other person. Further, the communication carried on must be understandable and acceptable to both parties.

- Communication has been defined in many ways, and there is no simple, all-embracing definition. It could, however, be said to be the transmission and reception of a message or idea from one party to another in such a fashion that it is mutually understandable. The key words here are 'mutually understandable' because unless both parties to a communication are of one mind as to what the communication means there is no communication at all. This definition also implies that the sender of the communication is quite clear about what the message is intended to convey; much communication is 'non-communication' simply because the transmitter's mind is imprecise on the subject of the communication. It follows, therefore, that unless management can make itself properly understood throughout the undertaking then the proper functioning of the organisation will be impaired.
- It is usual to think of communication in an organisation as being vertical or horizontal. **Vertical** communication is that which flows downwards from the top and upwards from the bottom of the organisation, and **horizontal** communication is that which flows across and between departments at more or less the same management level.

14.1 Vertical communication

- In the past, when the authoritarian approach to management was the prevalent one, vertical communication was predominantly, if not entirely, downward. Decisions were made at the top levels of management and instructions were passed down the line until they reached the level at which action had to be taken. Any upward communication came about through necessity; for example, responses to questions put from

above. The attitude was that management managed and their subordinates did as they were told; there was no right of question or to
information. Instructions were issued to be carried out, not explained.

- Times have changed, however, and workers at all levels, including
  junior and middle managers, are not content blindly to accept edicts
  from above. They are aware that many management decisions and
  instructions, particularly the more significant ones, may have an effect
  on their livelihoods or on their working conditions, and they therefore
  demand the right to be heard before such decisions are put into effect.
  There has developed, therefore, the concept of **two-way vertical communication** which is almost universally accepted by modern management. Hence an organisation must provide a formal channel for the
  upward flow of communication as well as the traditional channel for a
  downward flow. In fact, if there is a failure to provide a means of
  communication from the operating level upwards management may well
  find itself making important decisions that will be thwarted by the
  work-force simply because of non-consultation. Many unofficial 'light-
  ning strikes' can be traced to this cause.

- An important result of the acceptance of the need for two-way vertical
  communication is the increased burden that has fallen on middle
  managers and on supervisors. In addition to their traditional task of
  receiving and interpreting communications coming from the top and
  passing them on in an understandable form to their subordinates, they
  have the additional and onerous task of doing the same thing in reverse.
  If these upwards communications are handled reluctantly or are dealt
  with tactlessly or without understanding the effect on the would-be
  communicators can be unfortunate. Management–worker relations can
  be soured and morale damaged. Fortunately, at the lower end of the
  communication chain there is usually personal contact between manager
  and managed, or supervisor and supervised, and so, given goodwill on
  both sides, misunderstandings can be prevented or resolved.

- However, good staff relations are in greater danger further up the
  management scale. Inevitably the upwards flow lines will come together
  on some senior executive's desk and at this level the person concerned is
  unlikely to have the advantage of personal contact with the originators
  of the communications. Unless, therefore, the middle managers and
  supervisors have been whole-hearted and effective in relaying these
  communications there is the danger of misinterpretation and a consequent breach in good management–worker relations. In addition, of
  course, a senior executive is burdened with an ever-increasing flow of
  information which leaves little time for detailed study of any individual
  communication. In consequence such an executive has to rely to a large
  extent on the ability of subordinate managers for proper interpretation
  of the communications received.

14.2 Quasi-vertical communication

- Vertical communication within an organisation used to be confined to that organisation. However, nowadays there is another channel which runs parallel to the official internal one but which is strictly speaking external to it, and could be called the '**quasi-vertical**' communication channel. This has been brought about by the increasing influence of trade unions, staff associations and the professional bodies, and is most marked in large undertakings where workers and functional staff are well-organised. The trade unions and staff associations exist for the purpose of protecting and improving their members' pay and conditions of work, and the professional bodies are concerned with professional ethics and practice.

- It has become customary for trade unions, and to a lesser extent staff associations, to speak for and negotiate on behalf of their members direct with the higher levels of management. In doing this they by-pass middle managers and supervisory staff and so superimpose their own line of communication over that of the formal internal vertical flow. Similarly, the professional bodies establish standards of professional practice which they require their members to comply with, entirely without consultation with individual managements. By virtue of the strength of these outside bodies, particularly the trade unions, this quasi-vertical upward flow often carries a weight of authority far superior to the established formal internal upward flow. At times its weight equals that of the downward flow from top management.

- One of the results of this condition is that some of the authority over their subordinates is taken out of the hands of the middle managers and supervisors and usurped by internal union representatives such as shop stewards.

14.3 Horizontal communication

The need for effective co-operation and co-ordination between the various sections of an organisation demands a high level of communication between them, and is satisfied by the establishment of an effective horizontal communications network.

- This system operates through internal communication channels such as the internal telephone, memoranda or face-to-face consultation. It takes place between staff of about equivalent status in the different departments, for instance between the factory manager and cost accountant, or sales representative and sales account clerk. There is no authority flowing along the lines of horizontal communication, and it is tactless for the manager of one department to communicate direct with a subordinate in another department.

- Where requests, orders and instructions have to flow horizontally any implied authority to have them carried out is contained in the established procedures covering the operation and is not a delegation of authority to the giver over the receiver. Thus, in a procedure in which a sales representative demands information about a customer's account from a sales account clerk, this request has within it the authority for the sales representative to make this demand, but any authority over the sales account clerk's actions is in the power of the latter's supervisor and not in the power of the sales representative.

14.4   Difficulties in vertical communication

- The most common failures in communications occur in the vertical flow: this is especially so of the flow upward. Proper provision must be made for the flow of information both ways and the appropriate methods must be pressed into service and known by all concerned. Further, some method must be established, where necessary, within these lines of communication to obtain feedback, to ensure that communications are known to be received and understood. The provision of practical systems is a matter for the communications expert; the concern of this section of this chapter is how difficulties arise.

- In all probability the commonest cause of problems in vertical communication is that of lengthy chains of command. This is particularly prevalent in large organisations where a large number of management and supervisory levels exist. Two problems arise: first because of the number of levels concerned the communication takes a long time to reach its ultimate receiver and, second, some distortion tends to occur at each stage so that at the end of the chain the message can be quite different from the original. This is a particular danger where the communication is verbal at any point in the transmission. While written communication can avoid misquoting, this is often too expensive or too difficult, particularly where speed is necessary.

- Geographical location also causes vertical communication problems, particularly upward. Where the decision-making centres of an organisation are divorced from the operating centres, as happens in concerns with many depots or branches, delays and frustrations can occur in the communications network. A particular example of this is where either the transmitter or the recipient is constantly on the move. Such circumstances obtain in communicating with travelling sales representatives, in keeping up communication with a working group that changes sites frequently and whose movements are dictated by work conditions (a street-lighting gang is a good example here), and many others.

- Management style has a decided influence on the effectiveness of vertical communication. If it is authoritarian then there is likely to be a reluctance willingly to accept communications coming down the line and such instructions may be grudgingly complied with. There will certainly be an unwillingness to attempt any significant upwards communication.

Unco-operative attitudes may have already developed at the lower levels of the chain, producing a grudging response to communications from management. This is often symptomatic of poor industrial relations which have caused workers to set up obstructive emotional barriers to the acceptance of management communications.

This authoritarian attitude may also obtain at middle management and junior management levels, though where this occurs it is often a reflection of attitudes higher up. Such managers may see no reason to inform subordinates of many aspects of the organisation's affairs even though these have a bearing on their working conditions. Often such communications come to a stop at a particular manager's desk instead of being passed on. This lack of sensitivity on the part of such managers gives rise to resentment by the people lower down the chain and makes normal communication in either direction that much more difficult. It must be admitted, however, that sometimes communication stops at a certain level simply because the manager concerned is overburdened and neglects this aspect of his duties in favour of what he considers to be more pressing matters. Horizontal communication has higher priority because without it the organisation would slow down unacceptably or stop altogether. Vertical communication is rarely so urgent and thus is likely to be neglected at times of pressure. Naturally, such an overburdened manager should examine the possibilities of delegating some of the overload, perhaps even the communication task.

- The problems so far discussed have been concerned principally with downwards communication. Difficulties also, of course, obtain in the upward flow often because there is simply no provision made for it despite the fact that it is accepted as being highly desirable. Where upward flow is lacking management cannot be properly aware of the attitudes and feelings of their subordinates and are thus unlikely to be able to couch their communications in such forms as will encourage their work-people to accept them willingly and to implement their decisions ungrudgingly. The effectiveness of all communications depends to a large extent upon the willingness of the receiver to participate.

- Merely providing the means for upward vertical communication will not, however, ensure an effective flow in that direction. Such a flow is normally channelled through the line hierarchy and an unco-operative foreman or supervisor, or a manager with no real commitment to communication from work-people upwards, may cause distortion of the communication or stop it altogether. Such attitudes by those in authority eventually discourage lower-level workers even to attempt to communicate, to the eventual detriment to the well-being of the organisation.

- Misunderstanding through different uses of language also affect the effectiveness of vertical communication. The language of the boardroom is not that of the factory floor, and this may lead to lack of understanding.

14.5   Difficulties in horizontal communication

- Because of the common interest in dealing with internal matters it might be thought that horizontal communication would be free from too many difficulties. This is not so, however. The effectiveness of horizontal communication relies very largely on the attitudes of the departments to one another. Where this is good, communication will be good, but where there is an atmosphere of non-co-operation, for whatever reason, then communication can be poor. As efficient communication between all sections of an organisation is necessary for its proper functioning, the non-co-operation of even one can lead to loss of efficiency.
- There may be, for example, specific demarcation lines between departments and the crossing of these lines can cause resentment and a non-co-operative attitude. An example will clarify this. It is not uncommon for a customer to discuss his account with a sales representative, and the representative may take up the customer's queries with the accounts department on the customer's behalf. However, the accounts department may take great exception to this action and may point out to the sales representative in no uncertain terms that accounts are their prerogative and should not be discussed by members of the sales force. Such an occurrence may sour relations between the two sections of the organisation, especially if repeated, and cause difficulties in regard to future communications.

   It should be pointed out in connection with this example, that in many organisations the sales force does play a part in the collection of customers' debts and the accounts department sometimes seeks the assistance of sales representatives in connection with particularly difficult customers. However, this collaboration is by no means universal.
- So-called 'empire-building' is another example of a cause of interference in free horizontal communication. Where the head of a department is determined to increase the department's importance, and the head's own position in consequence, there may be a reluctance for that department to pass on information to other departments unless it is specifically requested, thus indicating how important that department and its head are to the running of the organisation. Such practices lead to severe difficulties in co-ordination and co-operation and slow down the work of the organisation as a whole.
- Finally, horizontal communication also suffers from the two problems of distortion and language. Distortion is a particular danger because so much inter-departmental communication is by internal telephone or verbally face-to-face, and messages passed from mouth to mouth are subject to unconscious alteration. In this respect horizontal communication suffers in the same way as vertical communication. The language problem arises principally where a line department and a specialist department are trying to communicate. The specialists are prone to use their own particular jargon, much of which is not really comprehensible

to the line staff, who are lay people in that respect. For example, the computer department may tell the accounts department that last year's accounts records have been dumped. The accounts department may immediately imagine that the records have been destroyed whereas the computer people simply mean that the records have been taken out of the current computer files and stored elsewhere.

14.6 The mechanism of communication

To improve communication and make it as effective as possible it is necessary to understand its basic mechanism.

● Essentially, communication requires a source (the sender or transmitter), a signal or code, a channel which is the means of transmitting the communication, and a receiver. In the ideal situation action will result, which may mean anything from simple understanding by the receiver to some actual activity performed at the receiving end. In addition, it is advisable if some form of feedback is available so that the transmitter can see that the communication has been received, understood and has produced some reaction. If there is no feedback future action by the sender which is dependent upon the correct receipt of the communication may be hampered. A simple example will clarify this. If a company writes to a job applicant offering employment, with a specific starting date, unless the company receives an acknowledgement and acceptance by the applicant agreeing the starting date, the company will be quite unable to plan the day's activities which depend on the arrival of the applicant to take up the post.
● The mechanism of an effective communication system is best illustrated in a diagram, as in Figure 14.1. It will be seen from this diagram that Stage 4 indicates decoding by the receiver; in other words understanding. This is the area where most breakdowns in communication take place, and may remain undiscovered without some form of feedback.

14.7 Reasons for breakdowns in communication

In order to achieve effective communication throughout an organisation it is necessary to understand the obstacles that occur to prevent it. In doing this it becomes possible to reduce or avoid these barriers and so lessen the risk of breakdown.

(a) Physical obstacles

These have been dealt with in **14.4** above and relate to all forms of communication. Thus long lines of communication and moving locations increase the practical difficulties of communicating efficiently. So do defects in mechanical and electronic apparatus, including faulty telephone connections, breakdowns in teleprinters and so on. Inefficient, reduced or entire lack of service may be included under this

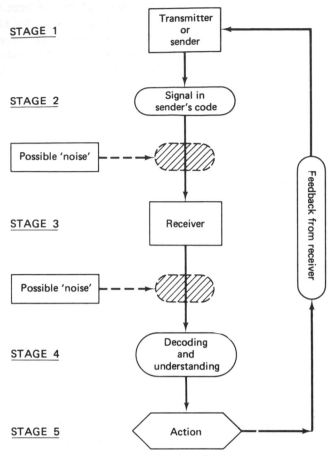

Fig. 14.1   A diagram of the mechanics of communication

heading. These breakdowns include poor postal services, electrical power failure affecting word processors and similar apparatus, and the simple absence of a competent telephone switchboard operator. Such physical problems suggest their own solutions, examples being a thorough overhaul of the lines of communication, proper maintenance of mechanical and electronic equipment and not being totally reliant on electric typewriters or word processors. No organisation should have only one skilled telephone operator; a standby should always be trained and available in emergencies.

Other physical obstacles include background noise such as noisy machinery and equipment (word processors and teleprinters are constant culprits) and aircraft flying overhead, which interfere with telephone and face-to-face conversations.

(b) Coding difficulties

The most common communication code is language. Care should

therefore be taken to ensure that the language used in any communication is within the understanding of the intended receiver and will be interpreted as the sender intends. Different words mean different things to different people as has already been suggested in **14.5** above with the use of the word 'dump'. Common words such as 'capital' and 'profit' have quite different meanings to accountants, economists, politicians and to those with particular political views. Where there is any doubt at all that the message may be misinterpreted, unintentionally or intentionally, then the communication should be worded so that this does not happen.

(c) **Difficulties with a psychological basis**

Much misunderstanding is caused by the communicator's failure to appreciate the receiver's background and attitudes.

- A person's understanding is conditioned by the social, educational and work-environment in which he or she has been raised. If a worker has been conditioned by family distrust of employers generally, or has been subjected to constant anti-employer propaganda, then management's attempts to communicate will be beset by the difficulty of obtaining an unbiased hearing. Any communication from management, however well-intentioned, will automatically be treated with suspicion. More unfortunate, in cases where management/worker relations are at a very low ebb the workers may see every communication as an attempt to deny them fair play even though, in fact, management is being absolutely honest. Of course, the reverse can be the case and managers can also be guilty of an adverse attitude against their workers, with the same unfortunate results in communication.
- Managers also sometimes forget that most of the work-people on the shop-floor have not had the benefit of an education that enables them to think in abstract terms and so all communications, to be properly understood, must be in concrete terms. Neither have they been taught to think a long time into the future; their interests lie in the present. Communications which try to put into effect plans that will not bear fruit for some considerable time are not likely to capture the interest of the work-force in the same way that they might capture that of junior or middle managers.
- Even between one level of management and another there may be difficulties of attitude and prejudice. This is particularly so where a junior manager or a supervisor has developed a certain resentment against a superior. This may have come about because of a need, at some time in the past, for a reprimand which the junior manager felt to be unjust, or because suggestions made by the junior manager were completely ignored or were the subject of tactless remarks. Some middle and senior managers can be guilty of an autocratic or arrogant attitude which generates animosity in their subordinates whether managerial or

in the work-force, and this can have a very deleterious effect on the way their communications are received and acted upon.

(d) Overload difficulties

Where, as is often the case, managers become subject to an excess of communication – and this is particularly true of middle managers – then an arbitrary system of priorities may be applied which may not help to ensure an effective communication system. In such circumstances telephone messages may take precedence over written communications simply because the telephone is more immediate and seems to be more urgent than a letter or a memorandum, both of which demand more time than a telephone call. Equally, face-to-face verbal communication may rank in priority not in accordance with its relative importance to the organisation, but rather to the importance of the person being addressed.

Where this problem of overload exists the managers concerned should urgently delegate those duties that do not require their personal attention, including those appertaining to communication, in order to ensure that no blockage in the communication flow occurs.

14.8   Formal communication

It is important that there should be an effective formal communication system. With external communication this poses few problems. The methods used for external communication, the letter and the telephone, are firmly established and few significant decisions have to be made as to when to use the one instead of the other. This will normally be dictated by the circumstances of each case. Similarly, telex, fax and other electronic communication devices are now firmly established and in current and effective use.

With internal communication, however, the picture is a little different. Where a tight organisation pattern obtains with few levels of management, particularly if it is line organisation, the communication network may be very clearly defined. However, few organisations fall into this category and so some rules must be formulated.

● An important first step is to establish who may, formally, communicate with whom. This is important in order to avoid bad relations building up between different people within the organisation. The question of demarcation lines has already been referred to in **14.5** above. Thus it is essential to lay down specific rules on the subject. May, for example, a stores controller communicate direct with a buying clerk or must he go through his own manager, who will go through the chief buyer? In what circumstances is direct contact allowable? Again, may a sales representative communicate direct with the production department or must this communication go through the sales office?

- The second step is the even more important one of determining who may communicate orders and instructions to whom. May, for example, the credit controller give instructions direct to a sales representative on a matter to do with a customer's account or should this be done only through the sales office? Much uncertainty and umbrage may be saved if firm and certain rules are established on this matter throughout the organisation.

The actual means of internal communication will vary according to circumstances. Normally memoranda and the internal telephone will carry most of the load with, possibly, the telex and fax being used where external depots and braches are involved. Personal contact also plays a large part in formal internal communication, both person to person and the holding of formal meetings. The methods used for purely staff matters, however, should be examined a little more fully.

14.9 Formal staff communication

Where matters of personnel policy are concerned various means are employed.

(a) **Staff meetings**
These can be simple meetings called by management to provide staff with information and to evoke discussion or may be joint consultative meetings which are formally set up with proper constitutions and comprise members from management (mostly appointed) and worker-members (mostly elected), or may be meetings falling between these two extremes. Joint consultative meetings, in particular, may be concerned with any aspect of working conditions and practices from productivity and pay through to welfare and safety. They work to a properly drawn up agenda and accurate minutes are kept.

(b) **Notice boards**
These are one-way communication, in effect a way of purveying information on decisions already taken or announcing the holding of meetings or other appropriate subjects. They are not a channel for discussion and are often ignored by a large proportion of employees. One particular golden rule in regard to notices is that they should be short and to the point, as well as being in appropriate language. A second golden rule is to date each notice and take it down immediately the business to which it refers has been completed. A board of out-of-date notices does more than anything to discredit this form of communication.

(c) **Staff journal or magazine**
This is an attempt both to encourage a corporate feeling in the workers and to provide a channel of active communication. By publicising the undertaking's successes and future plans it generates staff goodwill and a pride in belonging; by announcing promotions and

various social and welfare improvements it helps to generate positive motivation in the work-people; by including articles, letters and various personal matters such as engagements and weddings it provides a voice for the work-force at all levels.

(d)   Staff handbook

Not to be confused with the staff magazine (or house journal) this handbook provides new members of staff with all the information they should know about the organisation and their jobs. It also sets out both the legal and domestic rules concerning conditions of employment, pay, holiday benefits and similar matters. All employees, whatever their status, should be in possession of a staff handbook, and if it is produced in loose-leaf form it can easily be up-dated as conditions change.

14.10   Informal communication

Any management ignores at its peril the channels of informal communication that exist within its organisation. They are principally concerned with the organisation's internal affairs but there are some channels of informal communication which exist externally. Where formal lines of communication are firmly established and positive, informal communication is not present to a significant degree, but it does abound where the organisation does not provide adequate formal channels.

(a)   The grape vine

Sometimes known as the jungle telegraph, this is a network of channels for rumour and gossip. It is most active horizontally but can also exist vertically.

- As it is essentially verbal it is very much prone to distortion by its very nature, but the messages it carries are also embellished at various stages with exaggeration. Because of this, even if the information at the start is substantially correct it may be far from the truth before very long.
- Such a method is, of course, an attractive vehicle for malcontents to use to spread rumours and falsehoods that can damage the organisation. In fact it is true that the grape vine usually carries more bad news than good. There is normally little possibility of checking the veracity of the information being carried and the false gossip can have a disturbing effect upon workers.
- The grape vine can be truly effective only where workers are not kept fully informed of management's intentions and decisions; thus the best counter to the subversive activities of those who use the grape vine to the disadvantage of the undertaking is to ensure that all employees are aware of management plans. Undoubtedly the greatest difficulty concerning gossip and rumour is that it is normally impossible to trace the source. The answer lies in building up complete faith in the management by providing fully adequate formal lines of communication and releasing

information at the earliest possible moment through these lines. Thus rumours are less likely to be believed, and trust in management will be maintained.

- There is one circumstance where the existence of the grape vine can be of use to an organisation, however. Where it is not considered prudent to make a formal announcement on a matter without first gauging employee reaction, this reaction can be to some extent ascertained by leaking an appropriate rumour into the grape vine.

(b) The canteen lunch

Where an organisation provides canteen facilities then much informal communication takes place over the meal tables. Remembering that such meals are also a channel for the grape vine, an astute manager or supervisor can acquire much information as to the way work-people are thinking, and as to their attitudes or grievances.

Similar to the canteen lunch is the working lunch, where suggestions and plans may be discussed without any formal record being kept or any firm commitment entered into. Such working lunches can be used for both external and internal communication.

(c) Social occasions

Any type of social gathering can be a vehicle for informal communication, both external and internal, from rounds of golf to a reception dinner, from membership of a church to a visit to the local public house. Many of these occasions are engineered deliberately for information-gathering purposes, but in many cases information is passed on quite unwittingly and its importance quite unrealised by the giver.

Communication is a vital tool in the successful management of an enterprise and its use should not be left to chance. Proper efforts must be made by every management to utilise it to the full.

Questions

1 (a) Describe the principles of the communication process indicating the objectives to be achieved.

(b) What are the factors which can lead to failure in the communication process? **(IAM)**

2 Describe in some detail *three* important psychological barriers which can act as obstacles to good communication. Illustrate your descriptions from your own experience or reading. **(IAM)**

3 Outline the important characteristics of internal communication systems within an organisation. What is the significance for management of the concept of 'information overload', with special reference to internal management information flows? **(ACCA)**

4 What actions can management take to stimulate the upward flow of communication within an organisation? **(ICSA)**

5 What are the minimum functions fulfilled by an organisation's 'house journal'?   **(IComA)**

6 The management of business organisations often ascribe the cause of problems experienced to 'communication breakdown' or 'communication failure'. Examine a case of communication failure, in an organisation familiar to you, identifying its causes and suggesting means by which such problems may be prevented from recurring.   **(CIM)**

7 What are some of the difficulties experienced in organisations as far as vertical communication is concerned?   **(IComA)**

⬡15 Communication and people

15.1 Meetings

Meetings have been defined as 'the gathering together of two or more persons in order to discuss matters of common concern, in order to arrive at a decision or promulgate a policy'.

- This definition covers all types of meeting – the formal, the informal and the statutory meeting. It also explains the principal purpose for holding a meeting: that is, to have discussion about a matter or number of matters, and if necessary to come to a decision about any action to be taken. A meeting, therefore, has the same aims as an interview. Where it differs is that all participants at a meeting have equal status and that group decisions or opinions are required to be formulated.
- Many company meetings are statutory, being required by the Companies Acts. Such meetings include the Annual General Meeting (AGM), perhaps the best known of company meetings. Here the shareholders are given information about the progress of their company over the previous financial year, are asked to elect or re-elect members of the board of directors, and are asked to approve the rate of dividend, if any, the directors have decided to declare. The Annual General Meeting is the only time that shareholders can voice their opinion about the directors' conduct of the company without taking specific action under the various sections of the Companies Acts giving them rights to call special meetings.
- Outside the requirements of general law or of statute there are many other kinds of meetings, some of which have executive powers and others that possess only the power to advise or to suggest action. Except for the very informal meeting, which is often completely unstructured, every meeting should have some sort of framework within which to work. The rules that govern a meeting will normally be laid down by the body responsible for convening it, but in some cases power is delegated to the meeting to formulate its own rules.

15.2 Categories of meeting

- Before looking at the ways in which meetings are governed, we should examine the four important categories within which most meetings fall, and which may affect the way in which any particular meeting is conducted.

(a)   The meeting to inform

Some meetings are called not to discuss a problem and seek a solution, but rather to inform the members of a decision already made and, possibly, to obtain their consent. Often the meeting takes place to ratify what has already been done, just to regularise the situation. It is highly likely that discussion will take place about the problem and explanations given for the decision, but it is unlikely that the decision will not stand. It may seem that such a meeting is autocratic. Very often it is. However, in other cases it may be that a decision has had to be taken in an emergency that arose before the meeting and there was no time to call a meeting. In such instances it may still be necessary to inform the members and to obtain their formal approval.

(b)   The meeting to persuade

A persuasive meeting is one called in order that a member may put a proposal, which he then seeks to persuade the meeting to adopt. The point before the meeting may be one of policy or of strategy, and it is the intent of the proposer to influence the members to accept his proposition. His role is that of persuasive advocate and his aim is to 'sell' his idea.

- The two types of meeting mentioned above are positive meetings. In both there is a single-minded purpose: to inform or to persuade. Alternative propositions have really no place at such meetings. We have now to consider the two other categories, which are far less clear-cut.

(c)   The consultative meeting

Here there has been no previous decision taken, neither is it intended to persuade the members to a particular point of view. Instead, a problem is put to the meeting for discussion. In this way the knowledge and experience of the members can be called upon and brought to bear on the problem so that a satisfactory and generally agreed solution may be found. A good chairman is essential to this kind of meeting in order that all members may have a reasonable opportunity to put their views and have them properly considered, and so that the meeting is not dominated by just one or two members.

(d)   The enquiring meeting

This type of meeting seeks to acquire information, and so may be said to be an extension of the consultative meeting. Here the convener searches for ideas and information, and he may very well act as a catalyst to bring out suggestions. Discussion and debate will be freer than at a consultative meeting, and usually more wide-ranging.

15.3 Making a meeting effective

To be of any value a meeting must be fully effective. If it is not fully effective it has been a waste of the time of several people. If these are salaried officers of a company, a considerable expense may have been suffered as well. In order to avoid failure or only partial success there are certain steps that can be taken by the leader and convener of a meeting:

1 The objectives of the meeting must be made quite clear to those invited. The topics to be dealt with must be given in precise terms so far as this is possible so that members are quite prepared for proper discussion.
2 Members must be given adequate notice of the meeting, and a prepared agenda should be provided.
3 The accommodation chosen for the meeting must be suitable; it must not be cramped for the number expected, it must be comfortable and as free from noise as possible, and efforts must be made to avoid interruptions. Such items as writing materials and drinking water should be provided.
4 The time of the meeting must be convenient for all concerned, and its probable duration specified.
5 The leader of the meeting must be adequately prepared. He should have in advance all the information and material he knows he will need to deal with the proposals to be put, and he should anticipate possible questions and arguments so that he can meet them with confidence.
6 He should acquaint himself with the kind of people who are to take part in the meeting and try to gauge their likely attitudes so that he is prepared for their response and likely participation. Of course, in the case of very many meetings, the members will already be known to each other through previous acquaintance.

If these six points are given proper attention, then the meeting should start off in the right way and there is every chance that it will be successful and effective.

15.4 The conduct of a meeting

The actual conduct of the meeting whilst it is in progress is equally important. It is upon the leader of the meeting that the burden of successfully running it falls. He may or may not be called the chairman, depending upon the size and type of meeting it is, but whatever his title he should pay attention to the following points:

1 The chairman's authority must be unquestioned. Where a member seeks to dispute this authority or defy it then the chairman must be firm and not allow himself to be overruled.
2 It is up to the chairman to set the tone of the meeting. Members should be at ease with one another, and it is the chairman's duty to ensure this. If necessary he must ensure that members who have not met before are introduced to each other.

3 The purpose of the meeting must be outlined right at the start, despite the notice and the agenda, by a short speech by the chairman.

4 The chairman must do his best to ensure that members make useful and positive contributions to the matters being discussed. Unhelpful and unconstructive remarks and criticisms must be checked, but useful criticism should be encouraged.

5 Discussion should be kept to the point. Members' interest will be lost if the chairman allows irrelevant argument to develop, and loss of interest will lessen the value of the meeting.

6 Useful discussion can take place only in an atmosphere of good humour. The chairman must, therefore, prevent any sense of acrimony or bad temper from developing. The way he does this will depend upon his own temperament and personality, but in the event of serious bad feeling he must be seen to be completely impartial.

7 A meeting must move forward all the time, logically, from point to point. Too much time must not be spent on one aspect of a discussion to the detriment of the time available for other aspects, neither must aspects already discussed be allowed to be revived later in the argument. One of the skills demanded of the leader of a meeting is to be able to keep discussion flowing logically and at a pace commensurate with the arguments put up and the previously agreed duration of the meeting.

15.5 The chairman of a meeting

(a) Appointment of a chairman

There is no standard procedure for the election of a chairman for a meeting: this will depend entirely on the regulations of the body concerned.

- If the meeting is an informal one comprising only a very few people it is highly probable that no formal chairman will preside. In such cases leadership of the group often arises naturally, or one person takes on the task at the invitation and mutual agreement of the remainder.

- In the case of formal meetings, however, a properly appointed chairman is essential, and the Courts have ruled that a meeting is not legally constituted unless a correctly appointed chairman presides over it. Failure in this respect would lead to all the business conducted at such a meeting being invalid. In some cases the chairman holds office by virtue of his being chairman of a superior body – for instance, the chairman of a company is usually also chairman of the board of directors. In other cases the chairman is elected by the members at the first of a series of meetings and holds this office for a prescribed period – for example, the chairman of a social club.

- Where the office is a continuing one, it is usually provided in the regulations that the members may vote for the resignation of an unsatisfactory chairman before his term of office has expired, and for the appointment of a new chairman. Similarly, it is also usual to find that the regulations require the meeting to choose a chairman from among its members present if the official chairman has not arrived at the meeting after a predetermined time (sometimes as short as five minutes). The term 'chairman' is, of course, merely a description of the office, and a woman may act in this capacity. In this case she may be addressed as 'madam chairman' but increasingly the term 'chair' is used for both men and women.

(b) Duties

To act as an effective chairman of a meeting is not a light task, but there are certain recognised duties and powers possessed by a chairman to help him in his duties. The chairman should:

1 Be satisfied that his own appointment is valid.
2 Ensure that the meeting is properly convened, validly constituted, and that those present have the right to attend.
3 Make sure that a quorum is present.
4 Ensure either that the minutes of the last meeting have been circulated and read, or that they are read at the current meeting. This having been done, he should seek the agreement of the members present that the minutes are a true record of the last meeting and then sign them.
5 See that items are taken in agenda order. This does not, of course, prevent the meeting altering the order if it so wishes provided the majority of members agree.
6 Give those who wish equal opportunity to speak on any subject on the agenda as it arises. In doing this, the chairman should try to encourage shy members to voice their views, at the same time curbing those who are verbose.
7 In the case of dispute, act fairly and impartially.
8 Reject matters that may be introduced that are outside the agenda or not within the jurisdiction of the meeting. The last item on practically all agendas is 'any other business'. This should not be permitted to be taken as an excuse to bring up matters quite outside the business of the current meeting, unless of a very trivial nature.
9 Maintain proper order during the proceedings and break up any unruly disputes between members. Most rules allow the chairman in such cases to adjourn the meeting for a short while for tempers to cool.
10 Insist that all motions, amendments and remarks are addressed to the chairman. No direct communication between different members of the meeting should be allowed and offenders should be asked to put their remarks 'through the chair'. By this means the meeting as a whole is kept in the discussion and also some of the heat is kept out of arguments.

11 Put motions and amendments to the vote of the meeting and pronounce the results.

12 See that voting is carried out in strict accordance with the regulations of the meeting. Where there is no formal vote, as often happens at informal meetings, the chairman will pronounce the 'sense' of the meeting.

13 In the event of equal voting, and where the regulations allow, use his casting vote. Contrary to popular belief, a chairman does not have a casting vote as a right: this has to be given him by the regulations. Where such a vote is allowed and is used the chairman must exercise the utmost discretion. It is, in fact, usual for the chairman to vote in such a way as to retain the status quo.

14 After each discussion, summarise the sense of the arguments for the benefit of the meeting.

15 If another meeting is to be held obtain the agreement of the members as to its date and time. This is, of course, not necessary where a series of meetings is planned to be held on specific dates.

16 Declare the meeting closed at the end of the business, or if a valid quorum has ceased to exist through the departure of one or more members. The chairman has the prerogative to close the meeting, though the members may request that he does so.

17 Make sure that adequate notes are taken during the meeting so that proper minutes may be written up. These notes may be taken by the chairman himself, but are more often made by the secretary, who will be responsible for actually writing the minutes.

In addition to the points mentioned above, the chairman also has power to have disorderly members expelled from the meeting and to adjourn the meeting if he finds it impossible to restore and maintain proper order.

The role of chairman, clearly, is a very onerous one. On him falls the full responsibility for the success and smooth running of the meeting. Some chairmen are weak and allow discussion to ramble on, often without regard to agenda or time. In such cases frequently only the most vociferous members are heard. The opposite situation occurs when the chairman is domineering or arrogant, and imposes his own views on the meeting. In such circumstances it is impossible for balanced discussion to take place.

15.6 Standing orders

Many formal meetings are governed by specific regulations as to procedure, called 'standing orders'. These rules are designed to provide a procedural framework for the meetings concerned and are particularly helpful to members who may not be familiar with the conventions governing the conduct of meetings. Standing orders help to avoid misunderstandings, provide specific rules for most circumstances that may be met during a meeting, and generally assist in ensuring that the event will run smoothly and effectively.

Standing orders are usually formulated for the benefit of the particular meetings for which they are designed. However, there are some rules that are common to most standing orders:

1 The quorum

The quorum shall consist of . . . . members, entitled to attend and to vote.

No meeting shall be considered as valid unless a quorum is present continuously throughout the whole of the duration of the meeting.

If at any time a quorum is not present, or maintained, then the meeting shall stand adjourned on instructions from the chairman.

2 Notice of the meeting

Seven clear days' notice must be given in writing to each and every member entitled to attend at a meeting whether or not such member is entitled to vote.

3 Order of business

An agenda must be prepared and circulated with the notice of the meeting to every member entitled to attend.

The business before the meeting shall be dealt with in the order set out on the agenda unless it be altered by agreement of the members. Such agreement shall be signified by a simple majority on a vote by a show of hands.

No business not included on the agenda shall be considered by the meeting but by agreement with the members such business may be carried forward for the agenda of a future meeting.

4 Chairman's ruling

The chairman's ruling on any matter shall be final. However, should any ruling be challenged by not less than 25 per cent of those present and entitled to vote then the ruling shall be put to the vote on a show of hands. The decision shall be by a simple majority.

5 Speeches

Members shall at all times address the meeting through the chair.

No member may speak on any motion more than once, except with the permission of the chairman. Nevertheless, any member who has spoken on the original motion may also speak on any amendment.

Speeches must be addressed strictly to the content of the motion or amendment before the meeting, and shall be immediately terminated if so directed by the chairman.

6 Motions and amendments

All motions must be in writing and must be submitted to the secretary of the meeting not less than fourteen days before the date on which the meeting is to be held.

Amendments to motions before the meeting shall be put in writing and handed to the chairman, who will read them out to the members. All motions and amendments shall have a proposer and a seconder. The chairman may act in neither capacity.

Amendments must be put to the vote before the motions they seek to qualify. If an amendment is carried, the amended motion shall be put to the meeting as the substantive motion. If an amendment fails then the original motion must be voted upon without further discussion.

The chairman shall not allow any amendment that is merely a negation of the original motion.

A motion, having been carried, shall not be the subject of further discussion at the same meeting.

7 Voting

Voting shall be by show of hands and the chairman's decision on the result shall be final, subject to standing order **4** above.

A motion shall be deemed to have succeeded if it obtains a simple majority of the votes of those present and entitled to vote. There shall be no right of proxy.

In the event of a tie in voting the chairman may, at his discretion, use his casting vote. Should the chairman decline to use his casting vote in the event of a tie then the motion shall be deemed to have failed.

Any member entitled to vote may abstain if he thinks fit.

8 Unruly behaviour

If any member acts in an unruly manner, uses unseemly language or interrupts a speaker without permission of the chairman, or if he refuses to obey the chairman when called to order, then he shall be required to leave the meeting. Neither shall he be allowed to return unless and until he gives to the meeting an acceptable apology. Should this expulsion reduce the number of members to below the required quorum, the meeting must stand adjourned notwithstanding an apology.

9 The adjournment

The chairman may adjourn the meeting as and when he considers it necessary. Similarly, any member may move the adjournment, when the motion must be seconded and put to the meeting. However, if at the time the motion for the adjournment is put a previous motion is being discussed, no member who has already spoken on the latter motion may move the adjournment.

These nine rules are only examples of what may be found in standing orders. Many other regulations may be included, such as the selection of speakers, right to reply, procedure in the event of the non-arrival of the chairman and the action to be taken in any circumstances likely to be encountered by any particular meeting it is sought to regulate.

15.7 Committee meetings

Committees are a familiar phenomenon of most organised bodies nowadays. The reasons are not far to seek. First, a great deal of expert knowledge is required to deal with even the day-to-day work of large organisations, and second, the governing bodies of most organisations have little time to attend to detailed matters about which a fair proportion of their members have insufficient expert knowledge or experience. Hence, a board of management or other governing body may appoint specialist committees to deliberate on various matters for its information, guidance and counsel. Thus a large commercial enterprise may have a capital budget committee to advise the board of directors on matters of capital investment, a local authority may have a housing committee to deal with the specialist matters involved in housing the homeless.

(a) **Committee membership**

Members of specific committees may be members of the parent body which appoints the committee, or may be specialists directed or invited to the committee because of their particular knowledge, experience or qualifications. Generally speaking, then, committee members may be said to be expert in their fields and are appointed because of this fact. Committees, of course, operate by holding committee meetings and any authority they have is derived from the fact that they do conduct their business in concert at meetings. Individual committee members have, as a rule, no individual responsibility or authority.

(b) **A committee's authority**

A committee's authority is prescribed by the parent body that appoints it, and the limits to this authority are laid down by the terms of reference agreed at the time of the committee's formation. At no time may a committee exceed either its derived authority or its powers under these terms of reference. For the most part a committee's powers are limited by the simple reason that it has the authority only to consider, to report and to recommend; it has no executive power. Thus, usually a committee makes its reports to its parent body, together with its findings or its recommendations, and it is only the parent body that has the power to take action on the recommendations. A planning committee may recommend the demolition of a row of old houses and the building of a block of flats, but the power to put these recommendations into effect lies with the full council. Nevertheless, some committees do have executive powers, though these may be confined to non-controversial matters, or to matters on which specific limits may be set. For example, a finance committee may have the power to authorise expenditure up to a limited sum, but not beyond.

(c) **Standing committees**

Some matters for which committees are formed are of a continuing nature. Into this category would fall finance committees, planning committees, share transfer committees and many others whose business is part of the day-to-day work of the organisation to which they belong. Such committees are called 'standing committees' and are, of course, of a permanent nature, though their actual membership may change from time to time. As stated previously, individual members have no status; theirs is a collective power arising from their acting together in a committee meeting.

(d)   *Ad hoc* committees

Often, however, a committee is appointed to look into a particular problem or project, and when work on this matter is completed and reported upon, the committee is disbanded. Such a body is known as an '*ad hoc* committee'. The same rules apply to the *ad hoc* committee as apply to the standing committee in regard to authority and powers.

(e)   Control of committees

A committee is, of course, really an extension of the main assembly and the principal body remains responsible for the work of the committee. Consequently, it is essential that the main body has the means of exercising control over the committee. In very many cases this does not pose a significant problem, because the committee is composed of members of the main body, or has a majority of such members. Where, however, the committee is composed of persons who are not members of the main body, or where members of the main body sitting on the committee are in a minority, then some positive steps must be taken so that control is exercised by the responsible body. Particularly is this so if any of the committee members seem to be out of sympathy with the official policy of the main board. In such cases effective control of a committee can be exercised by following the suggestions set out below:

1 When the main body appoints the committee its resolution to put this into effect should state clearly and precisely the terms of reference under which the committee will carry out its duties. Equally, the committee's powers should be precisely defined, with limits to those powers clearly stated.

2 The chairman of the main body should be *ex officio* a member of the committee, preferably, but not necessarily, its chairman.

3 Care should be taken that members appointed to a committee are, on the whole, sympathetic to the aims and policies of the main body. However, it should be appreciated that a little dissent can be very beneficial in discussion.

4 Any person who is likely to dominate the committee, however well qualified he might be, should not be appointed unless his inclusion is unavoidable.

5 The committee should be required to submit promptly to the main body the minutes of each meeting as they are prepared. The same remarks apply to reports that the committee is responsible for preparing.

Committees are a very necessary aid to the work of principal bodies and they help very significantly in the making of well considered and effective decisions.

(f) Subcommittees

A committee is often helped by the appointment of a subcommittee. This is a subdivision of the committee. It is formed to deal with matters within the terms of reference of the committee that the selected members of the subcommittee are especially equipped to consider. Usually a committee has the power to appoint its own subcommittees, but where this is not so the necessary authority must be sought from the main body. Only very rarely has a subcommittee executive power; its function is to investigate the matter it is formed to consider and to report to the full committee.

15.8 Notice of meetings

All formal meetings require notice to be given to all those who are entitled to attend.

- Failure to do this leads to the possibility that the business conducted at the meeting may be declared invalid. Failure to give notice to even one person entitled to attend may invalidate the meeting and its business. This is, therefore, a very important matter.
- The notice that has to be given is laid down in the rules or standing orders governing the meeting, and such regulations must be rigidly observed. For example, if seven clear days' notice is required, this means what it says, and the day of sending the notice and of its receipt are not counted in the required seven.
- However, whilst the failure to give adequate notice, or any notice at all, to a few members carries the danger that the meeting may be declared invalid, if the members so affected attend the meeting they may waive their rights about notice. In this case the meeting will be considered valid. Similarly, if the notice to all the members of a meeting does not meet the strict requirements of the regulations and is, therefore, not a proper notice, nevertheless the meeting may be declared valid if all the members so agree.
- Finally, even the Courts do not construe the rules of notice absolutely rigidly, as was shown by a decision in 1961. In this case a company held a meeting of shareholders with a view to a reduction of capital. A few members were accidentally overlooked and received no notice, but the Court held that this did not invalidate the resolution passed to effect the desired reduction of capital. Nevertheless, it is very unwise not to follow the rules as to notice very carefully. Any doubt as to the validity of the business carried on at a meeting can cause delays in putting decisions into action and may, in serious cases, lead to expensive litigation.
- Meetings that are held regularly, such as directors' meetings, committee meetings and the like do not, strictly speaking, need formal notice. However, it is usual to send a notice, nevertheless, as this acts as a reminder at least. Similarly, if the date of a subsequent meeting is

agreed at a meeting, again no notice is strictly required, but is usually sent.

15.9   The agenda of the meeting

Every formal meeting needs a guide so that its business is carried forward positively and in an orderly manner, and so that no item that should be considered is omitted. The guide prepared for this purpose is the agenda. This is merely a list of the matters to be put before the meeting for discussion and decision.

- Tradition has given the agenda an accepted format, starting with, in most cases, 'Apologies for absence'. This is followed by 'Minutes of the last meeting' and then 'Matters arising'. Then follow the new items to be considered and the agenda finishes with two time-honoured items, 'Any other business' and 'Date of the next meeting'.
- Naturally, every agenda is not prepared precisely in this fashion. Many omit reference to apologies for absence, and others itemise the matters in the minutes of the last meeting to be considered, instead of requiring the chairman to go through those minutes item by item putting each to the meeting for consideration. The latter method can be a great time-waster, and often encourages discussion to start on a matter already decided at the previous meeting. Such discussion must be firmly stopped by the chairman. Again, if there is not to be a subsequent meeting, then the last item – 'Date of next meeting' – will not arise.
- It is usual for the notice of a meeting and its agenda to be combined, and a specimen is given in Figure 15.1.

15.10   Methods of voting

Except at very informal meetings, when the chairman may 'sense' the desire of the meeting and record this accordingly, all meetings need some method of voting so as to determine the will of the meeting. How voting shall take place will be laid down in the regulations governing the meeting.

- If a poll or a ballot is held after voting by acclamation or by show of hands, the decision by poll or ballot overrides the previous vote. As stated in **15.6**, point 7, if the voting is equal the chairman may, if he has one, use his casting vote to produce a decision, in which case he normally votes so as to leave things as they were. However, it must be stressed that a chairman has no right to a casting vote unless this is given him in the regulations. Where no casting vote is provided for and there is equal voting then the motion concerned is lost.
- The voting procedure is complete only when the chairman has declared the result. When a motion has been passed at a meeting by a valid vote, it may not again be raised in discussion, neither may it be rescinded, at that meeting.

```
┌─────────────────────────────────────────────────────────┐
│                                                         │
│                  NOTICE OF MEETING                      │
│                  ─────────────────                      │
│                                                         │
│                                                         │
│         A meeting of the Safety Committee will be held on│
│         14th May, 19 . . , at 3.30 pm in the Committee Room│
│                                                         │
│                      4th May, 19 . .                    │
│                                                         │
│                                                         │
│                        AGENDA                           │
│                        ──────                           │
│                                                         │
│                                                         │
│           1.   Apologies for absence.                   │
│           2.   Minutes of meeting held on 12th February, 19 . .│
│           3.   Matters arising.                         │
│           4.   Provision of fire extinguishers in Paint Store│
│           5.   Recruitment of Safety Officer.           │
│           6.   Any other business.                      │
│           7.   Date of next meeting.                    │
│                                                         │
│                                                         │
└─────────────────────────────────────────────────────────┘
```

Fig. 15.1   A specimen of combined notice of meeting and agenda

- Finally on voting, most rules provide for a simple majority to pass a motion. However, this is by no means universal and sometimes a specific percentage majority is necessary for a decision to be validly made.

15.11   Minutes of the meeting

Meetings are held to determine action, to formulate policy or to make decisions. This being so, it is essential that the business of the meeting be truthfully and accurately recorded. This is the function of the minutes. However, they are not a report of the meeting, and will not normally record argument and discussion, but solely decisions reached.

- Like the agenda, minutes have a conventional format. They are headed with the title of the meeting concerned, its venue and the date and time it was held. The names of those attending will be shown, with apologies for absences. In recording the business done, practice varies from body to body. Some minutes contain only the bare resolutions that have been passed, whereas others will include names of proposers and seconders. On occasion, though rarely, brief accounts of the arguments leading to the decisions are included. Where a resolution requires action by a named person this fact will generally be stated, as will any descriptions required to ensure the identification of sites, materials and so on.
- When minutes are written up, the agenda of the meeting is used as a

guide, and generally the secretary responsible for the minutes makes suitable notes on his or her copy of the agenda during the meeting. Each item in the minutes is numbered and, in order to ensure that all items are included from the very beginning, thus providing a complete historical record, they are often numbered consecutively following on from one set of minutes to the next. This is particularly important where minutes are kept in loose-leaf binders, as it is reasonable proof that none is missing.

- It is usual for the regulations governing meetings to provide that the minutes be signed by the chairman of the next succeeding meeting. This is perfectly proper and simple where meetings are held at dates not too far apart. However, where there are long intervals between meetings it is more sensible for provision to be made for the signing prior to the next meeting. In either case, once signed the minutes become the legal record of the business transacted at the meeting to which they refer and must on no account be altered. Where the minutes are signed at the next meeting it is usual for the chairman to have the secretary read the minutes, or to have them circulated previously and taken as read. He then asks the meeting to confirm that the minutes are correct before he signs them. By 'correct' he means a truthful and accurate record of the business transacted: this is not an invitation for any item to be reopened, which would be quite irregular. Should any member disagree with an item in the minutes it is for him, with the permission of the chairman, to put a motion to the current meeting so that the item concerned can be overturned by a proper vote if this is the wish of the meeting.

- Where meetings are held at regular intervals it is common for copies of the minutes of the previous meeting to be circulated with the notice and agenda for the next one. This gives the members the opportunity to study them and to formulate any questions necessary under the agenda item 'Matters arising'. It also provides a record of the meeting for those members who were unable to attend.

A specimen of a common form of minutes is given in Figure 15.2 based on the specimen agenda shown in Figure 15.1.

15.12   Interviews

An interview is a face-to-face verbal exchange which endeavours to discover as much information as possible in the least amount of time about some relevant matter.

- In business, interviews are used for a variety of purposes which include recruitment of staff, hearing staff grievances and complaints, disciplinary action and many other matters chiefly concerned with management/ staff relations. However, the term 'interview' may be used for any two-way verbal communication where one of the participants has some sort of authority over the other, or is in some other way in an

Minutes of the meeting of the Safety Committee held on 14th May, 19 . . , at 3.30 pm in the Committee Room.

Present: A. Dorritson   (Chairman)
                    B. Sideley
                    F. Bothamstone
                    S. Sydnie
In Attendance   J. Comely   (Secretary)

322. Apologies for absence were received from Messrs A. Anville and B. Burdock

323. The minutes of the meeting held on 12th February, 19 . . , having been previously circulated, were taken as read. They were signed by the Chairman as a correct record of that meeting.

324. Matters Arising
A tender has been accepted for the installation of sprinkler valves in the General Office and work is due to start on 1st June.

325 Fire Extinguishers for Paint Store
It was agreed that an additional four fire extinguishers should be purchased and installed in the Paint Store. Mr Sydnie was instructed to obtain tenders from three suppliers for consideration at the next meeting.

326. Recruitment of Safety Officer
It was agreed that a Safety Officer should be recruited as soon as possible. Mr Dorritson will instruct the Personnel Department to draw up a suitable job specification with a view to advertising this post.

327. Any Other Business
The low level of lighting on the stairway in the old building was brought up by Mr. Sideley. Mr Sydnie promised to look into this matter and report at the next meeting.

328. The next meeting will be on 30th July at 3.30 pm.

CHAIRMAN

Fig. 15.2 Specimen minutes

advantageous or superior position. This obtains, for example, when a sales representative sees a potential customer or a reporter visits a prominent or notorious person with a view to publishing a report of the conversation.

- Authority may be overt, as in the case of an employer interviewing an applicant for an appointment, or it may be by way of some special superiority over the interviewee, such as special knowledge as in the case of a counselling interview. In many instances the interviewer needs to have positive skills in diplomacy as well as social skills to carry off an interview successfully – for example, where the meeting is for the dismissal or reprimand of an employee, or where the other participant is an angry, complaining customer. Such interviews should not end with a feeling of rancour in either party.

15.13 The key elements of an interview

In order that the interviewer may derive the utmost benefit from an interview much care must be exercised before and during the meeting. It might be said that there are four elements to a successful interview: planning it, conducting it, making assessments during it and at its conclusion, and making a decision based on factors brought out by the interview.

(a) **Proper planning** must be carried out prior to the meeting, as without a clear plan the interview will probably be less than completely successful. The purpose for holding the interview must be definite and certain. What, precisely, do we wish to find out? What sort of questions should we put to the interviewee and in what order? How are we going to put them? Which is the most suitable place to hold the interview?

Many interviewers prefer to have a structured interview – that is, one in which a specific list of topics with, perhaps important questions, is prepared, probably on a form that can be completed as the interviewee answers. Others are content with a list of headings that act as a guide during the meeting, but which, nevertheless, keep the interview on course. Either method is preferable to an interview where the interviewer has no plan but asks questions as he thinks of them. Such an interview is likely to miss many important pieces of information that will allow of a well-considered decision.

The interview should be conducted in accordance with the plan that has been previously formulated. However, the plan must be viewed as a flexible guide rather than a rigid set of rules, and it must be modified as circumstances require during the course of an interview.

An interview is a human situation. This being so, the personality of the interviewee must be taken into account and accommodated so far as the other requirements of the interview will allow. Only in this way will the most benefit be gained from the interview. It must also be remembered that in most cases the interviewer is in a position of command, and this fact produces different reactions in different interviewees.

(b) **Assessment** is not, generally, something that happens at a particular point in an interview: rather is it the result of continuous appraisal from the moment the interview begins. Information will be gathered from the interviewee during the course of the meeting, adding to the knowledge being gained bit by bit. Gradually an assessment emerges based on this knowledge and on the impression made by the interviewee through his personality, his attitude and his apparent motivation. When this moment of final assessment is reached the discussion should be terminated; no useful purpose can be served by prolonging it and in some cases further conversation may interfere with the clear decision already made. In the case of the salesman/customer interview, for example, the customer may quite well be talked out of his favourable assessment of the product if the salesman continues to expound its virtues after the buyer has made up his mind to buy.

(c) **Decision** on the course of action to take normally comes very soon after the final assessment. Sometimes the decision comes simultaneously with the assessment. The temptation to arrive at a conclusion during the course of assessment, and before the termination of the interview, should be firmly resisted, because in such a case a verdict is probably being taken before all the evidence has been presented. The decision should be objective: if it is made without the full information being presented it will probably be in some measure quite subjective, perhaps influenced by the interviewee's dress, his accent or other personal trait.

Where possible, the interviewee should be informed of the decision at once, otherwise he should be given the result as soon after the meeting as possible. In the latter case it is courteous to tell the person concerned when he may expect to hear the outcome of the interview. However, if the announcement of the decision is to be delayed it is most unwise to give any hint as to the possible outcome in advance. In the case of an applicant for a job, for instance, hopes may be raised that subsequently have to be dashed to the ground.

15.14 Interviewing techniques

So important is the question of interviewing skills that it is advisable to look at some of the techniques that help to make a successful interview.

(a) The environment

Except for certain circumstances, such as a salesman/customer interview, all interviews should be held in private. All possible steps should be taken to avoid interruptions, such as informing the telephone switchboard operator to avoid putting telephone calls through, and asking colleagues to respect your privacy for the duration of the interview. Interruptions, even minor ones, can reduce the effectiveness of an interview by impeding the flow of thought and inhibiting conversation. Where a series of interviews has to take place, such as a selection of an applicant for a job from among a number of interviewees, sufficient time should be allocated for this purpose and be made sacrosanct.

The physical arrangements are also of extreme importance, and must be such that they put the interviewee at his ease. The room should be pleasant and evenly lighted. The chairs should be businesslike but comfortable, and preferably the same for each party. Both people should be able to see each other easily. The interviewee should never be at a disadvantage as against the interviewer. He should not be positioned so that he faces a window directly, thus putting him fully in the light whilst the interviewer is less well lighted. Such a condition simply makes the interviewee feel selfconscious and puts an obstacle in the way of the free flow of conversation. Where possible there should be no physical barrier between the two people, such as a desk, as this tends to produce a barrier against the free flow of thought as well as a barrier in the physical sense. Rather, if a desk is necessary to the interviewer, the interviewee should be seated at the side of it.

(b) The interviewer's behaviour

Because he is in control of the interview, the interviewer has a position of authority and this he must be at pains not to abuse. He must, therefore, be especially careful to put the interviewee at his ease and to give him confidence. The interviewer's attitude should be one of understanding and of wanting to be of assistance. Above all, the interviewer must not be overbearing, thus creating apprehension or nervousness in the mind of the interviewee. Neither must the interviewer abuse his position by putting personal and irrelevant questions. Unless the interviewee has a calm and relaxed mind communication will be hindered and the interview will be less than successful.

(c) Information flow

The purpose of an interview is the gathering and interchange of information, and this can come about only if a smooth, two-way communication is established from the very beginning. Mutual trust and confidence are essential, as is a relaxed and friendly atmosphere. One way to generate these conditions is for the interviewer to introduce a non-controversial topic of mutual interest at the start of the interview and so establish a rapport between the parties. This will make subsequent conversation much easier and will lessen any nervousness the interviewee may feel. The questions to be asked during the interview should have been decided upon during the planning stage; the form in which they are put will be governed by the circumstances that develop during the interview.

It must be remembered that it is desirable to check the answers and information that the interviewee gives during the interview, though this requires tact. There are a number of ways of doing this. For example, a question may be put in a different manner at a later point in the interview and the response checked with the previous answer. A response may be referred to again, casually, later and re-examined; or an alteration of approach may be adopted round a topic. It is important, however, not to give the interviewee the slightest impression that his integrity is doubted: his confidence must be maintained throughout.

(d) The theme of the interview

An interview is an exercise in the meeting of minds, as mentioned earlier. If this is successfully achieved, as it should be in a fruitful interview, then there may be a tendency to discuss interesting topics irrelevant to the objectives of the interview. This must be resisted firmly, except, perhaps, at the beginning of the meeting when it is necessary to induce a friendly and relaxed atmosphere. Thus, the purpose of the interview must be kept firmly in mind throughout the discussion, and no extraneous subjects allowed to intrude. If the interview has been carefully planned this should not be very difficult. An unstructured interview, however, may allow the conversation to wander off the point with the result that insufficient information is gathered about the interviewee and a conclusion come to based on inadequate data. More often than not such a situation results in decisions being taken that prove unsatisfactory.

(e) Behaviour the interviewer should avoid

The effectiveness and success of an interview depend almost totally on the behaviour of the interviewer. At the beginning of this section we looked at some of the things he should do, and we must now examine some of the things he should avoid doing:

1 He should not let his personal reactions to the interviewee influence his assessment. In particular, first impressions should not be allowed to colour the interviewer's attitude, otherwise a great deal of the objectivity of the interview will be lost. An open mind as to dress, accent, physical appearance and mannerisms must be maintained unless any of them is fundamental to the objective of the interview.

2 The interviewer should, at all costs, avoid asking leading questions which could indicate to the interviewee what answers are expected: not, for example, 'You can do a trial balance, can't you?', but rather, 'How far can you take the books of account?'

3 Too much talking by the interviewer is detrimental to the interview. This is not an uncommon fault, but must be resisted. The interviewee must be allowed to have his say fully and without having to compete for time with the interviewer.

4 Conversely, the interviewer must not be guilty of being taciturn. If he is uncommunicative the interviewee may be hindered from speaking freely, or may feel compelled to talk too much to avoid embarrassing pauses. In either case the interview will be less than effective. The interviewer is in charge of the interview and it is his responsibility to keep it flowing along his planned course; this means that he must make a reasonable contribution throughout.

5 Just as it is necessary to avoid putting leading questions, so is it important not to give information that can give an indication to the interviewee what sort of attitude and response are expected of him. At a job interview, for instance, if the interviewer extols the special virtues of the previous occupant of the post, the interviewee may be inclined to claim the same virtues.

6 The interviewer should very carefully avoid constantly interrupting the interviewee's answers and comments, or cutting them short. In addition to resulting in a less than fully effective interview, this practice may also cause the interviewee to feel that the interviewer has little interest in him or his views. A personal rapport must be generated and maintained all through the meeting, and this includes showing the interviewee that he has the interviewer's interest all the time.

7 No questions should be put that can be answered simply by 'Yes' or 'No': the interviewee should be required to express himself fully at all times.

8 The interviewee has as much interest in the interview as the interviewer, otherwise he would not be there. The interview should not be closed, therefore, without giving the interviewee the opportunity to seek all the information he feels he needs. Failure to do this frequently results in misunderstanding and subsequent grievance.

15.15 Staff selection interviews

A large proportion of the interviews that take place are concerned with the selection of suitable staff, and effective communication at such interviews is of considerable importance for both the employer and the potential employee. In order to try to draw from the applicant all the information that is necessary to make a wise staff choice the personnel profession has formulated a number of interviewing topics with this in mind. It is called the 'Seven-Point Plan' and is dealt with in **23.2** below.

15.16 Interviewing panels

Often interviews are conducted not by one person, but by a panel of two or more people; especially is this so when an important vacancy has to be filled. Usually, of course, the various members of the panel have differing interests in the applicant.

● In essence, the principles appertaining to interviewing by one person also apply to interviewing by several. However, it must be recognised that the presence of a panel makes the proceedings very much more formal and usually places a greater strain on the interviewee, who finds it much more difficult to relax in the presence of a panel than he would in the presence of a single interviewer. Greater efforts must be made, therefore, to relieve the increase in tension likely to be experienced by the applicant and to lessen his nervousness in this situation.

- Further, there is every advantage to be gained by structuring the interview. Each member of the panel will, in all probability, be expert in his own field and will be anxious to put questions on particular points appertaining to his special interest. Unless the interview is structured, and understood to be so by all concerned, there is the risk that the interviewee will be assailed by questions from all sides with little or no logic applied to their order or content. In such circumstances the applicant may quite easily become confused or, at least, tense and be quite unable to show himself in the most favourable light. Under such conditions, in a competitive interview, it is quite possible that a less than satisfactory decision may be made by the panel, with the reward going to the candidate with the strongest nerves rather than the one with the highest ability for the position. Undoubtedly, however, much can be done to ease the situation if the panel is under the control of a firm and understanding chairman.

15.17 Addressing an audience

It is often necessary for a manager to give a speech to a group of people, sometimes a large group and sometimes a small one. There are certain guidelines that can be followed to make this task easier than it may first appear, particularly if it is necessary to address a large gathering.

(a) Some general points

- The first step towards a successful speech is knowledge of the subject. A thorough grasp of the topic or topics to be dealt with is essential and gives confidence to the speaker. If necessary the subject should be researched to fill any gaps in the speaker's knowledge. This is particularly desirable if the subject or point of view is at all controversial.
- There are almost certain to be questions put by the audience or group being addressed and the speaker must be prepared to answer them. Any lack of knowledge displayed may lose the confidence of the audience. However, it is quite acceptable to admit being unable to answer a question that is very much outside the main theme of the talk. In the case of an intimate or informal group a promise to supply the answer later is usually welcome.
- Language can be a problem to a speaker and he should ascertain beforehand what kind of group he is to address, assuming they are not colleagues when he will know this. The kind of language used to address a board of directors is not the kind to employ when addressing a meeting of production workers.

(b) Notes

Very few speakers can deliver a first-class speech without notes in one form or another so there should be no reticence about taking notes on to the platform and to be seen to be consulting them. The problem lies in the manner of the notes. They are needed as memory aids and to keep the talk flowing logically from step to step, and to avoid omission of important points. There are four basic ways in which to prepare a speech, which are as follows:

1 **Writing the speech verbatim.** This is not to be recommended for various reasons. First, a read speech is almost always boring to the listeners, and the speaker is often more concerned to keep his place on the page than to keep his speech lively and vital. Second, he has to keep his eyes on his notes and loses the eye contact that is so important to keep an audience involved with the subject. Third, written language is more stilted than spoken language and the speech is therefore likely to lose freshness and spontaneity, especially if the speaker has taken time during the preparation to 'polish' his work. Fourth, if the speaker loses his place there may be an embarrassing pause whilst he finds it again, in which case the thread of the speech is broken, or he may, on restarting, omit a sentence or two and so cause misunderstanding.

2 **Writing out the speech and memorising it.** This is even worse than reading the speech. In addition to the disadvantages of a written speech as mentioned above, there is the additional hazard of forgetting part of it. Furthermore, even a written speech can be attuned to an audience if necessary, but this is exceptionally difficult with a memorised one and leads to complications in delivery when attempted.

3 **The extemporaneous method.** Here no attempt is made to write down full notes; instead, headings are prepared of the principal parts of the speech and brief notes are added below them. The actual speech is composed as delivery is made, the headings and notes helping the speaker to remember the items and facts he wishes to bring to the audience's attention, and ensuring that he presents them in a logical fashion. Speeches given in this manner are likely to be lively and vital and to retain the interest of the audience more fully than the two previous methods.

4 **Impromptu speaking.** Strictly speaking this should not be included in preparation of notes, because no notes are prepared. Simply, the speaker delivers his speech without benefit of any notes at all, and often without any preparation beforehand. Speaking in this manner can be successful only when attempted by a very experienced person who has absolute control over his subject. It is not to be recommended to anyone of only average ability, and certainly not to a beginner.

One note of caution; whichever method of note preparation is adopted, statistics and similar figure information should always be read from notes: the memory should never be trusted.

(c) Preparing a speech

Having looked at the question of the content of the speech, and how the notes should be prepared, the steps required in the actual preparation of the speech must now be examined:

1 Fix the purpose and aim of the speech. Is it to be informative, persuasive or evocative? Is it intended to offer new knowledge, to examine existing knowledge or to alter current thinking? Is it to instruct, to train or to further interest? Answers to these questions will set the tone and pattern of the speech.

2 Ascertain, or fix, the length of time of the speech.

3 Gather ideas, as suggested at the beginning of this chapter.

4 Write the main headings and fill in with the outline of the talk, as explained under **(b)** above.

5 Familiarise yourself with the main pattern of what you will say, guided by your notes as in **4**.

6 Set time limits to each section of the speech. This will ensure that each part is given its appropriate quota of time. More important, it will help to avoid over-running the total allotted time or, worse still, to avoid running out of material before the allotted span.

7 Consider whether the talk could be more informative or more entertaining if some form of visual aids were used rather than relying entirely on speech.

8 Leave time for questions.

A chart such as that shown in Figure 15.3 is a valuable aid to structuring a speech; where visual and other aids are to be used these are noted against the section heading in a column ruled for them. Inspection of this chart before the meeting will act as a reminder of what aids must be available, and the various times should be marked on the actual notes to be used for the speech. As a planning aid, this chart can be invaluable.

It cannot be overstated that the greater the care taken in preparing for a speech, the better the speech is likely to be.

15.18 Report writing

According to the dictionary a report is 'an account given or opinion formally expressed, after investigation or consideration'. It will be seen from this definition that a report is reckoned to be formal, and is required to give an account of the matter covered or to state an opinion on it: sometimes both are required. In most cases, moreover, conclusions have to be drawn by the compiler of the report and, often, recommendations given.

Generally speaking, there are two main types of report, though every report will not fall neatly into one or other of these categories.

● The first is the **individual report**. This is usually expressed in the first

Title: Communications

Date . . . .   Time . . . .   Venue . . . .

Timing	Topic	Aid
10.00 – 10.15	Introduction – Dictionary definition	—
10.15 – 10.25	Two-way nature of communication	Chart on O/H projector
10.25 – 10.40	Factors affecting communication	Hand-out
10.40 – 11.00	Perception and experience	2" x 2" slides

and so on . . . .

Fig. 15.3   A specimen scheme for a talk

person and is the kind used for internal routine reports and short reports on day-to-day matters. Examples of these are accident reports, organisation and method (O & M) reports, sales reports and so on. In some cases, particularly where a great deal of numerical information is included, a standard form is used so that variable data only has to be entered as in the case of the form letter.

- The second type of report is the **general report**. This is more formal than the individual report and is generally written in the third person though this is not always the case. Such reports are frequently composed for external or public circulation, and are often quite lengthy. Official reports of this nature sometimes run into two or more volumes bound in book form, with extensive indexes.

(a)   Basic principles

Whatever form a report takes it will be subject to a set of basic rules or principles. These do two things: they ensure that the report is logically constructed and they encourage the writer to present his report in an accepted format. The principles may be summarised as follows:

1 The report should have a title. This should be indicative of the content of the report, and clarity should not be sacrificed for brevity.

2 The report should be addressed to the person, or body of people, who are intended to study it. In a report destined for general public distribution, however, this is not considered necessary.

3 If the report is addressed as in **2** it should normally begin with a salutation, e.g. 'Dear Sir', or 'Gentlemen'. No such salutation is required where the report is a regular routine one nor, of course, if there is no specific addressee.

4 A statement of the terms of reference under which the report has been prepared is important, and this should be set out at the beginning of the report. In the case of regular routine reports, however, such terms will have been set down at the beginning of the series and need not be repeated unless, or until, they change. Neither are they required to be stated in a short internal report on any special matter, as the introductory sentence to the body of the report can cover this matter without undue formality.

5 Some sort of introduction to the body of the report is useful to present the problem dealt with and, usually, to state under whose authority the report has been prepared. Often this need not be more than one sentence.

6 The body of the report should contain the following:
   (1) The nature of any investigations carried out;
   (2) A statement of the facts discovered during the investigations;
   (3) Clear arguments and opinions arising from the investigations and the facts uncovered by them.

   In order to assist the reader to follow the report most effectively it is recommended that headings and subheadings are used for sections and paragraphs to indicate the various factors. This is helpful in all but the very shortest of reports. In long reports it is further recommended that the paragraphs be numbered for easy reference and as an aid to indexing in cases where the work is lengthy enough to warrant an index.

7 The conclusions of the author or authors are normally called for, and should be the subject of a separate section under its appropriate heading. The case leading to the writer's conclusions should be clearly and logically put in as succinct a manner as possible commensurate with conviction.

8 Frequently the recommendations of the writer are required to be stated. As with the conclusions, these should be put separately under the proper headings. Lengthy reports may have the conclusions and recommendations given at the ends of the relevant sections of the body of the report, particularly where the report is a substantial one and each section has a chapter to itself.

   At this point it should be mentioned that some authorities recommend that conclusions and recommendations be put immediately after the opening of the report and before the main body of the report. The argument here is that this is a position that enables the reader, especially one with limited time, to come to a quick agreement or disagreement with the report, and that he need then read only the body of the report on the investigations and the facts drawn out if he feels the need to substantiate his first opinion.

9 Inevitably, it will often be necessary to include in a report various charts, statistics, graphs and other supporting material, and the position of these within the work is sometimes a problem. The guide here should be the ease with which the report can be read. If the supporting tables and so on are few in number they may be positioned by the text to which they refer. If, however, there are a large number of them and they interfere too much with the flow of reading, then they may be put at the back of the report as an appendix and reference made to them in the text itself. However, sometimes constant reference to an appendix can be very irritating, if not difficult, and this should be borne in mind when arranging the layout of the report. This problem, of course, presents itself only in the case of long reports.

10 Where the report is of a meeting, the names of those present as members should be given at the head, under the title of 'Present'. Where there are non-members present their names should also be given at the head of the report under the title of 'In attendance'. Similarly, if the report is the result of the joint efforts of several people the name of each individual should be given.

11 Where the report is a lengthy one a table of contents, and possibly an index, should be provided so as to make reference to specific topics as easy as possible for the reader.

12 All reports should be signed by the author. If the report is the work of a team, the signature is usually that of the chairman. Most official reports, incidentally, are known by the name of their chairman, e.g. the Tomlinson Report 1992 on London's Hospitals.

13 A report must be dated.

(b) Planning and preparing a report

1 Terms of reference

A report, especially a formal one, is always commissioned for a specific purpose, and the extent of the brief must always be clearly known by the investigator. This is given in the terms of reference, and these terms must never be exceeded. Where, during the investigation, pertinent matters are uncovered that go beyond the terms of reference, these must on no account be included in the report, but must form the subject of a supplementary communication.

2 For whom intended

It is necessary for the writer of a report to know for whom the report is intended and why it is required. This information will help the writer to decide which parts of the matter he has collected should be included in the report and which should be omitted. Such discrimination is an essential talent for any investigator or writer, and is highly desirable in the sphere of report writing. For example, if a report is required on a new machine tool, the board of directors of the company will be interested in different data from the works maintenance engineer.

Similarly, the language in which the report is couched will be different according to its destination. Highly technical language will be in order for the works engineer, but not for the board of directors.

3 Headings

As with other written communication, the report should flow logically from one point to another, and should develop in an orderly and easily understood fashion. With this aim in view it is of great assistance if the headings and subheadings of the various sections of the report are laid down first so that a proper framework is constructed. The writing of the full account can then be undertaken in the sure knowledge that a logical arrangement has been established. Further, this method helps to avoid the accidental omission of important points that have to be made.

4 Drafts

For any report other than a fairly brief one, it is almost always essential to prepare a draft first, so that it can be carefully edited before it is produced in its final form. In fact, a lengthy report may require more than one edited draft before it is considered satisfactory. Where the report is to contain any statements or opinions by experts, it is very necessary to have these verified by the experts themselves, particularly in the context in which they are to appear. Drafts of these parts of the report will most certainly be required, therefore, to submit to the authorities in question for verification.

5 Meeting the required date

Not only is a report required for a specific purpose, it will almost certainly be required by a specified date. This must be known at the outset and must be met at all costs. A report that is not ready when needed is a valueless report.

6 Style

The style in which a report is written is important. It should be authoritative, and positive statements should be employed wherever possible. Negative statements should not be used unless there is no way of avoiding them. Particularly, if part of the purpose of the report is to stimulate action, positive statements will encourage a positive approach in the reader whereas negative statements are inclined to lead to apathy.

7 Presentation

The way the report is presented in its final form will depend upon its length, upon the number of copies required and, not least, upon the impression it is sought to have on its readers. It may be typewritten, duplicated or printed, therefore. A lengthy, formal report will normally be printed, and bound in book form, whilst a short, informal one may be duplicated and stapled together. If it is required to impress a potential client, a short, formal report on some project may be carefully typed, and bound in an attractive cover by one of the modern binding devices to be found in most offices nowadays. Presentation, then, is a matter of length and for whom.

Figure 15.4 is a specimen of a short, formal report. Examples of long, official reports are held at most public libraries and may be seen on request.

15.19   Sources of information

There are very many occasions when it is necessary to consult outside sources to gather information.

An ever-increasing volume of information is published nowadays on every subject from accountancy to zoology, and each has its own standard works which should be the first to be consulted for basic knowledge. So rapid is the advance of knowledge these days, however, that it is necessary to supplement basic reading of standard works with consultation of other writings on the same subject. It is also essential to consult the latest editions of all publications.

(a)   The Public Library

The most convenient source of textbooks and technical works is the public library. A member of the British public library system has at his command the written knowledge of all the experts on every area of study that man has engaged in, and what is not on the shelves of the local library can be obtained from any other library in the United Kingdom or abroad. On the rare occasions when the local library is unable to borrow a required book from another library then sympathetic consideration is given to the purchase of such a volume. Such purchases can be authorised, naturally, only if a sufficient demand can be established by the librarian.

Not all books are available on loan. Such volumes known as reference books, may be consulted only on the library premises. These include expensive publications such as encyclopedias, large dictionaries, all kinds of directories and, often, the more expensive textbooks. Examples are *Kelly's Street Directories*, *Wilson's Bibliographic Index*, *Encyclopedia Britannica*, *Kempe's Engineers' Year Book*, the *Annual Abstract of Statistics*.

Librarians have a vast amount of knowledge at their fingertips of where to look for information. They also have at their disposal a

The Nonsuch Company Plc.
Oldville,
 Anyshire, AY32 BOX
Phone: (0975) 29285
Fax: (0975) 810738
30th October, 19 . .

The Board of Directors.
Gentlemen,

Subject: Modernisation of Motorcar Fleet

As instructed I have investigated the condition of the motorcars now used by our salesmen, and have to report as follows:

Present position: The fleet of motorcars used by our salesmen comprises 10 vehicles. Of these, two are over five years old, six are three years old and the remaining two were acquired six months ago: all are Ford Escorts of 1300 c.c. capacity.

Condition of vehicles: The two oldest vehicles have done over 100 000 miles and are overdue for replacement. Of the six three-year old cars, four have done over 60 000 miles and the remaining two nearly 50 000 miles. The two six-month-old vehicles have both done under 15 000 miles.

Other findings: The six three-year-old cars are performing reliably at the present time, but are beginning to require constant maintenance to keep their performance up to par. Further, four of them will require an expensive major overhaul in the very near future, and in the opinion of our maintenance engineer the other two are likely to be in this category within the next three or four months.
All eight salesmen driving the oldest cars have expressed dissatisfaction that they have not been allocated up-to-date vehicles in line with those driven by their competitors.

Recommendations: In order to modernise our salesmen's motorcar fleet, the eight cars of three years old and older should be replaced by current models of the same make and capacity. Competitive quotes should be obtained from three fleet dealers, and orders placed on the basis of best selling price coupled with best trade-in prices for our existing vehicles. Immediate delivery is desirable but not essential provided the delay is not more than two months.

Car Fleet Manager

Fig. 15.4 A specimen report

number of specialised reference books that act as a guide to the most likely sources of information on any subject.

(b) **Specialist journals and newspapers**

Of necessity, however, all books on library shelves are out of date to some extent. (Two main reasons contribute to this: (1) the length of time it takes to write, print, check and publish a modern book; and (2) the rapid technological changes that nowadays take place outstripping the ability of writers and publishers of books to keep pace.) For most subjects, therefore, it is necessary to go to another source for the latest information, and generally speaking this is the technical journal. All professional and technical societies publish journals devoted to their particular speciality and, in addition, there are scores of such magazines put out by independent publishers catering for both the professional and the amateur practitioner. In addition, the so-called 'broadsheet' newspapers, such as *The Times*, *The Financial Times*, the *Independent* and *The Guardian*, often publish authoritative articles on technical, financial, social and economic matters. Particularly when consulting articles in the press, however, a watch for conscious or unconscious bias must be kept. Or, put another way, care must be taken to distinguish between fact and opinion.

Whilst all journals and newspapers can, of course, normally be purchased through the usual newsagents and bookstalls, though often only from the larger ones in the cases of very highly specialised journals, most can also be consulted at any large public library. Most libraries hold one or more of the current periodical indexes, such as *Willing's Press Guide*, the *British Technology Index*, the *Guide to Current British Periodicals* and the *Times Index*, and the librarian will be able to discuss precise requirements and to recommend selections.

(c)   Specialist bodies

It must also be remembered that the most up-to-date information on any special subject is most likely to be held by the professional or trade association or institution specialising in that particular subject. Thus, the very latest knowledge about accountancy is likely to be obtainable from the Institute of Chartered Accountants or the Chartered Association of Certified Accountants. Similarly, the current thought on industrial and personnel relations is likely to come from the Institute of Personnel Management. From such bodies, both fact and opinion will be obtained, as well as what are possible future trends. Most professional and trade associations are quite willing to provide information and advice to non-members provided that the applicant is serious.

Apart from the specialist bodies referred to, facts and opinions may also be solicited from government departments, local authorities, educational institutions and commercial or industrial undertakings having an interest in the subject under investigation. Experience shows, however, that information from these sources is usually more guarded and less forthright than that obtained from the other sources we have discussed. Other direct requests may, of course, be made to the specialist writers of textbooks and of articles in journals, addressing them through their publishers. Replies from such people are often very full and detailed, and sometimes they are willing to enter into limited discussion on the topic in question to the benefit of both parties. Care must, of course, be taken in such cases to watch for bias.

(d)   Abstract services

For the very busy person, however, the very wealth of current printed information, and the number of sources of information now available, make the task of investigation almost impossible. Fortunately, a number of abstracting services have been established that produce summaries of articles appearing in various specialist journals so that it is possible for the researcher to keep abreast of essential information without the need to read through long articles. Most of these services require the user to subscribe on a yearly basis, but there are many public libraries who subscribe to them and so the infrequent enquirer can make use of his library service.

15.20 Effective reading

A manager is often inundated with matters to read and it is important therefore that he does this efficiently.

- When discussing the question of reading many people first consider the speed at which the reading is done. An efficient reader, they say, reads fast. However, the activity of reading cannot be taken in isolation and must be related to comprehension. A shorthand writer may take notes at 200 words per minute, but this is pointless unless they can be transcribed. The average person reads at something like 200 to 300 words per minute and at this pace he will comprehend about 75 per cent of the content of what he has read. If he decides to read faster the chances are that his comprehension will fall because he will concentrate on raising his reading speed instead of concentrating on the content of the author's work.

  Therefore, efficient reading consists of a combination of speed and understanding, and increasing one at the expense of the other will not lead to efficiency.
- There is, of course, some relationship between efficiency in reading and the purpose for which we are doing it. We are more likely to read quickly and comprehend fully and promptly something that interests us greatly than something which is irksome to us. If we do not find what we are reading of interest, then our reading will probably be slow and our comprehension low. Other things that affect reading speed are style of writing, kind of typeface and, to many, even the kind of paper used.
- However, there are certain things we can do to enable us to read faster and to improve our reading efficiency. The most important one is to understand the physical activity of the eye when we read. The eye does not travel along the line of print in a continuous manner; if it did that we should see nothing but a blur of words. What it does is to stop, take in a word or phrase, and then move on, and it does this all the time we are reading. In fact, it acts in the same way as a movie camera or projector, where the film is constantly stopping and starting so that there is produced or projected a series of still images snapping on and off at speed.

At each rest the eye sees a segment of print – the visual span – and the segment is assimilated and passed to the brain for interpretation. One way to increase reading speed is not to move the eyes faster, but to widen the visual span. There are various devices that encourage this spreading of the span, but with practice it can be done without such assistance. Start with a piece of print in narrow format, such as a newspaper column. With practice it is possible to encompass the whole width of the column without sideways movement of the eyes, focusing them in the middle of each line. In such circumstances reading speed will increase to the extent that there is need to read only down the column. All the time, though, comprehension must be checked to ensure it does not suffer.

From the newspaper column the next step is narrow printed pages, such as paperback books, perhaps starting by dividing the lines up into two segments only. The wider the span the faster the reading without loss of comprehension.

Having increased the visual span horizontally, the next step is to try to assimilate two lines, and then three, vertically, because the eyes' peripheral vision extends upwards and downwards as well as sideways. This is, to be truthful, rather more difficult for the simple reason that reading horizontally means there is some relationship between the words and phrases whereas vertically this may not be so. It must be remembered that it is not only the eyes that are involved in reading – the brain has an important part to play in it as well. Therefore, what the eyes see and transmit to the brain must be decoded and processed by the brain. Where there is a relationship between words the brain can deal with the matter speedily; if there is little association, or none, the brain will not react so quickly.

- Many people, when they read, vocalise: that is, they say to themselves either audibly or inaudibly, the words and phrases they are reading. Some readers even mouth the words: such activity slows down the reading speed and is some hindrance to comprehension. In order to achieve greater efficiency in reading every effort should be made to assimilate the meaning of what is being read without repeating inwardly the actual images. Grasping, mentally, whole phrases and whole lines of writing is of great assistance in losing the habit of vocalising.

(a)   Concentration

To read with understanding it is necessary to concentrate. Concentration is the essence of comprehension, but is sometimes difficult to achieve. The reason is, very often, that the reader is looking at the words whereas he should be looking for the meaning. Vocalising, either inwardly or by mouthing the words, very often causes loss of concentration as more emphasis is being given to the words themselves than to their meaning. Aids to concentration, apart from freedom from outside distractions, are an interest in the matter being read, and a motive for reading it. Without one or the other of these, concentration is likely to be difficult to achieve.

(b) Skimming

Skimming is a skill that should be acquired by the person who aims to be an efficient reader. To skim does not mean to read carelessly or without motive. Essentially it is a practice to be indulged in as a prelude to the serious study of a written work. It consists of allowing the eye to move quickly over the page, picking out important words and phrases as it goes, and of skipping inessential statements and information.

The manner in which a reader skims is purely personal, and his success relies to a large extent on his ability to spot key words and phrases on sight. Some readers will move their eyes quickly down the centre of the page, using their peripheral vision to assimilate the beginnings and ends of lines, whilst others will glance down the page diagonally.

Skimming is not meant to replace serious reading but is used to obtain a general grasp of the sense of a piece. It is thus helpful in ascertaining whether the material is going to be useful and should be read thoroughly, or whether only parts of it will be of interest. In the latter case, during the skimming exercise, interesting passages can be marked for further study, whilst others can be skipped altogether. If the ability to assimilate two or more lines vertically has been acquired, this attribute will materially assist in successful skimming.

As with most activities, practice increases efficiency, and a deliberate effort to increase reading efficiency and comprehension will amply repay the work involved. Full exposition on how to improve reading ability will be found in *Read Better, Read Faster*, by Manya and Eric de Leeuw (Pelican, 1990).

15.21 Listening and hearing

(a) Effective listening

Everybody hears, but how many listen? Yet listening is a very important part of communication. It may be defined as 'conscious hearing', and it is this definition that points to the defect in most people's capacity to listen – consciousness.

The main cause of faulty listening is, in fact, mind wandering or loss of concentration. Allowing attention to lapse whilst listening results in an incomplete reception of the transmission.

1 Concentration

It is not easy to maintain concentration when listening: there are so many distractions around. In any event, it is difficult to maintain full concentration on a speaker for more than twenty minutes at a time. In the case of a formal lecture or talk, thirty minutes is the maximum time the speaker can expect to hold his audience's undivided attention, even if he is absolutely expert, and even during this period his audience's concentration will wax and wane at something like ten-minute intervals. The skilled speaker will, therefore, intersperse his talk with a small diversion every now and then. In ordinary conversation, or at an interview, the problem does not arise as there is variety in the content of the talking.

A positive attempt, therefore, must be made to maintain concentration when listening.

2 Interest

This is very much allied to concentration. If we have little interest in the subject we will not listen attentively unless we make a determined effort. In a formal situation it helps to prepare oneself with some foreknowledge of the topic to be dealt with, so that a mental challenge can be set up as the expected points arise. Equally, the purpose for listening to the speaker must be clearly appreciated, which will increase interest. An accountancy student may not find a lecture on company law intrinsically interesting, but the purpose of attending the lecture, to pass the examinations and become qualified, is a spur to interest.

(b) Barriers to effective listening

1 Emotional disturbance

It is very difficult to listen effectively if the mind is disturbed. A quarrel with someone, unpleasant personal news – such things upset the emotional balance and so upset concentration, which in turn leads to ineffective listening. The mind will be elsewhere, trying to deal with the emotional upset, and not in accord with the speaker. Great efforts must be made to forget the problem temporarily and to listen to what is being said. Even in informal conversations emotional upsets are likely to lead to ineffective listening.

2 Dislike of the speaker

If we like a person we are inclined to accept what he says and to evaluate it objectively: we will listen to him sympathetically. However, if we dislike a speaker we are likely to adopt a negative attitude to him and this will colour what we hear. Even an accent we do not like can cause us to look on a speaker with disfavour and so distort our listening. The way to overcome this pitfall and listen effectively in such cases is to try to hear the speech, and not the speaker.

3 Distractions

There are many ways in which a listener may be distracted. First it must be recognised that a good listener who has interest and concentration will not be distracted very easily. If extraneous noises or movement, for instance, cause distraction from what is being said, then it is evident that interest and concentration are not deep enough. The answer is greater effort to listen attentively.

4 Relaxing whilst listening

Listening is a positive activity, and can never be done in a passive manner. Therefore, the good listener does not relax when listening, but is engaged in a purposeful pursuit requiring his positive co-operation. The listener's mind is not a pint pot that can be filled by pouring in speech. The input has to be monitored, analysed and filed by the mind, and these activities cannot be carried out effectively in a relaxed state.

5 Speech lag

The average talking speed is 120 words per minute: the average possible hearing speed is nearer 400 words per minute or even faster. This means that the listener's mind has to slow down to keep pace with the speaker. Herein lies a difficulty, particularly to the active mind. What can the listener do about this speech lag which, if not dealt with, may result in mind wandering and loss of concentration? He can use it to question mentally what is being said, to analyse the substance of the speech as it goes along, or to anticipate what the speaker will say next and have a questioning attitude to it. He should not use this speech lag time to think about matters not appertaining to the speech. Neither should he dwell on the points of the speech long passed.

The path to effective listening is not easy. It needs attention and concerted effort. The unfortunate fact is that we so often do not realise that we are not good listeners and so make no effort to improve. The same could be said about breathing.

Finally, the points made above relate not only to listening at meetings but are also relevant to person-to-person situations.

Questions

1 'To be of any value a meeting must be fully effective.' What are the characteristics of an effective meeting?
  How can an administrator prepare and conduct meetings to ensure they possess these characteristics? **(ICSA)**

2 How important is the role of chairman in ensuring the effectiveness of a committee? **(ICSA)**

3 What are the roles of the meeting and the committee in the communication and decision-making process within the organisation? **(ACCA)**

4 What are the main characteristics of a properly organised and well-conducted interview? How can an interviewer apply these characteristics in order to monitor and improve his/her performance? **(ICSA)**

5 What are the basic problems which affect both the interviewer and the interviewee in a job regrading/promotion interview? How

would you as the interviewer ensure that the interview was fair and objective?   **(IAM)**

6 'What matters at an interview is not what is said, but how it is heard.' How far do you think this is true?   **(ICSA)**

7 Enumerate the essential features of a good report. Illustrate your answer by writing a brief report to your managing director on a subject of your own choosing.   **(IComA)**

8 Draw up a draft outline guide to writing reports to management and clients. This draft is required for discussion and eventual use in your organisation as training material in the induction of newly employed graduates and part-qualified staff.   **(ACCA)**

9 What do you understand by **either** 'effective reading' **or** 'effective listening'? Discuss how this skill may be acquired and developed.   **(ICSA)**

10 Explain what is meant by the terms 'visual span' and 'speech lag'. How can an understanding of these factors help us to improve our reading and our listening?

16 The manager

Management, which has been the subject of the preceding chapters, is carried out by people; these people are the managers. It becomes necessary therefore to discuss what a manager is.

The term itself has become somewhat debased recently in that many people who are given the title of manager are, in fact, not managers but supervisors and at junior management level the distinction can be a fine one. The main distinction is one of discretion. A supervisor will make decisions in accordance with rules that are laid down, little or no discretion being required or, indeed, allowed. Problems that cannot be solved within the established rules have to be referred to the supervisor's superior. A manager, on the other hand, will have the authority to use discretion in making decisions and the limits to this discretion indicate the manager's place on the management ladder. A person's title within an organisation, therefore, is not necessarily indicative of that person's real position from the point of view of management. Thus an accounts manager may be nothing more than an accounts supervisor having no authority at all to vary the terms of credit with customers nor to negotiate terms with suppliers. Someone in another organisation, with the title of chief clerk, may on the other hand have the authority and discretionary power of a middle or senior manager.

16.1 Management qualities

The question as to what constitute 'management qualities' and 'management potential' has been the subject of much discussion by many authorities over a very long period without any total consensus having been achieved. There is, of course, no specific answer possible because different people have different attributes and are able to learn to use them effectively often to the extent of overcoming any lack in other ways. For example, a person who lacks the desirable quality of stamina may develop a latent capacity for organisation so that his or her day's work is planned to conserve personal energy. The list of desirable characteristics is a long one if the suggestions of all the important authorities are taken into account, but among them are the following:

(a) **Self-confidence:** the belief in one's own power to succeed in solving problems and one's own ability to deal effectively with difficult situations.

(b) **Drive:** the urge and enthusiasm to stimulate action, both personal and in other people.

(c) **Initiative:** the ability to lead action without waiting to be prompted and to bring fresh thought to old problems.

(d) **Decisiveness:** the ability to think positively and without vacillation and to act in the same way.

(e) **Willingness to accept responsibility:** this includes the acceptance of accountability for one's decisions and the consequent acts of oneself and one's staff.

(f) **Ability to delegate:** this also includes (e).

(g) **Integrity:** this includes trustworthiness and loyalty to one's organisation and one's staff.

(h) **Judgement:** the ability to analyse a situation and formulate appropriate action. This includes choosing between different possible courses of action where choices present themselves.

(i) **Adaptability:** the ability to change one's outlook as circumstances change and to alter one's actions in the light of what is necessary in changed circumstances. This is a most valuable characteristic in the modern world which is subject to such rapid change.

(j) **Organising ability.**

(k) **Stamina:** the ability to work long and hard without undue strain or stress.

(l) **Emotional maturity:** includes self-discipline and self-control and the ability to analyse a situation without prejudice.

(m) **Human understanding:** the ability to work with other people with understanding and sympathy; the willingness to listen to staff problems.

(n) **Personality:** this is difficult to define, but the personality required in an effective manager might be said to include the ability to communicate easily at all levels, to exude confidence, to be approachable and open, and to be able to carry staff and other members of the management team with him. An open-minded approach to problems may be said to be part of personality, with no hint of vacillation on difficult questions.

(o) **Being supportive of staff:** ensuring that all are treated equally fairly; encouraging them and supporting them in their career ambitions.

(p) **Adequate educational standard:** this does not mean, necessarily, the holding of a university degree, but rather a development of the mind that enables one to think positively and without prejudging a situation, and also to communicate effectively.

This list of attributes is by no means exhaustive; neither are all these qualities likely to be found together in one person. Again, they are not necessarily conspicuous in everyone who is considered to have management potential. In fact most of the desirable attributes are likely to be latent at the beginning of a manager's career and develop through training and experience. Management skills are on the whole largely practical and virtually any man or woman can be effectively trained for management provided the necessary latent talents are possessed.

16.2   Leadership

This is the quality that enables a manager to exert a positive influence over the behaviour of his subordinates. It is difficult of definition but is, nevertheless, important to the success of any group activity whether this is a small group of workers in a department or the whole of an undertaking.

- The qualities that make a good leader will be determined to a large extent by the circumstances under which the leadership has to be exercised; or rather the attributes that are actually brought into play will be so determined. In other words different situations will require the display of different qualities from the same individual. Very generally the qualities that a leader needs to possess are those given under **16.1** above for a manager because to all intents and purposes being a manager also entails being a leader and equally a leader needs to be a manager. In point of fact, in management studies it is unnecessary and pointless to try to draw any distinction between the two.
- There is argument as to whether leaders (or managers) are born or made and the same answer can be given as that given earlier in this chapter – leadership can be developed provided that the latent capabilities are there. There are two elements that are acknowledged as being necessary to an understanding of leadership. The first is that it is essentially a group situation where members of the group have a common purpose, and the second that the authority of the leader must be accepted by all members of the group if that leadership is to be effective.
- The steps involved in the exercise of management or leadership skills can be illustrated in Figure 16.1.

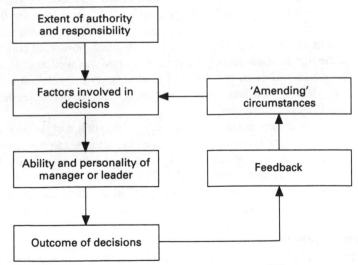

Fig. 16.1   Exercise in management and leadership skills

16.3   Styles of leadership or management

Leadership is the human aspect of management and so it can be said that the style of leadership is also the management style. In fact the trend in modern industry is that workers can only be led; they cannot be 'managed' in the old sense of this term, which was the imposition of the manager's will upon the workers. So what is management style?

- There is no simple answer to this question because every leader or manager will have a different approach depending upon his personality traits, early training, abilities and experience. In addition a particular style may be forced upon a manager because of circumstances occurring in the situation or in the group. The style of leadership needed to manage a group of untrained school-leavers in a production shop will be different from that required to manage a co-ordinated team of skilled technicians all expert in their work and accustomed to working together. In the first case close and sympathetic attention will be required, whereas in the second case leadership will probably consist only of general guidance and acceptance of ultimate responsibility.
- The extent that a manager 'knows himself' and recognises his own weaknesses and strengths will do much to characterise his management style and will reinforce his self-confidence in his powers of leadership and the form it should take. Nevertheless it is customary to try to define various styles of management, and because of their infinite range it is usual to divide them into three groups, through which individual styles can be identified.

(a) **Authoritarian management**

This is the traditional view of a leader or manager where power is in the hands of one authority whose word is law. Orders are issued and are expected to be obeyed without question. All decisions are those of the leader: little or no discussion takes place with subordinates, not even with executives at high level. This absolute power, of course, can be in the hands of an autocratic governing body as well as in the hands of one person, though members of such a body are often subservient to their leader. In fact such a person is not really a leader or a manager, but is a dictator.

If the person concerned is extremely able such a style of management may be very successful for a while (in fact in some rare cases may do a great deal of good to an organisation), but eventually it fails because of the leader's human fallibility. It also has the two disadvantages of producing a resentful work-force and difficulties in regard to succession. Such a style of management is unlikely to be tolerated by modern work-people except in very rare circumstances.

(b) **Paternal management**

Common, even in these days, chiefly in small concerns, paternal management endeavours to create a family atmosphere where the leader likes to be regarded by the workers as a parent figure. While sanctions are available to be used with unco-operative staff, they are kept in the background and the manager guides workers with instruction and advice. In a suitable organisation this style works very well and in most cases motivation of staff is excellent. As with any human enterprise, abuses will take place but staff generally become very loyal to their management and do not take kindly to those who seek to infringe the rules. This form of management is well-nigh impossible to apply in very large undertakings since the sheer numbers of operating staff make personal contacts with managers very difficult.

(c) **Democratic management**

This is the nearest a large organisation can really come to the paternal style of management. The leaders or managers share their decision-making activities with their subordinates as much as possible while not relinquishing their ultimate responsibility or authority. Much decision-making is, therefore, done by discussion, either formally or informally, and where this is not possible for one reason or another then the managers are at pains to explain matters to those concerned and who would, in the normal way, have been consulted.

The democratic style of management must not be made an excuse by the leaders to abdicate their responsibilities. Rather they must maintain their proper authority while carrying their staff along with them to assist in the management process. It is in this style of management that effective delegation is of enormous help as it frees the leaders from much routine detail so that they can devote more time to developing the personal relationships so necessary in this form of management. Such managers, however, must be seen to lead and not to be led.

In its most advanced form democratic management becomes participative management, where a majority of decisions are made by consultation. This has dangers in that decisions may take a long time to be arrived at and then may be compromises that do not fully fill the bill. Self-interest may motivate some groups and conflicts may arise between members of groups making effective decisions very difficult.

16.4 The Leadership Grid®

Whilst it is true that leadership must concentrate on the problems of human relationships to achieve set goals, it is also concerned with the question of non-human resources.

- To a considerable extent the style of management adopted will result from how much emphasis is given to one or the other. Recognising this dichotomy, Dr R. R. Blake of the University of Texas conducted research into the problem, the results of which he first published in 1964, and he defined two main concepts of management: (a) concern for people and **(b)** concern for results or production. These two aspects of management he expressed on a graph which he originally called the Managerial Grid® or as it is labelled in its latest form, the Leadership Grid (Blake and McCanse, 1991), where points 1 to 9 are plotted vertically for concern for people and similarly points 1 to 9 are plotted horizontally for concern for results. Concern is weakest in each case at 1 and strongest at 9. Concern for production is conventionally stated first so that a manager whose rating shows 1,9 has very high regard for people and one whose rating is 9,1 shows an extremely strong concern for production and little for people.

- Dr Blake actually defined five leadership styles from 1,1 which indicates minimum interest in both aspects to 9,9 which indicates high production achievements from dedicated staff. Rating 5,5 on the Grid shows an adequate and balanced management performance with both human and material resources of equal concern. A specimen of the Leadership Grid is given in Figure 16.2.

- The concept of what is now known as the Leadership Grid is the first step of a programme of management training developed by Dr Blake and his colleague Dr J. S. Mouton, and it shows how management styles can be depicted to indicate the basic philosophy of the management concerned. A full exposition of the concepts surrounding the management training programme involving the Leadership Grid can be found in Robert R. Blake and Anne Adams McCanse, *Leadership Dilemmas – Grid Solutions* (Gulf Publishing, 1991), which also explains the five basic management styles identified by the authors.

16.5　Management by objectives (MBO)

Management by objectives is a method of control which measures performance against individual objectives set. As a control mechanism it could probably have been included in Chapter 12 on Control, but since it also reflects upon a manager's own performance it seems more appropriate to discuss it as part of management performance and development.

- Management by objectives differs from the usual control techniques in that the objectives to be achieved are not imposed, but are set by consultation. The system has two principal aims: first, to provide strong motivation for managers to perform at a high level of efficiency, and second, to integrate corporate goals with a high measure of job satisfaction for the managers. All managers have a basic need for job satisfaction and consequent self-development, and management by objectives provides the basis for such self-development in that it closely associates the achievements to be made with the personal efforts of the manager who is responsible for attaining them. This is done through the fact that the managers themselves are intimately involved in setting the

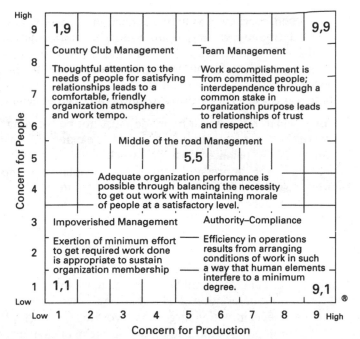

Source: The Leadership Grid®. Figure from *Leadership Dilemmas – Grid Solutions*, by Robert R. Blake and Anne Adams McCanse. Houston: Gulf Publishing Company, p. 29. Copyright © 1991, by Scientific Methods, Inc. Reproduced by permission of the owners.

Fig. 16.2   The Leadership Grid®

targets to be aimed for, and are thus self-motivated to endeavour to achieve them.

- The mechanics of the system can be simply stated as:

(a) The clarification of corporate objectives.

(b) The setting of departmental objectives, with the assistance of the departmental managers.

(c) The agreement by the departmental managers, through consultation and discussion with their superiors, of individual departmental managers' targets.

(d) Continuing the process at (c) down the management line, each manager suggests and agrees with his immediate superior his own targets and has them made part of his individual work-plan. Targets at all levels should be realistic and not over-optimistic or unattainable, as this leads to discouragement, but they must, nevertheless, be challenging.

(e) Drawing up plans for the achievement of individual objectives; this operation is left entirely to each individual manager at each level.

(f) Establishing a review mechanism which will indicate the progress achieved by each manager in the attainment of the agreed targets. This review system should also include giving advice where targets have not been reached, even to the extent of suggesting further management training or development so that performance can be improved.

(g) Providing a procedure for modifying targets or plans in the light of experience.

(h) Providing some means of overt recognition of personal achievement.

• Periods over which reviews will be made must not be too long, though the nature of the work being done will, to a large extent, determine the review intervals. A balance must be struck between short intervals which may give the impression that the participants are not being sufficiently trusted by their superiors, and long intervals which may allow too great a divergence from targets before corrective action can be taken.

• The technique of management by objectives is important because it requires the personal involvement of each participant, it requires the key areas of each job to be identified and a satisfactory level of attainment agreed, and above all because it is more interested in results than in mere job descriptions. The personal involvement of each manager at each level in setting targets and working out work-plans is an important factor in positive motivation and in the management development process. Lastly, all managers remain responsible for the activities of their subordinates and also remain accountable to their own superiors for the achievement of the mutually agreed goals.

• In order to set up and maintain an effective MBO system it is helpful for there to be a system to provide past management information so that objectives can be easily arrived at, and to provide a basis for the setting up and implementation of a control or monitoring mechanism. This is most profitably done by means of a formal management information system: this is described in **24.3** below.

16.6   Management training and development

The management trainee is a common phenomenon both in private industry and in the public sector, and is a sign that the training of future managers is being taken seriously by an increasing number of organisations. Some confusion, however, is likely to be experienced in trying to differentiate between three terms used almost interchangeably by various authorities on management: these are management education, management training and management development. The differences between these terms are subtle and it is as well to define the distinctions.

(a) **Management education** deals with the theoretical aspects of management. Usually it is acquired through formal courses of study, either by short concentrated programmes or by longer continuous courses. In these courses many real-life management problems are simulated but, of course, are devoid of the day-to-day circumstances appertaining to the live situation.

Sandwich courses, where students spend part of their time at college sandwiched with periods of actual work experience, are an attempt to overcome the difficulty of unrelated theory.

In 1992 polytechnics became universities and colleges of higher education may choose to become polytechnics or may choose to remain as colleges of higher education. It is hoped that the courses in these newly-formed institutes will continue, as now, to include practical management experience.

(b) **Management training** concerns itself with the practical aspects of management and is heavily committed to ensuring that the trainees are exposed to the day-to-day problems assailing managers. It is essentially a practical exercise and relies very heavily in most cases on the trainees learning the application of management techniques. This is not to say that managers must be expert accountants, mathematicians or operational research practitioners. What it does mean is that they must be aware of these techniques and their uses and be able to use the services of the experts in these techniques to assist them to make their decisions. Management training also involves the trainees gaining experience of the different functions in their organisation – accounting, marketing, production and so on – so that they gain a balanced view of all the facets of the enterprise. Most of the larger employers provide this varied experience by insisting that new recruits who are deemed to be potential managers enter into what some term a 'commercial apprenticeship'. Under this scheme each trainee spends a specified minimum time in each department, often supplemented by a part-time external education course.

Where the goal of a recruit's future is functional management it is often required that the trainee take steps (usually sponsored by the employer) to acquire the appropriate professional qualification. Other general training includes improving the so-called managerial social skills of communication and discussion, and improving the intellectual and creative skills such as thinking analytically, problem-solving and so on. Attention is also paid to improving interpersonal attitudes.

(c) **Management development** carries on where education and training leave off. It utilises the benefits of these two to develop the managers' potential as leaders and to enhance their latent abilities and attributes which will be made evident during their education and training, and which can be steered towards benefiting the organisation as well as their own personal career development.

Management development is now widely recognised by all major organisations as being of great importance to the future of the undertaking. Specific steps are now taken to ensure the formulation and execution of properly structured programmes for the development of managers. Among the goals such programmes seek to achieve are:

1 To create conditions which will enable present managers at all levels to recognise and so realise their own potential abilities. This entails giving them scope for using their initiative and reducing the limiting rules and prohibitions so common in the past: in other words extending their responsibilities and authority as much as possible and so providing the conditions through which self-confidence can grow.

2 To increase the competence of managers by providing training and education programmes, organising seminars and encouraging managers to attend conferences arranged by outside agencies whose business it is to teach management skills.

3 To ensure that the potential for promotion among junior managers is recognised and that such staff are given opportunities to show their capabilities whenever possible.

4 To measure the growth of management skills by regular appraisal.

5 To ensure that managers understand the importance of recognising management potential in their subordinates, and to encourage them to develop this. This, of course, is an important aspect of the problem of providing for management succession.

16.7   Management development programmes

(a) Functions

- A management development programme starts at recruitment. The possible future requirements of the organisation must be constantly reviewed and planned for. Future management staff must be recruited and given the necessary education and training programmes in accordance with the forecasts of future requirements.

- In addition existing managers will be required to keep themselves aware of management potential in their subordinates so that proper attention can be given to such staff to develop their latent managerial abilities. Where the organisation's policy is to require regular appraisal of all staff performances the necessary attributes should be discovered during such appraisal exercises. Staff recruited specifically as management material will also be subject to periodic appraisal to ensure that the promise shown at their recruitment interview is being fulfilled.

- In this way most of the promotion to management posts will be done internally. Because existing staff are considered equally with those engaged specifically as trainee managers, there should be a minimum of ill-feeling between the two groups, as can happen if ambitious existing staff are not given the same opportunities for promotion as are given to the specially recruited trainees.

- It should be emphasised that managers have a duty to develop their subordinates and this should be seen as part of the management development programme. More especially, managers should ensure their own succession by appointing deputies from the ranks of their subordinates. The abilities of each manager's deputy should be nurtured by the manager concerned and the deputy must be given every opportunity to be associated with all aspects of the work carried out by the manager. In this connection the frequently guarded attitude of some managers and their unwillingness to share their knowledge and expertise must be recognised, and persuasion must be used by their superiors to ensure that the deputies are given the insights needed for their development. Such subordinates should also be given every opportunity to join courses on management education and training and encouraged to translate their new-found knowledge into day-to-day practice.
- It follows that management development must be a properly planned operation, and that it involves all levels of management from the very top down to junior managers. It also follows that it is very much influenced by the corporate plans of the organisation, since the type of managers and style of management may have to change as the corporate plans unfold: this must be taken into account when designing the management development programme. This is achieved by periodic reviews of the management needs of the organisation, both immediate and for the future, and comparing these with the existing force of managers at all levels from senior executives down to junior managers. By this means provision can be made in good time for proper training and development for the future, ensuring adequate management succession throughout the undertaking.

(b) Difficulties

While a properly instituted management development programme should result in improved management performance and ensure proper management succession, there are dangers that should be recognised so that steps may be taken to mitigate them. The main difficulties are:

1 Lack of proper support from top management. It is important that the governing body of the organisation approves and actively supports the management development plans.

2 Uncertainty as to precisely what the programme should contain and what its ultimate objectives are. If there is not the necessary expertise within the undertaking to produce a sound programme then outside help from an appropriate consultant or professional body should be sought.

3 The programme is too restricted as to the number of staff it includes. The opportunities for development should be available to as many staff at all levels as could benefit from it.

4 The limits of the potential of certain managers and staff are not

recognised at the right time. This may raise aspirations that cannot be realised.

5 Adequate appraisal reviews are not instituted. Serious attention must be paid to this aspect of the programme.

6 Insufficient attention is paid to wastage, that is, staff quitting, thus leaving gaps in the succession plan. This is a problem not easy to solve as over-recruitment to the plan may cause disappointment through there being insufficient management posts ultimately available if wastage is less than allowed for.

7 Management development schemes envisage self-sufficiency in management succession. This can cause an inbreeding in management ideas and a conservative management outlook. Outside talent can bring in fresh ideas and a more radical outlook, so essential to the organisation's continued success. Some provision should be made, therefore, for some external recruitment of management ability from time to time.

8 Resources are devoted to developing managers who then leave the organisation for other employment. This is unavoidable in any programme of training and development. Attempts to hold the services of such people by restrictions in their contracts are likely to be resented and could possibly be unenforceable at law. In any case a manager forced to remain in a post unwillingly is unlikely to perform effectively.

The success and continued survival of any organisation depends upon the quality of its management team. Management development schemes are an important step in producing managers of the right calibre and of ensuring proper management succession.

16.8 Appraisal

Some form of control is essential to ensure that all training programmes throughout an undertaking are achieving their objectives and to measure to what extent the staff involved are performing adequately. Management training and development programmes are no exception, and all staff who are involved in such programmes must have their performances assessed to ensure that expectations are being achieved and that their potential is being suitably developed. Such appraisal will also indicate where a manager or potential manager has reached the limits of performance, and whether some revision of the individual's career development might be advisable.

- Such appraisals cover two areas – achieved performance and future potential – and are carried out by continuous assessment by the subject's immediate superior supported by records of work. Almost always appraisal interviews are also conducted at regular intervals. This is virtually essential to assess the changes in attitudes, social skills, managerial skills and increased technical knowledge which should be brought about by a successful programme and work experience. Performance record and improvements in managerial qualities will indicate the potential for promotion and the route of the subject's future career within the organisation. At the same time the need for changes in the individual's programme to improve the subject's capabilities can be discerned.

- The areas most likely to be covered in the appraisal are:

(a) The ability to recognise, isolate and solve problems.

(b) The ability to plan and organise work programmes, both personal and for subordinates.

(c) The ability to communicate effectively both vertically and horizontally.

(d) The ability to create and maintain good relations with superiors and with staff, and to establish and sustain a co-operative attitude with other sections of the organisation.

(e) The development of personal qualities such as decisiveness, ability to lead, willingness to listen, ability to accept responsibility for errors, a positive attitude to change and so on.

(f) The extent of the individual's technical knowledge and ability and the improvements that have taken place since the previous appraisal.

- The areas subject to appraisal will be dealt with in depth, and in many cases organisations use appraisal forms which include scales of performance and potential. This structured approach seeks to eliminate too much reliance on the subjective judgements of the appraisers, endeavouring to make the exercise more objective. Nevertheless, all judgement will be subjective to a certain degree, especially where career potential is concerned.

16.9 Stress

Before leaving this discussion on the manager it would not be out of place to look at the question of stress, which is increasingly in evidence in those having to take managerial responsibilities.

- The incidence of stress seems most commonly found in those in middle management positions. These are the managers who are subject to pressure from those at the top to achieve targets and objectives, and from real or imaginary threats from those for whose performances they are responsible. That is not to say, of course, that other levels of management and supervision are immune from stress.
- Stress manifests itself in many ways, the most noticeable being anxiety, worry, nervous tension, irritability, loss of self-confidence, difficulty in concentrating, a feeling of inadequacy and, often, an unwillingness or

inability to delegate. Extreme cases of stress can lead to physical distress such as chest pains and even to a heart attack.

- Like the symptoms, stress can have many causes. It is not possible here to give a long list of the factors which may lead to stress, but among these factors are fear of not being able to cope with the work, work overload, unsatisfactory personal relations with staff or superiors, changes in routine for which the manager is not adequately prepared, lack of sufficient information on which to base sound management decisions, perhaps one serious decision error which has been exaggerated disproportionately in the mind of the manager, indecision and many others. It could be argued that the now almost universal use of the mobile telephone may be a potential cause of stress in that there is no relief from the minute-by-minute demands of the job even when away from base.

- Of course, domestic problems can also lead to stress at work but these are not for discussion here.

- There is no short or easy solution to the diminution of stress, but it is certain that the longer it goes on the more difficult it is to overcome. Thus, at the first signs of stress action should be taken to reduce it; what action to take is obviously related to the cause or causes. Generally relaxation is suggested as a starting point, as is the pursuit of outside interests – and to resist taking work home.

- More specifically, where the cause is too heavy a workload an endeavour should be made to delegate more or to redesign jobs so that they take less time. A feeling of not knowing enough (common when there is a change of routine and especially when there has been a promotion) can be reduced by taking positive steps to increase knowledge. If there is a lack of sufficient information attempts should be made to have the system altered so that sufficient relevant information is forthcoming in adequate quantity and quality and in good time. Indecision should be combatted by positive thinking. It is also important to remember that one wrong decision is not a disaster: consider the number of right decisions that have been arrived at during a year.

- Where unsatisfactory personal relationships are a cause then a positive effort must be made to put things right.

_ Questions _

1 The size of an organisation is often considered to influence managerial style, organisational climate and employee attitudes. Do you accept this view? State your reasons?   **(ICSA)**

2 What do you understand to be the special skills required in management to-day?   **(IComA)**

3 (a) What are the potential disadvantages of a participative style of management?
   (b) How could such disadvantages be overcome or minimised?   **(IAM)**

4 You are required
   (a) to describe the structure of MbO (Management by Objectives);
   (b) to assess its advantages over other methods of direction;
   (c) to suggest reasons for its comparatively rare use.   **(CIMA)**

5 'The word "leadership" is sometimes used as if it were an attribute of personality, sometimes as if it were a characteristic of certain positions within an organisation, and sometimes as an aspect of behaviour.' Discuss.   **(ICSA)**

6 In a changing world, senior managers face many pressures and uncertainties. Why do managers keep on managing? What motivates people to perform effectively in senior management positions?   **(ICSA)**

7 (a) Identify, with brief examples, **four** organisational causes of individual stress.
   (b) Make recommendations for the management of stress in the work situation.   **(IAM)**

8 Making the transition from sales representative to sales manager can be traumatic. Explain the tensions involved and suggest ways in which such personal promotion can be achieved effectively.   **(CIM)**

9 Six supervisors from accountancy departments are on a management development course. *A*, one of them, has reported his proposals about a case which they have been studying. The other five have rated *A* by placing crosses on Blake and Mouton's

Managerial Grid [now known as The Blake and McCanse Leadership Grid]. The results are as shown.

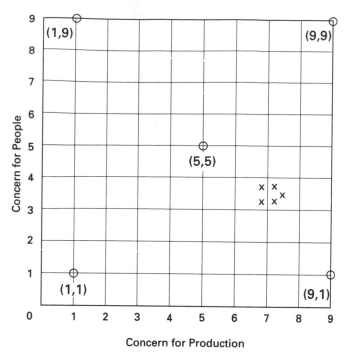

You are required to
(a) explain what the consultant in charge should tell the group about the significance of the result;
(b) make **seven** suggestions as to how *A* could improve his management style. **(CIMA)**

⟨17⟩ Functional management

So far this work has concentrated on general management, its theory, practice and some of its techniques. Many managers, particularly senior executives, are certainly concerned with these areas exclusively. Their working days are devoted to planning their organisation's future, setting objectives and generally concentrating on survival and progress. When they are members of the board of directors or other governing body they are responsible for formulating policy and making the final decisions on corporate planning and corporate strategy. Yet all the planning and strategy is of no account without the work of the functional departments of the organisation. These are the sections of the undertaking which actually make it work on a practical basis.

It is at the functional level that management expertise has to be married to technical expertise, and where functional technical knowledge is as important as managerial skills: this was pointed out in Chapter 1 where it was suggested that at the level of principal officer, or senior manager, the proportion of skills should be somewhere in the region of 50 per cent managerial and 50 per cent technical.

17.1 The need for managerial expertise

Although the operation of functional departments requires function knowledge and expertise it does not follow that a person highly qualified in the technical sense will necessarily turn out to be a good functional manager. An efficient factory superintendent, highly effective in the mechanics of running a factory, may not prove a success as a production manager where much more managerial skill is needed. A competent sales representative may prove quite unsuccessful if promoted to the position of area sales manager. In fact, it is the transition from the purely technical level to one where a certain amount of true managerial skill is needed that is frequently the most difficult. Years of study and of practice in a purely technical capacity can narrow the view of many people in this situation, and it often demands a real change of attitude and outlook for such a person to become a competent functional manager. Here the term 'technical' is used in its widest sense and includes such areas as accounting, marketing, purchasing and so on. Once any sort of supervisory or managerial element is present in a job then the occupant of that post must start to practise management skills in addition to technical skills. A foreman bricklayer on a building contract is responsible for managing his team of bricklayers, of planning their work-load, their activities and their material resources and equipment. The element of management is small, but is there. Such a foreman may be less of a craftsman than his best bricklayer but his managerial capacity, though relatively small, makes him a better foreman than his best bricklayer who has no managerial talent or skill.

17.2　The need for technical expertise

Nevertheless, a functional department will not be most efficiently managed unless the manager has technical knowledge of a high order. This is for two reasons. Subordinate staff have more respect for a manager who is fully competent in the technical aspects of their department, and a properly qualified manager is able to solve technical problems with authority and confidence. Unless subordinate staff respect their manager's technical skill they are unlikely to respect him in his managerial capacity.

- It is a fact that practically all functions are now served by professional bodies who lay down minimum standards of knowledge and experience for membership and who require qualification by examination for their members. They also require a minimum standard of ethical conduct in order to maintain public confidence in the work of their members. In Britain some professional bodies have gained statutory recognition while others are so highly regarded that senior posts in most organisations are reserved for members of those bodies. Among the functions so circumscribed are accountancy, purchasing, marketing and personnel.
- In countries where independent professional bodies have not gained the same kind of recognition it is usual to find that statutory qualifications are required of people aspiring to certain functional management positions.
- The role of the functional expect has become increasingly important as new techniques and new concepts have been introduced, and to which management must pay attention to stay successful. Even top management, where the requirement of technical expertise is at its lowest, must be aware of technical problems and understand what they are about. In consequence, Chapters **18–23** will introduce the principal functions to be found in most organisations.

17.3　The scope of the functional manager

The manager in charge of a functional department, for example purchasing, should have total control of his function and be responsible for all aspects of its operation in respect of its technical performance. However, the department must be operated within the framework of the organisation as a whole and thus the functional manager is subject to the constraints set for the general running of the undertaking.

Examples are working within the requirements of the corporate plan, adhering to budgets, co-ordinating the department's operations with the needs of other functions, and working with the advice of staff officers such as the personnel department when recruiting staff.

Questions

1 What is meant by 'functional management', and how does it differ from general management?
2 Why is it important that a functional manager should be seen to be technically competent?
3 Would you say that an expert craftsman would make an efficient supervisor? Give reasons for your answer.
4 In many jobs where technology changes rapidly a manager may have subordinates who have greater technical competence than he possesses. How can you reconcile this apparent conflict between knowledge and authority?   (ICSA)
5 What are the main organisational and environmental factors which limit the managerial discretion of the manager of a functional department in an organisation?   (ICSA)
6 What are the main managerial issues to be faced by a functional manager wishing to achieve effective control over **one** of the following:
   (a) a production or operations department;
   (b) a marketing department;
   (c) a research and development department;
   (d) a sales department (**either** in manufacturing **or** service **or** retail).   (ICSA)

The marketing function

Marketing is the function of a profit-making enterprise that is vital to its success. Without effective and profitable marketing the enterprise will die. It can be described as the function that identifies the needs of the buying public, assesses the extent of these needs and endeavours to satisfy them in the most effective and profitable way. It is sometimes argued that marketing creates needs, but this is disputed by most authorities on marketing. According to these authorities the marketing function merely draws attention to unsatisfied needs but cannot create new needs.

This point of view is debatable. There is a need expressed nowadays for colour television sets, for example, yet this need did not exist fifty years ago: or did it? Was there a latent need that was awakened by the present availability of equipment able to show coloured moving pictures in the home without effort? Or was this need created by expert marketing? Perhaps it is fair to replace the word 'need' in most cases by the word 'desire'. Marketing can certainly create the desire to acquire products, and this is the continuing function of marketing.

18.1 The marketing concept

Marketing is defined by the Chartered Institute of Marketing as 'the management process responsible for identifying, anticipating and satisfying customer requirements profitably'.

The idea of a producer first investigating and then producing goods for customer requirements rather than endeavouring to sell goods already produced is a rather lately arrived one, certainly in the United Kingdom. It is covered by the term 'Marketing Concept', which simply means a management style that puts emphasis on the marketing aspects of the organisation's operations.

The marketing concept has in turn given rise to various ways of assessing consumers' needs and wants, among them market research and dynamic advertising.

18.2 Marketing and selling

In the popular view marketing is often equated with selling, so the relationship between the two must be made clear. Marketing embraces every activity required to find customers for, introduce, inform about, create a desire for and actually supply the goods or services an organisation provides. Thus, it is involved in market research to determine the probable extent of the market, advertising to introduce and inform about its goods and services, public relations to promote a persuasive public image and selling to ensure the satisfaction of the demands created by its other activities. So it can be seen that selling is, in fact, only one facet of marketing; the part of marketing that actually places the goods or services in the hands of the customer. Selling involves the effort of finding the actual customers and then persuading them actually to buy. The rest of the many facets of the marketing function are investigatory (that is, researching possible demand), informative and persuasive.

18.3   Marketing and the non-profit-making sector

- The function of marketing is normally associated solely with profit-making ventures, be they private enterprise or publicly owned industries. However, this is not really so, particularly in view of the high proportion of the gross national product (GNP) that is now absorbed by the public sector in education, social services and other related activities. Whether such services are paid for out of general taxation or out of local taxes the public at large resents the high proportion of disposable income it has to pay to finance them. In consequence it has become necessary to explain to taxpayers the reasons for and need for the services provided. In effect, the exercise of explanation is one of public relations which comes within the marketing function. Similarly, it is a fact that many people who are entitled to social benefits of one kind or another do not take up their entitlements, often through ignorance or pride. These benefits range from supplementary payments to special grants such as are provided for insulating domestic premises. Such services have to be marketed to the people concerned, both to inform them of the existence of these benefits and to persuade those entitled to them to make their claims: a very expert public relations exercise has to be put into operation here.
- The other important non-profit-making area where marketing techniques are widely used, though they may not be obvious as such, is in the business of fund-raising. Practically all the important relief organisations such as Oxfam engage in expert marketing, particularly public relations activities, to raise funds for their special projects. The persuasion has left the realms of merely appealing for funds and has gone into the realms of well-planned marketing.

18.4   The marketing mix

The various elements of marketing need to be carefully employed in order to achieve the greatest success, and it is necessary to combine them in the most effective way given the circumstances at any particular time. The

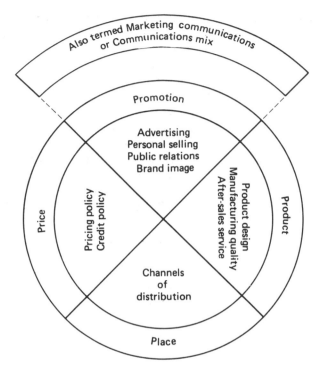

Fig. 18.1   The marketing mix

combination of these elements is known as the marketing mix, and is
graphically portrayed in Figure 18.1.

- There is no universal list of the particular aspects of the marketing
  function that go into the marketing mix, but they fall under four main
  headings with subdivisions providing an analysis of the mix. The main
  headings are:

(a) Promotion
   This includes advertising, selling, public relations and the creation of a
   brand image where this is advantageous. Promotional activities are
   often referred to as 'marketing communications'.

(b) Product
   This includes product design, the quality of manufacture and, where
   the product requires it, after-sales service.

(c) Price
   This must relate to product quality and the particular market aimed at.
   The policy on granting credit also falls under this heading.

(d) Place
   This involves the channels of distribution to be used, e.g. sales
   through agents, wholesalers, direct, and so on.

- The particular marketing mix used at any one time will depend upon many circumstances such as the economic climate, the strength of the competition and sometimes the need for an improved inflow of revenue. Different organisations, even in the same industry, will use different mixes successfully because their particular circumstances demand a particular mix. For instance, in an intensively competitive industry, where there is very little difference between the various makers' products within a general price range, heavy promotion on a particular aspect of its product may be engaged in by a manufacturer to emphasise a particularly attractive feature which may or may not be present in the products of competitors. A typical example comes from the photographic industry where the Pentax camera was, and still is, heavily promoted on the basis of its handling qualities. 'Simply hold a Pentax' created a brand image of a very desirable camera, though it is probably no better or no worse than other cameras of its class in other directions. However, it is a feature most potential buyers now examine carefully in all cameras they handle with a view to buying.
- Similarly, pricing may be an important marketing feature where quality is not of paramount importance. It is generally conceded that intending customers equate low prices with low quality and are likely to question the quality of a product selling for substantially less than its equivalent competitors. If a top-quality product is offered at a very low price suspicion is aroused as to whether a new and improved model is about to be introduced. Often a manufacturer or supplier may price a product or range of products at substantially reduced prices simply because of a fall in cash intake and this is the only way to generate revenue quickly.

These two examples are sufficient to show how a marketing manager may constitute the marketing mix to suit prevailing objectives or conditions.

18.5 Market research

Before launching a new product or improving an existing one it is desirable to discover its potential sales volume in order that the resources to be devoted to it may not be wasted in a vain attempt to find a substantial enough market. The activity used to try to establish whether the potential customers are likely to buy, and to discover the best form the product should take, is market research.

- By various means the market researcher endeavours to establish what is likely to attract buyers in a particular product line in sufficient numbers, in regard to design, size, price and other relevant features that go into a customer's buying decision. For instance, if it is decided by a radio manufacturer to launch a new portable radio on to the popular market, it will be necessary for him to know as accurately as possible what physical size the equipment should be, its frequency range, its output volume and quality, and so on. If this receiver is to replace an existing model, it will also be useful to know what the public's opinion is of the present set, what improvements should be made and what features should be retained. By researching these matters the chances of a successful launch are better than if no such research is carried out.

- Similarly, if an organisation is in the retail trade the opening of a new store will be contemplated only after research into the population of the selected area, the proportion of these likely to become active customers, the average income of the area, the normal buying habits of the potential customers, their particular tastes and so on. Only if it can be shown by this research that enough people will be likely to patronise the potential store, and that its revenue will thus be sufficient to justify the required capital expenditure, will the project proceed.
- Even in the non-profit-making sector similar research should be carried out. Thus, for example, a local authority should set up an advice bureau only after having assured itself by proper research that there will be enough clients to justify the costs of establishing and running it.
- Market research can be divided into desk research and field research.

(a) **Desk research**

This involves researching past records, both internal and external, on matters relating to the proposed project. Past sales and other records, past reports from sales representatives and other data are used to form an estimate of possible sales based on past sales volume, customer complaints, and suggestions gathered by sales representatives during their calls. Information can be gathered from external sources such as government publications and statistics, technical and trade journals and the sales literature of competitors to give indications of market trends, technical innovations and what competitors have to offer.

(b) **Field research**

This involves active fieldwork in interviewing potential customers, preparing questionnaires and having them completed by the public at large or by selected sections of the public, offering samples, or having selected categories of potential customers carry out tests by using the product or prototypes of the product and reporting on specially prepared questionnaire forms.

- How the active or field research is done will depend almost entirely on what type of product is to be launched. The distribution of free samples is common in research on foodstuffs (new breakfast cereals, instant tea and the like) and cleaning materials such as washing powders, whereas high-cost capital equipment requires research through personal contact with potential buyers, the preparation of detailed specifications and analysis of the reactions of the potential buyers.

Market research is very highly statistical and requires expert knowledge and experience if it is to be at all reliable. The public is notoriously fickle in its behaviour: the reasons for behaviour changes are not fully understood and changes are hard to predict. Only a person highly skilled in market research techniques can be relied upon to reduce as far as possible the imponderables in consumer behaviour and thus produce from such research results of practical value.

18.6 Marketing research

Market research is concerned with the assessment of the market for a new or existing product or service, and confines itself strictly to this. Marketing research, on the other hand, takes a much broader view and concerns itself with all the factors bearing on marketing policy and plans. These factors include research and evaluation of marketing opportunities, investigating various promotional and selling methods, evaluation of advertising media and their effectiveness, research on a broad scale into customers' desires and needs, consideration of different methods of distribution, the organisation's public image compared to its competitors' and other factors bearing on the general marketing problems of the organisation. Market research is part of marketing research, but the latter has much wider implications. In many undertakings marketing research also includes investigating its own existing marketing methods, product research and sales policy, assessing their effectiveness and suggesting improvements. This particular activity is properly termed a 'marketing audit'.

18.7 Market segmentation

- To market successfully an organisation must first know what the total potential market is for its products or services and then try to identify the various divisions or segments of the market. Having broken down the market into segments it can then decide its best policies in regard to exploiting either the total market or desirable segments of it. For example, the total market for lamp-posts for street lighting includes columns made of steel and of concrete, to supply them and to erect them, wherever they can be sold. In Great Britain the total market spans the whole of England, Scotland and Wales, and customers include local government authorities, building contractors and concerns needing lighting for yards, transport depots, wharves and similar areas. A street lighting column manufacturer can, therefore, decide to undertake to carry out all the activities concerned with the total, or whole, market or can decide to try to serve only one or more sections, or segments, of it. In one instance a maker of concrete lamp-posts serving the supply-only segment to the local authority section decided to embrace the erection segment as well. Eventually this same concern covered the total market. The ability to serve the total market, however, is very difficult unless the possible market is fairly limited (as it is for street lighting) or the undertaking has enormous resources.

- Market segmentation is, properly, the term used for dividing the market into categories according to type of customer, by age, by sex, by income, by region, or by any other logical division that suits the product or service. In the example above, for instance, local government authorities are a particular category of customer. Additionally, such general classifications can be further broken down or combined so that a manufacturer may make clothes for girls between the ages of 5 and 10, a shoe manufacturer may produce shoes for both sexes up to the age of 11. However, 'market segmentation' is the term often used to cover product segmentation.

18.8   Product segmentation

- This is a newer classification than market segmentation, which explains why the latter term is often used instead. Product segmentation follows market segmentation in that, having classified the customer categories to aim for, the undertaking then classifies these segments according to the products which it can exploit within each customer category. An example of this is the publishing of women's magazines. A publisher may decide to serve the segment of the market containing young women between the ages of 18 and 30. Some will be single, some married, some with low incomes and some with high incomes. In consequence, a single publisher publishes magazines that interest the single and low-paid, the career girl, the young wife on a low income, the young middle-class home-maker and so on throughout the range of categories.
- Often manufacturers use reputations gained at the quality end of the market to exploit the cheaper end offering, perhaps, a simpler product bearing the same brand name. Others exploit different segments by different qualities of product, but with dissimilar names seemingly having no connection: often this is done so as not to damage the brand image of the more highly priced product.
- However segmentation is done, by market, by product or by both, it is essential that continuous research is carried out to ensure full exploitation of opportunities. Customers move between categories, their buying behaviour is not constant in many cases, and these changes must be reckoned with all the time.

18.9   The product life-cycle

- It is an established fact that practically all products have a life-cycle, which means that they have a span of useful existence passing through the various stages of conception, development and growth, a period of stable or relatively stable sales and then suffer a decline and eventual disappearance from the market. A very simplified graphical representation of this phenomenon is given in Figure 18.2. This also illustrates the

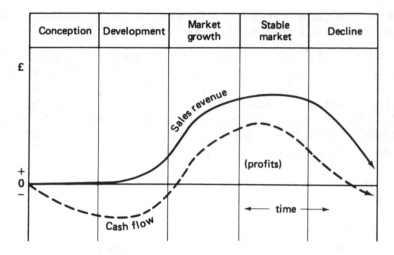

Fig. 18.2 Product life-cycle

initial outflow of cash and subsequent inflow of profits during this time.
These stages can be described as follows:

(a) **Conception**

It is at this stage that careful research has to be conducted into market
potential, and expense is incurred against which there is no revenue.

(b) **Development**

This second stage also demands the investment of considerable
resources with a view to returns in the future. Product development
will lean heavily on the findings of market research, technical innovation and design expertise.

(c) **Market growth**

Assuming a successful product, sales increase and the product becomes increasingly accepted by the market. If it is completely innovative, once its novelty has been accepted and it proves dependable,
market growth may be very rapid and highly profitable because of the
absence of competitors. The introduction of zip-fasteners and ballpoint pens are cases in point.

(d) **Stable market**

Often termed the 'stage of maturity', at this time the product has
become established and competitors have entered the market with
similar products, often offering some improvements. Profitability
tends to fall even against level or rising sales because of the additional
costs of selling, advertising and promotion required to challenge
competing products.

(e) **Decline**

At this point the market has become saturated both because demand has been virtually satisfied and because of the intensification of competition for a contracting market.

- This concept of the product life-cycle can be only a general one because there are many factors which can influence it. Some of these are the application of the product to new uses, improvemenets to the product by restyling or adding technical refinements, and finding completely new markets. The life of a product can also be extended temporarily by price reductions made possible by the fact that all the development costs have already been recovered, and perhaps by reducing marketing expenditure.

- The real solution to the problem of the product life-cycle is, of course, to have new products ready to take the places of those in decline, and also to endeavour to avoid the simultaneous decline of several product lines at the same time. Many manufacturers anticipate the decline by actually launching new products well before this stage occurs: in fact artificially killing off the existing product. This is very usual in mass-produced manufactures, cameras and cars being particular examples.

- It must not be forgotten that services as well as goods also suffer this life-cycle. The professional laundry, for example, is a very much reduced activity and invisible mending is a service very hard to find indeed, having reached its peak when clothes were in short supply and expensive. Launderettes also appear to be in the stage of decline.

- The rates of growth and of decline in the life-cycle of a product or service are affected by both demand and supply, with the emphasis on demand. Demand will change according to the availability of competing products, whether they offer something better in the way of technical or cosmetic design, and according to prices. Customer buying behaviour is also not constant and may influence the decline. On the supply side, demand may be persuaded away from the existing product by the introduction of a new one satisfying the same consumer needs more cheaply or more easily. In this case the new product may be that of the same undertaking or of a competitor. An example of this is the introduction of the automatic camera which has led to the decline of the manual camera. Most manufacturers appear to be very largely neglecting the manual camera in favour of the automatic one even though available evidence seems to show that there is still a significant demand for a manual camera. In this case the decline is because of the supply position.

18.10   Pricing

An essential feature of marketing that must be examined is pricing, which can have a profound effect upon the success of a new product and the continued life in the market-place of an established one.

There are three considerations to be made when setting a price for a product, the economic price, the market price and the psychological price:

(a) **The economic price**

This can be said to be the lowest price that can be demanded to cover all costs involved in the production of the good and its distribution, and to show a reasonable profit. This is the true economic price that will make production worthwhile. However, the true economic price is also defined by some authorities as the price 'the traffic will bear', that is the highest price that the consumer will pay and which will yield a satisfactory sales volume. As the definition suggests, it is higher than the purely economic price but is one the market does not consider unreasonable. This price is likely to obtain until either sales begin to fall off or competitors enter the market with a similar product at a lower price.

(b) **The market price**

This is the price that the customers expect to pay and may be at either of the levels discussed in (a) or, more probably, somewhere in between. The term 'expect to pay' is significant, especially when the product is competing with similar goods. If it is pitched higher than the figure demanded by competitors it may cause sales to suffer; if pitched lower, particularly if the difference is significant, consumers may question the quality of the product, perhaps unjustifiably.

An instance is the case of a calculating machine marketed by a very well-known manufacturer of office machinery. The calculator's price was significantly lower than that of its competitors, and although the machine itself was at least equal to if not superior to its rivals, sales were unexpectedly poor. Investigation of the problem established that potential customers thought the machine must be inferior because it was too cheap.

(c) **The psychological price**

There are two sorts of psychological price. The first is that pertaining to luxury goods or goods generally thought of as generous presents. These are such things as jewellery, perfumes, high-class watches and similar goods most often bought as gifts. Here the buyer expects to pay high prices because the gifts are high class. Similarly, such quality goods as top class motor cars, top class cameras, top of the range hi-fi equipment and *haute couture* fashionware can command much higher prices than the economic price.

The second psychological price is the one which sounds lower than it really is. Thus an article marked £99.99 sounds cheaper than if it were marked £100 and £9,975 sounds much cheaper than £10,000, though the difference is relatively insignificant. Similarly, a verbally quoted price of two hundred and fifty thousand pounds sounds significantly less than a quote of a quarter of a million pounds, although the amounts are identical. Is this dishonest? Perhaps not, as it is up to the buyer to see through the device. It is, of course, in almost universal use in the retail trade.

18.11   Pricing a new product

A new product that is in competition with existing similar products will have little margin for manoeuvre as its price will be immediately compared with its competitors. It would be expected that enough market research would have been done to ensure that there is capacity in the market for an additional product to be able to establish itself and its price must bear favourable comparison.

- At its initial launch there may be a price incentive offered in the expectation that the product will commend itself to users and so establish some level of brand loyalty: subsequently it is almost inevitable that the price will rise to a common level with its competitors. However, in the event of a reduced launch price it may be that competitors will reduce their prices so that a price war ensues. This will depend upon how much a threat the other providers see in the new product. In such a case such a price war could damage the chances of the newcomer.
- The other tack is to enter the market at an average market price but to have something in the product that can be said to be clearly superior to its competitors. This device was mentioned in **18.4** above and Pentax have remained one of the market leaders ever since.
- The pricing of a completely new product is of especial difficulty, particularly if it is an innovation. In such a case initial pricing is often very high and will be reduced only when competitors enter the field. An example is the ballpoint pen, a completely revolutionary writing instrument. At first the Biro pen was as expensive as a high quality fountain pen. Now, after many years of competition, it is one of the cheapest writing instruments available.
- Another element to consider in pricing a brand new product is the question of recouping research and development costs: can these be recovered in the first period of the launch, should they be spread over a predetermined period of time or should they be spread over the expected life-cycle of the product?

18.12   Advertising

(a)   Function
Advertising is concerned with selling an organisation's goods or services. It can be said to perform three main functions:

- **To inform**
  Advertising's first task is to make the public aware of an organisation's products or services. On the launching of a new product it will introduce

the product to the potential market and will give all the information considered necessary to generate the interest of potential buyers.

- **To persuade**

Advertising's second task is to generate a desire for the product being offered and to turn the desire into a need that must be satisfied. This is the most controversial aspect of advertising and one that has led to much adverse criticism of advertising practice. In this area the appeal is very much to the emotions rather than to reason and to the practical worth of the product. Thus using a certain washing powder may be shown to make a woman a better mother or housewife, or the use of a certain brand of after-shave lotion will make a man attractive to women. This is sometimes known as 'selling dreams'.

- **To convince**

Having attracted attention and created the desire, advertising's third task is a twofold one: first, to convince the potential buyer that the product advertised is the only one that will satisfactorily fill that desire, and, second, to convince the customer that future purchases should be of the same brand as the only way of achieving continued satisfaction. This is the long-term goal of advertising.

Advertising is a direct effort to create sales and makes use of many media.

(b) Common advertising media

The traditional medium for advertising is the press, comprising daily and weekly national newspapers, local newspapers, magazines and journals. Other media are commercial television, commercial radio, direct mail advertising, and slides and films in cinemas and occasionally in theatres. Increasingly the latter two media are shown in long-distance public transport, such as airlines and coaches, by means of video recordings.

Posters on hoardings and other sites are also a much used medium, their function being more to remind than to persuade. Which medium to choose depends upon a number of factors including the market aimed at and the type of product being promoted.

1 The market aimed at

Food products will be advertised in women's magazines and papers read by women; contractors' plant will be advertised in building trade journals and investment opportunities in the financial papers. An advertiser could expect little response from an advertisement for excavator hire appearing in a fashion magazine.

2 Is the market local or national?

A local newspaper or local commercial radio will serve the local market quite adequately in most cases: commercial television, national newspapers and national magazines will serve the national market.

3 Section of the public aimed at
Where specialist products are advertised this is best done in specialist publications, e.g. angling anoraks in angling magazines. Products of general interest will be advertised through media with general appeal.

4 Availability of names and addresses
Where up-to-date and reliable lists of the names and addresses of potential customers are available direct-mail advertising may be used. Often these lists provide details of specific segments of the market, enabling the advertiser to aim precisely at the people he hopes to influence.

5 Would a moving advertisement be advantageous?
Where a product or service lends itself to a moving presentation then television or moving film may be considered.

6 Past effectiveness of the medium
A successful medium will obviously be used again and again. The problem is how the response from any particular medium can be measured. Coupons, department numbers or names and other devices are pressed into service in this connection but there is as yet no really reliable and accurate way of assessing the effectiveness of any particular medium.

7 The budget allocation for advertising
A careful assessment must be made of the expected gain in sales and profit against the proposed advertising expenditure. Again, however, measurement of sales gain against advertising cost is incapable of accurate measurement.

8 What type of sales are aimed for?
It must be determined whether increased sales are expected to come from the existing market or whether a new market is the target. A case in point is the advertising of wines in photographic magazines rather than, or in addition to, advertising them in food and related journals.

18.13   Advertising and consumer interest

The role of advertising is seen by many as having a detrimental effect on the interests of the consumer. It is argued that it increases prices because the cost of advertising must inevitably be passed on to the customer, that the scale and high cost of advertising of brands already on the market may prohibit the entry of new brands thus diminishing competition, and that repetitive advertising can so influence a customer's mind that it is made difficult to consider a competitor's product objectively.

The counter arguments to these objections are that advertising helps to create high demand, thus allowing the economies of large-scale production resulting in lower costs and thus lower prices, that advertising costs will be absorbed by greater demand, that competing advertisements encourage more careful examination of competing goods by consumers, and that advertising does, in the long run, cause poor quality goods to be withdrawn from the market because of widespread customer dissatisfaction.

- The claims that the high cost of advertising discourages new brands from entering the market must to some extent be admitted. However, this objection cannot be sustained in the case of large-scale producers where their already well-known names can persuade the buying public to try a new product even if it is outside their normal range.
- Nevertheless, complete newcomers who are willing to take the risk of a high-cost advertising campaign can successfully challenge established products provided they have something positive to offer such as price advantage, or design or performance advantage.

Advertising is a specialist undertaking and should be done only by the expert. If the organisation itself does not have staff competent to undertake the task it should engage the services of an advertising agency, otherwise much money can be wasted on unfruitful advertisements.

18.14 Public relations

- Fostering good public relations now plays a very important role both in the private and in the public sectors. It has been described by the Institute of Public Relations as the 'deliberate, planned and sustained effort to establish and maintain mutual understanding between an organisation and its public'. This definition has been taken a stage further by many organisations who consider that good public relations must also be maintained with their employees at all levels.
- Goodwill and a good reputation are not easily acquired; they take a good deal of time and trouble to build up. Conversely they are very easily and quickly destroyed and once gone take a much longer time to rebuild. Confidence, once lost, is not easily regained. Even relatively minor incidents, such as an impolite representative or an unhelpful telephone operator, can mar the organisation's public image. The need for special attention to public relations is, therefore, obvious.
- Public relations can be in the hands of a senior member of the organisation, usually a member of the marketing team, or can be handled by an outside public relations consultant, but however it is done it must be done effectively. A large part of the work of a public relations officer is to deal with complaints and criticisms from customers and from the public at large. Great skill is required to provide satisfactory answers and explanations so that criticisms are accepted as being explained and not explained away. Public relations has the reputation of being an excuser and is not entirely trusted in many quarters: this attitude must be carefully countered and defeated so that trust is built up in the work of the public relations activity.
- However, public relations is charged with more than simply protecting the organisation's reputation. It is also responsible for informing the

public about the organisation's actions and policies where they will be likely to affect the physical and social environment. The rise of numerous pressure groups which raise objections to so many plans and projects emphasises the need for careful and expert public relations work to pacify these objectors, or to meet their objections with suitable compromises.

- Fortunately, public relations is not always on the defensive. Much is done to enhance the organisation's image, particularly in the realm of industrial and commercial undertakings, in a positive way by the sponsoring of social and sports activities such as the arts (music and CD records for instance), and sporting events such as championships in golf, cricket and many others. In fact, in a way this form of public relations, in which considerable sums of money are donated, has taken the place of the wealthy patrons who used to encourage and support the arts and sports.

- Though part of marketing and promotion, public relations is not directly concerned with selling, though indirectly it can be expected to have a positive effect on sales. Its function is to show the world that the undertaking concerned is socially aware and socially responsible, and to show customers that it has their interests at heart.

18.15   Distribution channels

The marketing function's ultimate objective is to ensure that the product ends up in the hands of the customer: if this does not happen all else has been in vain. It is essential, therefore, to use some form of distribution channel to achieve this. There are four main ways in which distribution is accomplished.

(a) **Direct sales**

In these cases products are sold direct from the producer to the consumer. This is the common method adopted for capital goods of high value or made to individual specification such as aircraft, machine tools and similar goods. It is also used by many manufacturers of retail consumer goods such as household requisites which are sold door-to-door by sales representatives. One of the world's largest cosmetics firms sells its products this way.

Another method of direct selling is by the establishment of retail outlets by manufacturers themselves. Footwear is a common commodity sold direct by the makers in this way and the major boot and shoe manufacturers have numerous high-street shops.

Services such as insurance have always been sold direct through agents and intense competition has led to the opening of what are really retail shops in many busy shopping areas.

(b) **Through a third party**

In this case the supplier uses an intermediary to channel his wares, usually an appointed agent. This is common in the retail area and some examples are domestic equipment such as washing-machines and refrigerators where the manufacturer appoints special retail shops to act as agents. In this way the manufacturer retains some control over the quality of the service the ultimate buyers obtain. A service example is that of insurance, which is often sold through agents such as banks and through brokers. Supermarkets who buy direct from food manufacturers form part of this pattern of distribution.

(c) **The distribution chain**

This involves more than one party between the source of the goods and the consumer and is the traditional way in which many staple goods such as food and household requisites are sold. The chain usually consists of producer, wholesaler, retailer and consumer, but on occasion there may be more than one party between the producer and the retailer.

(d) **Retail mail order**

Though really part of (a) and (b), the retail mail-order business is so large that it warrants separate mention as a distribution channel. It takes two forms:

1 Direct sales by the manufacturer to the user, an important example being footwear. Other examples are double-glazing and central-heating installations.

Many services also use this method, examples being insurance, mostly specialised cover such as hospital insurance, and motor insurance. Contact is made with the customer mainly by display advertisements in the press and magazines or by direct mail advertising by circular or inserts stuffed into newspapers and magazines.

2 Sales by mail-order houses which are, in fact, retailers who sell exclusively through the mail; they are not manufacturers. There are two main methods: the first uses advertisements in the press and magazines and the second uses catalogues held by agents who are often housewives on housing estates. Goods offered through adver-tisements usually have some novelty value or some price advantage: those sold through catalogues cover almost all the items to be found in any well-stocked department store.

The method of distribution chosen will depend very largely upon the type of market aimed at and the type of goods or services offered. Many producers, in fact, find it profitable to use more than one method. The cost of holding stocks can also pose problems and the use of wholesalers means less stocks on hand at the factory and conse-quently less capital tied up. On the other hand, a wholesaler stocking goods from several manufacturers is unlikely to be such a persuasive salesman for a particular manufacturer's good unless there is some profit advantage. Tradition also plays a very large part in choosing the method of distribution in many industries.

___ **Questions** ___

1 Explain the marketing concept. Discuss the factors which have caused companies to become marketing oriented.   (CIM)

2 Explain the concept of the marketing mix and write a brief account of each of the **four** elements into which it may be divided.   (IComA)

3 Define market research. Write an account of the activities which are covered by the term.   (IComA)

4 Distinguish, with examples, between market research and marketing research.   (CIM)

5 How might increased consumer concern about environmental issues affect markets and market segmentation in the future?   (CIM)

6 Assess the contribution of market segmentation to marketing mix planning.   (CIM)

7 Describe the stages in the product life-cycle.   (CIM)

8 Discuss the value and limitations of the product life-cycle concept.   (CIM)

9 A marketing director is planning to launch a product into a competitive but growing market. It is claimed to be of superior quality to the existing products. What factors should he bear in mind when setting the price?   (IComA)

10 You are required

   (a)   to explain how a marketing specialist may have regard to the benefits which potential buyers perceive in a product when determining its selling price;

   (b)   to assess the importance of product quality to a buyer of consumer goods;

   (c)   to explain why a direct relationship between the costs of production and a selling price may be inappropriate as a pricing strategy.   (CIMA)

11 Discuss the role and purpose of the public relations function.   (IAM)

12 What do you understand by the term 'an organisation's image' so far as it relates to the local community? How may a positive image be developed?   (ICSA)

13 Is advertising in the public interest?   (ACCA)

14 'Ensuring a high quality of service to the client or customer is the key to the success of any enterprise.' Discuss.   (ICSA)

19 The production function

In Chapter 18 it was stated that effective marketing is vital to the survival of an organisation, in whatever sphere it operates. If goods are to be sold or services provided, however, then it is essential that they be available. So far as goods are concerned in the manufacturing industries, whether in the private or public sector, this involves production, the conversion of raw materials into usable commodities. In this sense the term 'raw materials' is used to indicate the basic input to a production process, though this input may be anything from a primary material such as iron ore to a finished component such as a length of cloth. In the first instance the iron ore is the raw material for the manufacturer of iron and in the second the cloth, already a finished article in its own right, is the raw material for a manufacturer of garments. In fact it is commonly the case that the finished output of one manufacturer is the input, or raw material, for another.

19.1   Types of production

Production methods are conventionally divided into three types: job or unit production, mass or flow-line production, and batch production.

(a)   Job production

- In this type jobs are carried out individually and usually to the specific order of a customer. Job production can range from small units such as the production of an individually designed piece of pottery to the building of a large cargo ship, from made-to-measure clothing to bridge-building.
- Job production is usually very labour intensive since it does not easily lend itself to mechanisation. Further, the labour employed has to be highly skilled for the most part, and supervision must be constant and very technically competent. There is little opportunity for the use of highly specialised machinery, and the machinery that is used must be versatile and able to cope with varying work.
- It is unusual for an organisation to be able to make for stock as each order will be different from previous orders and from future ones. In many cases, such as a bridge-building or in road construction, there can be no question of making for stock. Continuity of work for both labour and equipment depends, therefore, on effective marketing and under this heading must be included competitive tendering.
- Where jobs of high value and extended time-span are the rule problems

are often experienced with financing the projects, especially in view of the high labour content which means that large sums for wages have to be regularly found.

(b)　Mass production

- This method, which is also known as flow-line production, is a process of continuous production where large numbers of more or less identical units are manufactured continuously. It is the exact opposite of job production. Little or no individuality can be introduced into the product, and the processes are extremely capital intensive. The labour content is relatively small compared to the capital investment, and most of it is unskilled or semi-skilled. Highly specialised machinery is used and in the most modern mass-production plants practically all of the work and machines are controlled by computer. The small proportion of skilled labour required is employed to set up the machines for production, and is highly paid. This small, very skilled, work-force is a vital element in continuing production and disruption of their operations normally causes severe setbacks in manufacturing volume, and can cause production to cease altogether.
- Mass-produced products, which range from such items as breakfast cereals and paper products to motor-cars, are manufactured in advance of sales, and sales forecasting and marketing of a high order are essential for the success of the manufacturing enterprise.
- A distinction is usually made between two aspects of this method of production. The term 'mass production' (or flow-line production) is used for the continuous production of manufactured goods such as those just mentioned. Where the nature of the product is the result of formulations such as petro-chemical products, adhesives and jams, process production or continuous-flow process production are the terms normally used.
- In order to remain profitable it is necessary for enterprises employing mass-production methods to utilise machinery to virtually full capacity. When orders fall short of full capacity it is often more advantageous to keep the plant running and to produce for stock rather than to reduce the volume of output. An example of this is the stock-piling of motor-cars when sales are low. This situation cannot, of course, continue indefinitely. In the case of domestic consumables, such as washing-powders, attempts are made to stimulate sales by a variety of means including 'special offers', competitions and free gifts.
- Mass production is often criticised because of the poor quality of life it imposes on the workers. The content of the individual job of a worker may be severely limited, sometimes even being reduced to one repetitive operation. The use of a conveyer belt gives the worker no control over the pace of his work and diminishes opportunities to communicate with his fellow workers. This has an adverse psychological effect on the workers leading to boredom and lack of job satisfaction. The result is a

high rate of absenteeism, general work stoppages and possibly defective work owing to a low level of interest in the job. Group working as set out in **19.2 (c)**, **(d)** and **(e)** below is practised by some manufacturers to obviate or alleviate these problems, and the increasing use of robots is advantageous in this respect, though it has the social disadvantage of causing redundancies.

(c) Batch production

- This is a method that falls between job and mass production, and may be said to be repeated production but not continuous production. It is employed where orders consist of a significant number of similar items but these orders are not sufficient to justify continuous manufacture.
- Industries offering choices of design or sophistication in their products make use of batch production, a notable one being the furniture industry. A batch of one design will be made and then a batch of another, and then perhaps the first will be run again. Labour is more skilled in this method of production than in mass production because of the variety of the work entailed, and machines are more versatile. It uses more labour, proportionately, than mass production and less machinery.
- Whether goods are made in advance of orders or subsequent to them depends not so much on the type of production method as on the situation in the market. A manufacturer using batch production will set up a production run when orders for a particular item are received, but has the problem of making the run economically viable; in other words producing sufficient quantity to make the run profitable. He does this by adding a stock quantity to the ordered quantity. One of the most difficult problems in batch production is, in fact, this one of deciding what is the economic batch size.
- Batch production can offer some of the cost saving advantages of mass production, but also allows the manufacturer to satisfy individual job orders if necessary because of his more versatile machinery and skilled workers. At no time, however, can the user of batch production methods compete in price with mass-produced items.

19.2 Determining production conditions

- The first decision a manufacturer has to make is to choose the factory site. This used to be done either on the basis of proximity to raw material and power, where the raw materials were bulky or heavy or, in the case of metal ores, where the usable content was small compared to the total volume, or on access to the market. These simple criteria now apply to a much lesser extent first because of better transport facilities and communications and second because of government intervention by way of grants and other inducements to industry to move to areas of high unemployment and economic stagnation. In addition there are

legal restrictions placed on where industrial development may take place.
- The method of laying out the factory, however, is still the prerogative of the manufacturer and there are some basic ways in which factory layout is organised, determined by the type of production used:

(a) **Layout by process (functional layout)**

This is the method most favoured in batch production. All the machines carrying out the same operations are located together in groups, and sometimes even in separate production shops. The product moves from work-station to work-station progressively until it reaches the final finishing shop. This style of layout favours specialisation in operations and can make more efficient use of high-capacity, versatile machines, as well as better use of labour. In the case of machine breakdown work can be easily transferred to another nearby machine and so production will suffer minimum interruption. The same remarks apply to machine maintenance requirements. Such a layout, as noted in **19.1 (b)** above, does have social repercussions on operating staff, creating monotony and boredom.

(b) **Layout by product (flow-line layout)**

In this method machines are grouped to perform the total sequence of processes needed to make a complete product or component of a product. At each work-station, therefore, there will be all the various machines needed for the complete operation and staff of various skills will work together at these stations. Control of the production process is easier than in process layout because the progress of complete units can be ascertained, which is not possible in the process method. It also gives the advantage that workers are more involved in the manufacturing process and can have greater interest in their work.

- These two types of layout are the traditional ones, though it is unusual to find either used entirely on its own. In practice there will be a combination of both in most factories. Following the work of industrial psychologists a further method, known as group working, has been evolved and put into effect by some major manufacturers.

(c) **Group working**

In this arrangement, which is very like production layout, machines and workers are arranged in self-contained groups which make complete units or components, but they enjoy considerable autonomy not provided by the production method. Thus, each group is, in effect, a small self-contained factory with virtually full control over its own planning and control. Experience shows that this method provides considerable social benefits to the workers and encourages them to identify themselves more completely with their organisation. It is also claimed that production control is facilitated.

(d) **Group technology**

In this instance the term 'group' refers to manufacture rather than to workers. It involves grouping parts or components into 'families' by way of design, shape or production requirements, the aim being to improve production efficiency by increasing the utilisation of each work-station. Machines are divided into groups each appropriate to a given 'family' of components. An advantage of this method is that more economical production becomes possible because of the increased output of each work-station and consequent reduction in unit costs.

(e) **Cell production**

Group technology often gives rise to cell production which, like group working, is a form of worker grouping. It becomes necessary because group technology involves some flexibility in operation, for instance workers being required to operate more than one machine. Again, like group working the operatives enjoy a measure of autonomy.

- The choice of which type of production line to adopt will depend upon many factors such as the need or otherwise for highly specialised machinery, the need for or availability of an adequate supply of labour with the right skills, the ability to operate long continuous runs, the form of the product, such as whether it is for the mass market or to special order, whether various processes can be treated as highly specialised, and many others. In some cases the physical aspects of the factory building may play a large part in the decision; whether it is a single-storey or multi-storey structure will often determine the choice. In practice, of course, a mixture of methods is usually to be found.

- While this discussion has centred on the actual making of products, it must be remembered that many factories are really only assembly plants, assembling bought in components into saleable items, but the same remarks apply to assembly lines as to production lines. In fact, practically all manufacturing undertakings buy in some of their components and assemble them into their completed products. The motor-car industry is a case in point where dashboard instruments, sparking-plugs and many other components are made, not by the motor-car manufacturer, but by an outside concern.

19.3 Production management

- Production management has the overall responsibility to ensure that the materials, labour and equipment resources of the organisation are utilised to the best and most economic advantage.

- Manufacturing undertakings fall, generally speaking, into two broad categories: those that are marketing-orientated and those that are production-orientated. The marketing-orientated organisation will require those responsible for production management to plan production to fit in with the requirements of the market and the sales forecasts that the marketing function has prepared. The whole of the organisation's efforts will be directed to this end.

- This is in contrast to the production-orientated philosophy which, in effect, says that production will make what it most conveniently can and the marketing section must sell those products. This philosophy is very much in evidence where the top management team has a good deal of expertise in production techniques and problems and lacks a depth of experience and knowledge of marketing. It is generally conceded that in present-day conditions success comes to those who are marketing-orientated and there is much evidence to show that production-orientated concerns have far less chance of success.
- Production management is, therefore, very much influenced by what the market is persuaded that it wants by the marketing people.
- The four main headings under which production management functions are:

(a) The type of production-line and assembly-line methods and layouts, dealt with under **19.1** and **19.2** above.
(b) Production engineering.
(c) Production planning.
(d) Production control.

19.4   Production engineering

This occurs principally at the pre-production stage and upon the quality of the decisions made at this point depends the success of the production runs. Though usually under the ultimate control of the production manager, the work involved in production engineering is normally delegated to a production engineer who has high managerial status. The production engineer is responsible for

(a) deciding the most effective way of carrying out each manufacturing process required in the total production runs;
(b) detailing the methods of manufacture to be used and selecting the machinery and equipment required; this may include actually drawing up specifications for machines and equipment;
(c) defining the standards of quality and tolerances to be worked to at each manufacturing stage;
(d) designing special tools and jigs for use on the machine tools to be utilised in production;
(e) constantly monitoring the manufacturing processes with a view to improvements and the introduction of newer technology as it develops.

So important is the work of the production engineer that it is now the subject of special study and is recognised as a profession in its own right.

19.5   Production planning

This follows the production engineering decisions and covers the requirement to plan the actual manufacture of the products. Production planning
may be under the control of a production planning manager, often given
the title of production planning engineer, or may be combined with the
function of the production engineer.

The activities covered by production planning are

(a) to determine when the production should be put in hand and the
time-scale involved;

(b) the preparation of work and materials schedules to ensure labour and
materials are available at the right times and in the right quantities;

(c) the preparation of machine utilisation schedules, commonly termed
'machine loading', to ensure machine and operator availability and the
most economic use of plant and operators;

(d) to maintain close liaison with the design and sales sections, with actual
production runs and with production control.

Effective production planning ensures smooth production runs with
reduced possibilities of disruptions due to material shortages, non-
availability of machine tools and unexpected staff shortages.

19.6   Production control

- Production control is an extension of production planning and has to
work closely with it. In many organisations both sub-functions are
combined under one manager, particularly in the smaller concern. It can
be said that production planning says what is to be done and production
control ensures that it is.
- The principal form of production control is progress chasing, which
entails monitoring the passage along the production lines of the items
being manufactured, and ensuring that time schedules are being maintained. If any delays or deviations are discovered then corrective action
has to be taken to remedy the situation. Progress chasing is a positive
activity and the most common form it takes is by the use of progress
slips. As work progresses along the production line it is accompanied by
job cards detailing what work has to be carried out at each work-station.
Each job card has attached a progress slip and when the operation has
been satisfactorily completed the slip is sent to the progress office, which
is thus apprised of the stage at which the work has been completed. The
slips are recorded on the planning schedule and any discrepancy is then
immediately followed up. Increasingly, where long regular runs are
concerned, progress chasing is being automated.
- Other production control activities are checking machine utilisation,
ensuring adherence to materials delivery schedules (often done by the
purchasing department) and labour utilisation checks.

- Some organisations also involve the production control department in cost control by means of a costing section under the jurisdiction of the production control manager. However, it could be argued that this is properly the province of the finance function and should be carried out under the authority of the management accountant, who is answerable to the chief accountant.

19.7   Inspection

(a)   The function of inspection

Clearly factories cannot be allowed to manufacture goods without regard to the quality of the items produced, and therefore checking is required so that a minimum standard of quality is maintained. This is known as inspection and is an essential part of any manufacture to avoid waste, the production of unacceptable goods and thus loss of profits. Inspection really starts with goods received, be they raw materials or manufactured components, to ensure that the input to the manufacturing process is of the requisite quality.

Before inspection can effectively take place standards of quality must be set, and these will depend upon the precision with which the materials can be worked, what effect the part or materials in question will have on the finished article, and the standard of quality required in the finished product. The last will be largely determined by the market for which the goods are destined and the price range within which they must be sold. Except where expense is only a secondary consideration the maintenance of precise standards is impossible and so some variation is allowable, these variations being known as tolerances. The amount of tolerance allowed is such that the function or working of the finished product is in no way impaired. The closer the tolerances, of course, the better the product, but this will lead to higher production costs and a greater proportion of rejected units.

(b)   When to inspect?

It is important that defects should be discovered as early as possible to prevent faulty material or components being incorporated in the finished article, or additional processing being carried out on a defective part. Against this must be set the sensible requirement that the cost of inspection must not exceed the cost of the necessary remedy.

The principal stages at which inspection is normally carried out are as follows:

- On receipt of raw materials or bought-in components.
- Before a production run to ensure the correct setting up of machines.
- During the production run to ensure that the machines are maintaining their correct settings.

- At the time of pre-assembly, where parts for assembly are inspected for quality before being incorporated in the final product.
- Final product testing, which is carried out on the completed products ready for sale.

With regard to inspection before assembly, it is most important that any defects which will be hidden by subsequent work shall be discovered before the fault is hidden. Such a case would be where a flaw in a metal part will be covered by paint and subsequently invisible.

(c) Quality control
- The best and surest check is, of course 100 per cent testing, but this can be highly expensive and is normally reserved for products where public safety is at risk or those goods destined for the highest-quality market where price is a secondary consideration.
- In other cases inspection of samples is carried out. This may be done on purely random samples taken at regular intervals, on spot samples taken at irregular intervals or, more scientifically, on statistical random samples, technically termed 'statistical quality control' (SQC) and more popularly simply as 'quality control' (QC). This last method is suitable only when conditions of mass production obtain – that is when large quantities are being manufactured under relatively unvarying conditions. The incidence and trend of faulty components are determined over a period by constant inspection. From this information the size of the samples and the number and frequency of the checks needed for effective control of quality are calculated statistically. Quality control is then instituted on this basis.
- It is claimed that statistical quality control provides a means of forecasting the trends in poor-quality production so that remedial action can be taken before quality falls below the limits of acceptability. Unfortunately it is not a foolproof system and despite these techniques faulty specimens can still fall into the hands of customers.

(d) Where to inspect
There are two main places to carry out inspection: on the floor of the factory and at centralised inspection points. Both have their merits.

1 Floor inspection
This is carried out by roving inspectors, who check at the actual point of production. It is a particularly valuable method because it prevents the faulty items receiving any further processing and enables remedial action to be taken immediately. It is adopted where relatively unskilled labour is employed to operate automatic machines, and where the product is too bulky or too heavy to be transported economically to a central inspection point.

2 Centralised inspection
This obtains where there is a central inspection shop to which parts,

sub-assemblies and complete assemblies are brought for testing and checking. The advantages of this method are that there can be a better supervision of the inspection function, more precise measuring machinery can be developed and used and more automatic machines can be utilised. The use of centralised inspection usually involves more movement of goods and the accumulation of more work in progress than occurs with floor inspection, and to minimise this inspection shops are set up at various logically determined points along the production line.

Whether to use floor or centralised inspection will depend upon circumstances. Usually there will be a mixture of the two, with floor inspection for individual vital components and centralised inspection for less vital components and for sub-assemblies and final assemblies.

(e) Responsibility for inspection

Opinions differ as to whom the inspection team should report, some preferring reporting at a managerial level closest to the production process involved, while others contend that inspection should be divorced from actual production operations. On the whole it would seem wisest to adopt the latter policy, the inspection team being under the direct control of a chief inspector who is responsible direct to the production manager. In this way actual production and inspection activities are kept entirely independent of each other. Experience shows that where inspection reports direct to a manager intimately involved with actual production persuasion can be brought to bear on inspectors to pass slightly substandard units so as to show favourable production figures. This happens particularly where a factory is hard pressed to meet sales demands and production targets.

19.8 The make or buy decision

- One of the major production decisions that has to be taken in connection with certain components is whether they should be made in the manufacturer's own works or whether they should be bought in from an outside supplier.
- There are a number of factors which need to be considered before a decision can be made. The advantages of making components internally are that the manufacturer has complete control over their quality, so ensuring finished products of acceptable standard, delivery times are completely in the hands of the production team as are the costs of manufacture, and additional earnings may be generated which may bring increased profit. It is thus possible to have components which relate precisely to production plans in quality, delivery and cost. Further, it may be a marketing advantage to be able to claim that a product is made in its entirety by the manufacturers of the complete product.
- There are, however, some disadvantages. These include the need to

finance this aspect of the product in regard to design costs, manpower and machine availability. In some cases additional machinery and work-people may be required. Having engaged in the manufacture of the components some flexibility in supply is lost. Where the market fluctuates it is easier to stop placing orders with outside suppliers than it is to run down production when there is a reduction in demand. Equally, should there be a sudden increase in demand it is more difficult to restart production to satisfy manufacturing requirements than it is to go into the market and buy.

- Ideally, it is probably advantageous to make components internally only if there are spare facilities available, and then only if these facilities include appropriate design and development capabilities.
- Finally, to an organisation with a social conscience a decision to make internally may be made on the grounds of avoiding redundancies among loyal employees should components be bought in from outside.

It is necessary to stress that production practices differ very widely from industry to industry and from enterprise to enterprise, particularly in relation to size and market. What is presented here is a general picture as an introduction to the subject of production and as a basis for understanding and appreciation of this function.

Questions

1 What are the four main divisions in the work undertaken in any company under the general heading of Production Administration? **(IComA)**

2 What are the principal responsibilities of the production planning and control department in a manufacturing concern? **(IComA)**

3 The use of the assembly line for a manufacturing operation is justified in terms of specialisation and higher efficiency achieved. Examine the factors which a company should evaluate before introducing an assembly-line system of production, or when considering the abandonment of an existing assembly-line system. **(ACCA)**

4 Flow or assembly line production has been the subject of considerable criticism. Explain the difficulties to which this system of production gives rise and consider suggestions which have been made to overcome them. **(IComA)**

5 A manufacturer is faced with a decision whether to produce components for his product within his own organisation or to buy them from outside specialist suppliers. Discuss the points which he should consider in arriving at a decision. **(IComA)**

6 (a) What may the advantages and disadvantages of cohesive work groups be?

   (b) How can managers reduce or avoid the disadvantages? **(CIMA)**

7 Explain how the level of demand for a company's products influences the way in which its production system is organised.   **(CIM)**

8 In manufacturing industries, inspection takes place to ensure a satisfactory standard of quality in the finished product. Such inspection is not concerned only with the finished article. Describe **four other areas** where inspection may take place in a manufacturing process.   **(CIM)**

20 The purchasing function

The purchasing function used to be part of the production function and enjoyed very little status in the organisation. Over the past few decades, however, the purchasing activity has grown in stature through recognition of the contribution it makes to the success of any enterprise and it is now recognised as a separate function in its own right.

- It is salutary to consider the enormous impact efficient purchasing (or procurement as it is sometimes called) has on the costs of an organisation. Many figures of comparison are quoted, but it is safe to say that by judicious buying the purchasing department can save as much in a week as the sales department can generate profit in a month. The heavy weight of responsibility falling on those concerned with purchasing is, therefore, very evident. This has come about because of the increasing size of organisations, the increasing complexity of materials and components and the extreme competition met in the modern market.

- The purchasing function differs from most others in that those carrying out this work are to a large extent tied to their own industry. With little adjustment accountancy work, personnel work and even marketing are much the same from industry to industry. An accountant from the wool trade would have little difficulty in transferring to the building industry; fundamentally he would be handling similar problems. No such relatively easy transfer is available to the buyer. Purchasing wool requires expert technical knowledge of a high order to ensure that the correct wool is being acquired, each batch varying from sample to sample. In addition buying will be done by auction in a highly competitive atmosphere with rapid on-the-spot decisions having to be made.

  A buyer in the building industry, on the other hand, will be operating in an environment where prices are relatively stable, even if for only short periods of time; spot decisions are rarely called for and quality is fairly uniform from whatever source the materials are acquired. Portland cement from one manufacturer is indistinguishable from Portland cement from another, and the same condition applies to paints, bricks, glass and the very many other materials and components the building contractor uses.

  Where natural materials are concerned, such as timber or ballast, standards are relatively uniform and do not call for technical knowledge of a very high order. In the main it can be said that manufactured materials and components will have a reasonably constant quality, particularly if made to strict specifications, whereas natural raw materials may vary considerably from sample to sample.

Nevertheless there are many activities within the purchasing function that are common to many industries and other types of enterprise.

20.1   Common purchasing activities

Activities common to most industries are:

(a)   All buyers will need to have a wide knowledge of the markets from which they have to make their purchases, whether these are raw materials, manufactured components or, as in wholesale and retail trading, finished goods. The knowledge will extend to how the suppliers perform in regard to reliability and delivery performance.

(b)   In manufacturing and kindred industries buyers will have to liaise closely with the production department to ascertain their precise requirements. In retail selling the buyer has a key role in the success of the enterprise in that he or she must be closely attuned to consumer taste and demand.

(c)   Though stock control may or may not be the direct responsibility of the purchasing officer, he is primarily responsible for ensuring that sufficient supplies of materials or components are available to maintain continuity of manufacture or sales. The buyer may do this by contracts with suppliers for regular deliveries or by building up stocks to be called off as required. The former keeps a minimum of capital tied up in stores and storage space but entails the risk of suppliers not keeping to delivery undertakings, while the latter does tie up capital but ensures that materials or components are readily available.

It is probably true to say that in the retail trade no one knows how many sales are lost to an organisation because of articles not being in stock. Most consumers nowadays demand instant satisfaction and are disinclined to wait even a short while for delivery, preferring to go to another retailer who can supply immediately.

(d)   In most organisations the purchasing department will be responsible for negotiating purchase prices and terms of credit.

(e)   Purchasing will also generally be responsible for ensuring that the goods ordered and invoiced are actually received and that the prices charged are those quoted. This is an area where fraud is not difficult and procedures should be instituted to minimise this risk, such as having the necessary checks carried out by different staff from those directly involved in placing the orders.

(f)   Purchasing will constantly monitor expected deliveries to ensure that suppliers adhere to their undertakings regarding quality and delivery dates.

(g)   Purchasing will constantly investigate the market
    1 to seek better products, prices, terms or deliveries;

2 to seek out alternative suppliers to ensure continuity of deliveries should the principal source unexpectedly fail for any reason.

20.2 Purchasing's relations with other functions

- The purchasing department probably has direct relations with more functional departments throughout the organisation than any other single department.
- Its primary relationship in manufacturing and similar industrial enterprises is with the three aspects of production, namely production engineering, production planning and production control. It serves production engineering by advising on the availability and costs of both equipment and materials. The buying department, by its constant investigations into all the appropriate sources of supply, has a wide knowledge and experience with which to advise on these matters. A similar service is provided for production planning where information concerning availability and continuity of supplies is vital if production is to be planned effectively. Equally, production control benefits from the activities of the purchasing department since this department is concerned with monitoring delivery performance of suppliers and seeking alternative sources of supply should delays or breakdown in the principal sources be experienced or even suspected.
- The purchasing department also has a direct relationship with the marketing function in that customers' remarks and complaints, especially in respect of material quality, have a direct bearing on what is purchased and, sometimes, where. A direct link in retailing is obvious, but the same influence is present in other activities. One example would be the country of origin of components in a finished manufactured article. A manufacturer exporting to certain countries may be required to ensure that some components made in the importing country are incorporated in his goods. Alternatively, there may be a prohibition of components made in a third country or group of countries. It is the responsibility of the purchasing department to ensure that these conditions are met.
- Purchasing is also very much to do with finance: the buying department is a major spender in any organisation. Its link with the accounts department is therefore obvious. Credit terms in regard to payment times and cash discounts are as important as the actual purchase prices. Again, judicious timing of purchases can have a beneficial effect on working capital. If, for instance, credit terms are for remittance at the end of the month following delivery, then orders for delivery in the first week of a month allow of two months' credit before payment is due. Many other similar devices are also used by the purchasing department to benefit the financial aspect of the organisation. Very often, for example, the buyer may be able to strike a particularly favourable bargain to the advantage of the organisation, and the enterprising

purchasing officer is constantly on the alert for such favourable offers. On the other hand prudence must always prevail in this connection as the costs of storage can easily absorb any savings made by favourable prices.

20.3   Purchasing policy

As with other functions, there must be a clear policy on purchasing laid down. This is, of course, ultimately the responsibility of top management, but the purchasing officer will have a great deal of advice to give on this matter.

- Perhaps the first item of purchasing policy to be considered will be the level of stocks to be carried. Will stockholding be restricted to goods for immediate and current usage or should a buffer stock be held? If the latter, what quantities should be held? The normal pattern of deliveries by suppliers may determine this. If supplies are generally constant then reliance can be placed on a continuing receipt of goods ordered, but if they are erratic it may be more prudent to establish a stock to ensure regular input to production. Costs of holding stores, quantity discounts, the possible financial implications of production stoppages, and vulnerability to deterioration and to theft will all play a part in making this decision.
- Second, is speculative buying to be indulged in? Certain raw materials in particular experience wide price fluctuations and it may be both prudent and profitable to purchase large quantities when they become available at low prices. There are two advantages in doing this. First, production gains the benefit of low-priced inputs which can reflect in lower selling prices, giving the final products a competitive price edge, or alternatively the lower cost can be seen as an opportunity to gain higher profits particularly where a sufficiently large part of the market is already assured. Second, when raw-material prices rise the organisation may be able to dispose of its surplus stocks at a profit, thus experiencing a gain just by holding the stocks.
- Third, is entering into short- or long-term contracts for the purchase of materials to be part of the purchasing policy or is it to be the policy to go to the market as and when materials are actually required? When prices generally are rising, or when supplies are difficult or uncertain, such a practice has its attractions. On the other hand being committed to one supplier at fixed prices may inhibit more adventurous buying and may also turn out to be detrimental if prices fall unexpectedly or supplies from the contractor fail for one reason or another.

These are by no means the only considerations that may be part of the buying policy, and it must be remembered that the type of activity or industry in which the organisation operates will determine the policy details.

20.4 Objectives of efficient purchasing

The objectives of efficient purchasing can be set out in the 'seven rights' which may be expressed to buy:

> the **RIGHT goods**
> at the **RIGHT price**
> in the **RIGHT quantity**
> of the **RIGHT quality**
> at the **RIGHT time**
> delivered to the **RIGHT place**
> on the **RIGHT terms**

These, the seven aspects of efficient purchasing, are self-explanatory and enter into all buying operations.

20.5 Centralised purchasing

- Purchasing is one of the activities of an organisation that lend themselves readily to centralisation. Where the operations of the undertaking are on a large scale and relatively uniform centralised purchasing has much to commend it. It should result in a consistent buying policy, which means fewer problems for both buyer and supplier because fewer queries arise that need special attention: in other words the practice of management by exception is easier to apply (see **12.9** above). Large single orders resulting in bulk buying result in more power in the hands of the purchaser to influence suppliers in regard to prices and terms in favour of the buyer. Suppliers are also inclined to give better and more favoured attention to those organisations placing large orders because a large customer is a valuable customer the loss of whose business may be a serious matter. The purchasing department itself can develop specialist buyers who can concentrate on different parts of the market and so build up greater expertise than if they were required to spread their activities over many different purchasing needs. Finally, buying procedures can be made uniform with consequent convenience in administration and greater control of expenditure and over stocking.
- There are, of course, some disadvantages to centralised purchasing. The first disadvantage is that of loss of flexibility. Where a large enterprise is spread geographically over a wide area, or where there are many diverse activities carried on centralised purchasing can become a rigid operation and special individual requirements have to be refused on account of this. This may result in certain activities of the enterprise having to substitute slightly less effective materials or components for those which would be ideal. Thus in reinforced concrete component manufacture, for example, a steel of slightly greater or less diameter may be supplied

by the purchasing department than that ideally specified because to buy an unusual size would cause greater expense or be inconvenient administratively. This in turn may necessitate an alteration to the specification of the concrete mix to accommodate the size of steel actually supplied.

- Where centralised purchasing is practised it is common to find that user departments have practically no control over the procurement of their requirements. Where particular suppliers are specified this is often ignored by the buyer for reasons of convenience, being contracted to particular suppliers or because of cost. Therefore the user departments can take no responsibility in connection with the purchase of their requirements other than informing the buying department of their needs.
- Often centralised purchasing procedures become unwieldy and bureaucratic. This is unavoidable in a large organisation but it does lead to delays in authorising and placing orders. This can be to the detriment of the user department concerned.
- Departmental buying avoids the disadvantages of centralised buying in that it gives individual users control over their material and component inputs and brings greater operational experience to bear on their selection and acquisition. Orders are placed more quickly and followed up more effectively. There is less bureaucracy and thus less paperwork. Against these advantages must be set the disadvantages of a probable increase in material and component costs, the inability to bargain from the strength of large orders and a possibility of a greater opportunity for fraud.

20.6 Stock control

- The question of whether stocks of materials and components should be the responsibility of the purchasing function has no universal answer. Some undertakings have such stocks under the control of production on the basis that the physical availability of these items is part of the manufacturing function. Others assert that as the purchasing department is responsible for procurement then it is this department's responsibility to control and account for stocks. There is yet another school of thought that believes storage and stock control should be a department separate from either, particularly as the financial value of stocks held is usually very considerable.
- These three points of view are really relevant only where operations are conducted on one site or on a very small number of nearby sites, and appertain principally in the manufacturing field. Other industries and activities, such as building construction, where operations are carried out on sites far removed from central administration, have the question answered for them. Every building site and every civil engineering site, for example, must of necessity have materials and components at hand

under the direct control of the site manager (by whatever name he is known).

- The main objectives of stockholding and stock control are to ensure an adequate flow of materials and components required for the organisation's operations, to keep minimum stocks commensurate with operational requirements, to ensure the good physical condition and safety of the stocks held and to reduce to the utmost the possibilities of fraud and theft. The procedures required to carry out these objectives will vary according to the types of stores held, their physical disposition and the rates of usage.
- Finally, there seems to be no common usage of the words stock(s) and stores and they are employed interchangeably most of the time.

Questions

1 What are the main objectives of efficient purchasing? To what extent is it desirable or necessary that the purchasing activity should be carried out by a separate department? **(CIM)**

2 With which other managers and on what facets of business would the Purchasing Manager normally concern himself in effectively carrying out his duties? **(IComA)**

3 The scope of activities of the Purchasing Department may vary from company to company, but there are a number of common activities which are essential. Describe these vital activities. **(CIM)**

4 What might be the objectives of a Purchasing Department? **(CIM)**

5 What are the main factors on which the purchasing manager of a manufacturing company would base his decision, in awarding his business to one of several competing suppliers of production materials? **(CIM)**

6 The purchasing function may be organised in various ways. It may also be a separate department or part of another department (e.g. accounts or production). Discuss with reference to the purchasing functions of centralisation or decentralisation. **(IAM)**

7 P Ltd is a company producing a number of different products and services from five sites which are located quite near to each other. At each site several departments are involved in creating the products and services of that site. All the equipment used, the materials and components for production as well as general purpose supplies, are bought for the whole company by a central purchasing department. The company's performance is below target. This is partly due to sales being lost because of long delivery dates and delayed deliveries, and partly due to quality problems. The operating departments blame these problems on the failure of

up-to-date and suitable supplies of good quality to reach them according to the agreed plans. You are required to

(a) describe what the objectives of a purchasing function might be;

(b) recommend how the purchasing of the materials and components could be re-organised to improve the situation described above.   **(CIMA)**

The research and development function

Because of continually increasing technological knowledge, the pressure of competition and the fact of the life-cycle of products, discussed in Chapter 18, in order that a manufacturing organisation can survive and remain profitable it is essential that it has new and improved products constantly available to the public.

- Manufacturers who rely on their existing range of products, however successful, will eventually find that they have been overtaken by others who have exploited new methods, new materials and improved designs. Even in the service industries an organisation cannot stand still and institutions such as banks now provide such facilities as electronic cash points for the withdrawal of money outside banking hours to compete with other types of financial organisations such as building societies that open longer hours. It is in the field of manufacturing of all kinds from the simplest to the most sophisticated products, however, that the pressing necessity for new and improved goods is most in evidence. It is the role of the research and development function to ensure the provision of such products.
- The research and development (R and D) function is often considered to be part of the production function and ancillary to it but, in fact, the scope of research and development goes much further than this. Upon the programme and the success of the research and development department depends the future of the organisation. It is therefore essential that it is under the control of an independent research and development executive who will report direct to top management. Nevertheless it is equally important that complete co-operation and confidence is established between both the marketing and the production functions, the views of each of which must be taken into consideration in formulating research and development programmes.
- The work of the research and development department will also be influenced by the organisation's corporate plans and strategy, which will be concerned with the further development of existing markets by improved products, the exploitation of new markets by the introduction of new products and the financial investment allocated to the research and development function.

21.1 Research

Research can be divided into two basic kinds, pure or fundamental research and applied research, though in practice there is often some overlap.

(a) **Pure research**

This is concerned, essentially, with furthering basic knowledge and is principally exploratory. It is not pursued with any idea of exploitation or specific practical application and seeks only to add to the fund of human knowledge. That is not to say that out of pure research nothing of practical or commercial value ever flows. In fact the origins of new materials, methods and applications that eventually become commonplace can be traced in almost all cases back to such research. What is true is that researchers engaged in fundamental research have no aims in the direction of exploitation. This being the case, nearly all pure research is carried out by government agencies and universities where no financial return is expected from the necessary investment. Industry, however, does make some contribution. Many of the very large industrial concerns do carry on some pure research in their laboratories while others make contributions by way of donations to universities.

(b) **Applied research**

It is in the area of applied research that industry is heavily involved. This research is concerned with investigating and solving an identified problem or project with a view to ultimate commercial exploitation. There is little scope for pure exploration in this type of research and interesting lines of investigation must not be pursued unless some positive outcome can be made apparent. It is, in fact, problem orientated, the problems arising through the need for improved products, entirely new ones, or simply the necessity to keep ahead of the competition. A good example of this is that of the electronic pocket calculator where all the successful manufacturers have found it necessary to carry out continuous research to make their product even smaller, lighter and with ever more functions. Those who fall behind in this effort just lose their markets.

21.2 Development

Research throws up the basic elements of a new material or product, or an improvement to an existing one: development is the process of translating these basic findings into practical application.

- Very often development is a long and expensive business and there is a temptation for a manufacturer to launch a new product before development is absolutely complete in order to be first in the field, particularly if it is known or suspected that a competitor is also engaged in a similar project. This action is understandable when it is realised just how much time and financial investment may have been expended on the project. However, the benefits of what is really a premature launch can be easily outweighed by loss of customer confidence if the product fails to live up to expectations.

- The amount of development and necessary testing required of a new product will depend entirely upon what kind of product it is, its cost and how it affects the health and safety of the user. Thus pharmaceutical companies, in developing new drugs, may engage in testing for many years in order to be satisfied with the safety and effectiveness of new products. A new motor-car may also take years to develop because of the considerable pressures on the manufacturer in regard to safety, economy and the minimising of pollution, in addition to taking account of what the customer demands and what the competition has to offer.

- Once a new product has been marketed other manufacturers will follow suit with as little delay as possible and a sort of 'leap-frogging' then takes place as minor improvements are developed and added as time goes on. This is well illustrated by the motor-car industry where the first really effective small car, the Austin-Morris Mini, set a new trend in car design. Most of the other major manufacturers followed suit with equivalent but better equipped models, and all added small refinements from time to time, each vying with the other to develop a car to beat the competition and be more attractive to the motoring public.

21.3   Design

Design is the ultimate stage in the development of a new product before it enters the production phase, while in an existing one it is a continuous process to effect improvements.

- The dividing-line as to where development stops and design begins is a very thin one, and in some organisations both terms are used interchangeably. Design is, in fact, recognised nowadays as a skill in its own right and can be studied separately. What it attempts to do is to translate the project as developed into a product acceptable to the market, and it does this by being concerned with the function of the product and with its appearance. In some cases function is the more important and in others appearance. An example of this can again be taken from the automotive industry. Owing to London's special road conditions, for the London taxicab function is of overriding importance and appearance second. However, a sports car must give the appearance of being very fast and aggressive even if performance does not match its looks.

- Much research has gone into design in recent years, especially in regard to functional products such as machines. For example, human physiological and anatomical characteristics are taken account of in regard to sizes, shapes and placing of controls. Industrial and office seating is ergonomically designed and the colour and material qualities of office furniture carefully selected on scientific principles. In some industries such as food and cosmetics the appearance of the actual products is important and colour in particular allies design with marketing (strawberry jam that was not rich red and had no pips would be unlikely to sell well, neither would margarine that was its natural white instead of butter colour). In many cases packaging is even more important. An enormous amount of design skill is engaged in designing packages for cosmetics to create an attractive and enticing image, to the extent that in some instances the package costs more than its contents.

- Just as good design can enhance a product both in performance and in attractiveness so poor design can damage a product's chances of success, and many a sound and effective product has failed in the market-place simply because its design was clumsy, unattractive or old-fashioned. It is often said that a book should not be judged by its cover; but it often is!
- While it is true to some extent that a designer can work on many diverse products, an instance being the designing of a modern camera by the designers of a famous sports car, nevertheless it is very necessary that a designer be well acquainted with the properties of the materials involved and the ultimate use to which the product will be put.

21.4   Innovation

The introduction of new products is a necessary element in the continued existence of an organisation in the manufacturing and allied industries. In fact it is sometimes stated that innovation is the only way to survival, but this must be taken as an exaggeration. Nevertheless very often unless new and adventurous thinking is applied to the products of an enterprise it will begin to run down and eventually fail.

- To some extent the type of industry determines whether and how much innovation is necessary. For example, the building industry is extremely resistant to innovation and the many projects put forward from time to time to increase the speed of construction or to reduce costs in house-building have failed lamentably. Only those innovations that have followed traditional patterns have superseded the old ways. An example of this is the use of plaster board for ceilings instead of traditional plastering and this is probably because plaster is still the basic material of plaster board, and this innovation was probably encouraged by the scarcity and high cost of skilled plasterers. Blocks of flats and office and industrial buildings have seen more innovations, but many of these have been only reluctantly accepted by building contractors on the grounds of speed and cost.
- On the other hand, if the photographic industry is examined it will be found that innovation is the order of the day both in regard to design and to materials. The development of integral exposure measurement,

automatic exposure, electronic operation, the use of advanced plastics for camera bodies instead of metal, and many other innovations have changed cameras almost out of recognition over the last two decades, and there seems to be no end to new developments and fresh design ideas. Any camera manufacturer who fails to keep pace with the innovations now going on will soon find failure ahead. In other spheres such as manufactured or processed foodstuffs innovation is necessary to maintain the required share of the market essential to ensure continued profitability. A prime example here is breakfast cereals where new, or apparently new, products are continually being offered to whet the appetite and to keep abreast of the competition. In fact the word 'new' is an overworked description used in connection with the promotion of very many household items in the struggle for increased sales.

- Innovation is also shown in the packaging of goods. New ways are found to present products so that they are more attractive or easier to use. A garden insecticide, for example, may be marketed in an ordinary bottle from which the liquid has to be transferred to a spray gun of some kind for use. The innovation of the aerosol can now enable this same insecticide to be presented in a container which allows of its immediate use without the bother of transfer to a spray. Innovations in packaging can be very important in promoting sales.
- The research and eventual development needed to bring about useful and sensible innovation can be considerable as can the normal and expected evolution of a product or range of products. The question of financial investment and support for research and development is therefore a difficult one and one that must rest with top management.

21.5 Financing research and development

So far as allocating financial resources to research and development is concerned there can be no hard-and-fast rules. In general the amounts to be spent will depend upon the type of product or products involved, the size of the organisation and its financial strength, and to what extent the industry itself is subject to technological change. So much of research, in particular, is unpredictable, both in regard to the amount of time required for it to bear fruit and the eventual outcome of the work. Further, in an intensely competitive industry one organisation's research in a certain direction may be overtaken by that of another organisation causing the efforts of the first organisation to lose impact, or even to be proved mistaken. Perhaps the classic example of this occurred in television, where the research and development work of John Logie Baird's team, who were working very largely along mechanical lines, was overtaken by those researching and developing purely electronic television systems (the type now operating) resulting in the ultimate failure of Baird's initial enterprise. Very rarely is an outcome so dramatic but nevertheless significant sums of money can be devoted to research and development that are eventually found to have been wasted.

- The provision of finance for research and development is, then, one of great importance but also one of considerable risk not found in other aspects of an enterprise. Judgement and foresight are necessary in those who have to decide what to finance and to what extent. Subsequent control of the sums allocated is equally difficult.
- As with other functions research and development should be subject to budgetary control. The difficulty of assessing the size of the budget is not an inconsiderable one, however, and is usually based on one or more of the following factors, modified by the persuasion of the research and development staff:

(a) How much can the organisation reasonably afford in this area? Often this is based on a percentage of the previous year's turnover or profit: in other cases, where a yearly budget has been established, an annual inflation percentage may be added to this.

(b) Provisional estimates may be made of current work in this area and a budget allocation made on this basis.

(c) The stages in the life-cycles of current products may be examined, assessments made as to where new research and development efforts are required to revitalise or renew selected products and finance allocated on that basis.

(d) Where it is possible to obtain information as to the research and development expenditure being incurred by competitors this may be used as a basis for a budget allocation on the grounds of the necessity to keep abreast of the competition.

(e) Is it possible or likely that some contribution may be obtained from interested outside sources such as universities, sponsoring businesses or relevant government departments?

- It must be remembered, however budgets are assessed, that the outcome of research and development work is rarely predictable and consequently there is unlikely to be a direct correlation between expenditure and results. Only a relatively small proportion of the work is likely to be put to practical use and there will always appear to be a high measure of wasted effort which can be translated as money wasted. However, unless promising avenues are explored, which is the function of research and development, their impracticability will not be discovered.

21.6   Other problems of research and development

Of the other problems besetting management in connection with research and development the following are the most important:

(a) Research staff, highly intelligent and mostly very dedicated, are not the easiest of staff to control. The nature of their work makes them independent-minded and individualistic, and often resentful of imposed rules and restrictions.

(b) Because of intense interest in a particular project a research team are tempted to carry on with their work beyond the point where the outcome of the research would be economically viable.

(c) Where several research projects are going on at the same time and it becomes necessary to curtail one or more of them it is often extremely difficult to agree priorities on what should be continued. Similar difficulties arise in the selection of projects from the ideas put forward for research.

(d) Where work has been going on for some time on a research project which seems to have reached stalemate there is often great difficulty in deciding when to abandon it. Are the resources already expended to be considered wasted or is it more sensible to spend more effort to try to bring it to a fruitful conclusion? The cold mind of finance is often at odds here with the inquiring mind of the research worker.

(e) Occasionally management, or a forceful member of it, will insist on research being done from a sense of prestige only, which may be wasteful of resources that could be more profitably used on other projects. This is often known as a 'management ego trip.'

Control can be exercised over the research and development function to some extent by the rigid application of budgetary control, though this is often condemned because sometimes valuable investigations have to be abandoned just when they appear to be on the verge of success. Flexibility is needed here. Other methods of control are by imposing time-limits on projects and by requiring regular detailed reports of progress stage by stage so that decisions as to the continuance of the research may be kept constantly under review. In addition the executive in charge of the research and development function should have had considerable experience in management as well as in the relevant technical areas so that his judgements are commercially sound. He should report directly to top management, probably through the chief executive. Nevertheless, it must be appreciated that the price to be paid for an effective research and development department is the risk that it will be, by its very nature, difficult to control.

21.7   Value analysis

Value analysis is a technique used to endeavour to reduce manufacturing costs without impairing the quality or use of the product, principally by cutting out waste of one kind or another. As such it belongs very much within the realms of research, development and design, particularly the last, although it is not generally confined within that function.

● In practice value analysis is carried out by a team comprising members from the staffs of the departments of research and development, purchasing, production and marketing. Every facet of the product under scrutiny is studied to determine its precise function and the existing design in all its aspects is examined. In this way alternatives of design, material, expected life and finish may be assessed to establish where more efficient or less costly materials and techniques can be applied. The incorporation of plastics into components in place of the more traditional metals is a case in point. Most lawn mowers for domestic use, for example, have a completely plastic casing and grass box: not only is this easier and thus cheaper to produce, but it is free from rust. Many handles and other controls in motor-cars are now of plastic materials instead of metal, which also means lower costs without loss of effectiveness.

- Traditionally, many of the components of some products have been designed and made without any reference to the expected life of the product as a whole. The consequence of this is that many parts outlive the total unit. Value analysis seeks to avoid this imbalance by determining the total expected life of the complete product and then redesigning its components to suit this expectation. Equally, it is hardly economic to manufacture articles that are going to last much longer than the period of their expected use as savings can be made in costs if they are designed and manufactured to endure only the amount of time they are going to be needed. The philosophy, especially in regard to motor-cars, has led to a charge of built-in obsolescence, but where value analysis has been applied carefully and honestly this charge is often unjustified.

- It is evident that properly employed the technique of values analysis can be useful and cost saving for both the manufacturer and the customer. It requires the design and performance of existing products to be carefully assessed in detail. This exercise not only enables beneficial modifications to be made, but also brings to light faults in design and materials that can be corrected in future production. It also generates in those responsible a consciousness towards costs which may not formerly have been present, and is also a spur to creative thinking which encourages a fresh approach to the design and material aspects of a product. Frequently the term 'value engineering' is used instead of 'value analysis', but strictly speaking value engineering properly applies to this technique at the design stage and before production.

21.8 Product standardisation

Whether or not a manufacturer uses value analysis some examination and revision of the design of products from time to time is necessary to reduce manufacturing costs and to simplify the holding of stocks and spare parts.

- One way to reduce both is by a system of standardisation. This is simply the reduction of unnecessary differences in parts and components going into completed units. A good example of this is in the manufacture of television remote control hand units. Different models of a maker's televisions will have various facilities, not all common, controlled by buttons on the hand unit. It is common for these hand units to be equipped with all the buttons that may conceivably be required even though individual sets may not have some of the facilities. The result is less necessary stock holding and the elimination of possible requisition errors.

- This philosophy is now common and has been extended to the standardisation of parts between products and product ranges. Thus, car handles tend to be common on most of the vehicles produced by one car manufacturer, and variation is limited usually only by the differences in price range.
- Standardisation also applies in industry overall. Thus it would be inconceivable for domestic light bulbs of any make not to fit the normal lampholder, or for any compact disc not to be playable on a normal CD-player. In fact where standardisation is not achieved in this sort of situation very often the industry concerned finds some difficulty in exploiting its products to the full. A good example of this occurred in the video recorder industry. Three recording systems were developed by three different companies, none compatible with the others. The result was that potential customers, except real enthusiasts, were inhibited from buying while waiting to see which system would become standard. It is interesting to note that universal standardisation does not always result in the adoption of the best system. In the video example, for instance, there is strong opinion among experts that the now accepted VHS system is inferior to the two it superseded.
- It is, of course, very largely a matter for the design team, a part of research and development, to ensure standardisation whether it be within components or within completed products.

21.9 Product simplification

'Simplification' may be taken to mean making a product simpler and less complicated.

- Simplification of a particular product is often the result of value analysis, though it may come about without such an exercise. Generally speaking, however, the term is normally associated with a reduction in the variety of the products manufactured and is sometimes referred to as 'rationalisation'. It may apply to the products themselves or to the ways in which they are offered. Thus a paint manufacturer may restrict the number of packing sizes of the paint produced or may reduce the number of colours. Both of these decisions will result in simplification. In the first case if the existing packing sizes are 0.5 litre, 1 litre, 2 litres, 2.5 litres and 5 litres the manufacturer may feel that the 0.5-litre and the 2-litre tins are superfluous. The elimination of these saves in costs and stockholding space, but in regard to the smallest size may inconvenience customers. In the second case the existing range of, say, 100 colours may be rationalised to 50. Again this will result in lower manufacturing and stockholding costs, and the inconvenience to the customer may be minimal since mixing of colours is possible to provide intermediate tints.

- It is not only manufacturers, however, who find simplification effective in saving costs and reducing stock varieties. Retailers, especially in times of recession, rationalise their stocks by reducing the variety held. Food producers, also, reduce the number of different varieties of fruit and other produce that they cultivate.
- Simplification is not specifically a function of research and development, being more concerned with marketing and production. However, it is closely associated with standardisation (from which it must be clearly distinguished) and so is best considered in conjunction with it.

Finally, in manufacturing industries in particular, research and development is crucial to their continued existence and progress. Resources for this function should never be begrudged. Where the financial burden is too great for the producer's own resources then recourse should be made to one of the many independent research establishments which offer their services, or to the research facilities provided by the industry's trade association where these are available.

Questions

1. Describe the key problems associated with assessing the benefits from research and development activities, and exercising financial control over the resources employed.   **(ACCA)**

2. What is 'value engineering' or 'value analysis'? Indicate the importance of this technique for a manufacturing concern. **(ACCA)**

3. Explain where the responsibility for 'innovation' within an organisation might be. Suggest how the performance of innovators could be measured.   **(IAM)**

4. How can the expense of innovation be justified when a company is struggling to survive?   **(CIM)**

5. (a) What is meant by the terms 'standardisation' and 'simplification', in relation to products and their components?

    (b) What implications would a greater emphasis on standardisation have for the marketing department of a company manufacturing fast-moving consumer durables?   **(CIM)**

6. Where do you see R and D (research and development) activities fitting into long-term and short-term planning and control in a company manufacturing consumer products? How would you implement accountability in these activities?   **(CIMA)**

7. Many companies regard a flow of new and successful products as

essential to their continued prosperity, and spend large sums on Research and Development and design. What are the main factors to be borne in mind in the design of a new product?   **(CIM)**

8 It is frequently complained that Research Departments develop new products without early consultation with other departments of the business. Explain, with reasons, the departments which should normally be involved.   **(IComA)**

The finance function

The survival or failure of an enterprise in the private sector sooner or later rests on how successful it has been financially, and it is increasingly the case that finance and its implications enter into the management of public bodies and corporations as well. The influence of the finance function is therefore all-pervading. Whoever exercises financial control of an organisation therefore, whether called the chief accountant, financial director, treasurer or some other title, bears considerable responsibility and wields considerable power. The subject of finance and accounting is specialised and highly technical and detailed study is outside the scope of any book devoted to general basic management. However the study of management would be incomplete without some acquaintance with the scope of finance and accounting, which is what this chapter is intended to provide.

22.1   The scope of the finance function

The primary occupation of the financial function is to ensure that adequate funds are available for such capital expenditure as new plant and equipment and for working capital to meet revenue expenses such as wages and salaries, materials and all the inevitable administration expenses.

The need for capital expenditure will be ascertained from the long-range plans of the organisation which will have set out the objectives and targets to be achieved and the strategies and tactics required for success. It is the responsibility of the finance function to prepare regular capital budgets to ensure that funds are available for such expenditure and to advise on suitable sources of funds if these cannot be generated from within the concern. Similarly, the finance function is very concerned with a continuing flow of working capital to meet the revenue and running expenses of the organisation, and so must prepare cash flow forecasts and cash budgets to ensure the availability of liquid funds for working capital purposes. Both capital and cash budgets must be subject to budgetary control. The question of budgets and budgetary control was discussed in Chapter 12 and need not be elaborated on here.

22.2   Sources of funds

The acquisition of funds resolves itself into three main categories: long-term funds which are to be applied to capital projects such as new buildings, plant and machinery; medium-term funds for smaller capital items; and short-term funds needed for use as working capital for expenditure on materials, labour and day-to-day expenses. While in practice some overlap is inevitable (current labour and materials, for example, being used to construct a capital project) separate consideration of the three is easier to present and understand.

(a) **Long-term finance**

This is usually considered to consist of finance that is permanent or will be repayable over a long period of time. In the private sector the most obvious source, particularly if the amount is a large one, is a share issue, either in the market and offered to investors generally or an offer specifically to existing shareholders, often in proportion to their existing holdings, when it is called a 'rights issue'. Such finance is, of course, permanent in that once issued shares cannot be bought back by the issuing company. Other forms of long-term finance, which all require repayment at some future time, are:

1 **Debentures.** These are really redeemable long-term loans at fixed interest and secured on the assets of the company. Debenture-holders secure certain rights over the borrower which in some cases involve the right to sell off assets to secure repayment in the event of the failure to meet interest payments when due.

2 **Ordinary loans.** These may be at fixed or variable rates of interest and are repayable at a specific date. They are normally secured either on some asset or assets, or on a personal guarantee of someone of substance. Such loans do not as a rule attract such severe rights to the lender as do debentures.

3 **Mortgages.** These are the same as ordinary loans, but are secured on property which can be realised in case of default.

4 **Sale and lease back.** This form of finance involves the borrower selling fixed assets such as buildings and then leasing them back from the purchaser for use. In effect it is the realising of a capital asset for funds and the regular expenditure of current revenue to pay for leasing.

In considering **1–3** above it must not be forgotten that the interest payments on this loan capital will be a continuing charge on the borrowing organisation until such time as the loan is paid off, and whether profits are earned or not. The proportion of loan (or fixed charge) capital to equity capital is known as gearing or leverage. A company with a high proportion of loan capital is high geared and, of course, it is low geared if the reverse obtains.

When trade in the company's industry is buoyant and high profits are earned this usually means that after the prior charges for loan capital are satisfied there remains a high proportion of the profits available for dividends to the equity shareholders in the cases of high geared companies. However, in times of recession the payment of charges on loan capital may absorb all the available profits leaving none for ordinary shareholders. Where no profits are earned the lenders have to be paid out of reserves. It follows, therefore, that in severe cases the burden of interest charges can be fatal to the organisation.

(b) Medium-term finance

This is usually interpreted as finance over three to ten years and generally involves funds for small capital projects or the development of new products or markets, where the return on the investment is expected to begin within two or three years. It is also used to finance the working capital requirements of a planned programme of growth. It is not considered suitable for the funding of normal working capital requirements. Funds are available as follows:

1 **Hire-purchase** from various finance houses. Hire-purchase relates to specific plant or equipment which is named in the contract. A common hire-purchase contract is that for a lorry or a fleet of lorries.

2 **Medium-term loans** from merchant banks, finance houses or commercial banks. Commercial banks tend to be less generous in the period of their loans than the other sources.

(c) Short-term finance

This is generally finance required for current working capital, to pay wages, current creditors and the like, when self-generated funds are short. In some industries revenue is cyclical although current expenditure continues all the year. An extreme example is that of arable farming where income is received perhaps only twice a year but farm workers have to be paid each week throughout the year. Sources of short-term finance are:

1 **Bank overdraft:** This is usually the simplest and cheapest external source of short-term funds, especially if the requirement is only very temporary. Short-term bank loans can be negotiated, and are sometimes insisted on by the bank, instead of taking an overdraft. However, two aspects of this course must be mentioned: (a) the time limit for a loan is finite and will need to be re-negotiated at the end of the term and (b) the sum represented by an overdraft varies with the intake and expenditure of funds, so that the average sum borrowed in this way is less than the total negotiated, so saving interest.

2 **Extended credit:** Special payment terms can sometimes be negotiated with suppliers to extend credit, thus conserving liquid funds. Careful timing of purchases can also help to provide temporary accommodation, as suggested in **20.2** above.

3 **Credit factoring and invoice discounting:** These related methods of obtaining short-term finance involve selling book debts to special finance houses who specialise in this practice.

4 **Bills of exchange:** In certain industries such as export and import trading bills of exchange can be negotiated and discounted to

provide funds in advance of the actual due date of settlement.

The sources of funds described are the main external ones available to an enterprise and it is within the skill and experience of the chief finance officer to guide the organisation to the use of the most suitable one in the circumstances obtaining when the necessity arises. However a prudent finance department should examine all forms of self-generated finance before going elsewhere, as such funds are cheaper and subject to fewer constraints than those from external sources.

(d) Self-generated finance

Funds generated within the organisation itself can be categorised as follows:

1 **Retained profits.** A prudent policy of retaining a proportion of the profits within the organisation instead of distributing them entirely as dividend or other earnings to owners can build up funds for working capital or short-term capital projects. These retained profits can be invested for a return until they are needed.

2 **Profitable use of funds.** The amount of stocks held, assets under-employed and unprofitable lines or ventures should all be examined to see how these can be reduced to free funds for more profitable use.

3 **Credit policy.** Clear and definite terms of credit should be agreed with customers and these terms should be strictly but diplomatically enforced. Debtors who delay payment are using their supplier's capital for their own purposes, usually free of charge. In fact it is an unfortunate common practice that large undertakings such as supermarkets delay paying their less powerful suppliers well beyond the due date, so providing themselves with what are in effect substantial interest-free loans, to the detriment of the financial health of their creditors. On the other hand the most advantageous terms should be negotiated with creditors and full advantage taken of them. There should be a rigorous credit control policy pursued to minimise bad debts. It is worthwhile to note that experience shows that the incidence of bad debts is lower where accounts are rendered to customers promptly than where there is a time lag between the order being fulfilled and the account being rendered.

4 **Surplus funds.** Surplus funds should always be put to profitable temporary use if they are not immediately required for the organisation's own operations. The earnings so derived are a useful addition to funds, and here the expertise of the finance officer will be invaluable.

22.3 Working capital

Working capital is the financial lifeblood of an enterprise and insufficient working capital is a frequent cause of failure. Maintenance of an adequate flow of working capital is, therefore, a first duty of the finance function to ensure funds for continued operation.

- The definition usually applied to working capital is that it is the excess of current assets over current liabilities. In other words it is the total of assets, liquid or easily made liquid such as cash, trade debtors, finished stocks of raw materials and semi-finished goods, over liabilities that have to be met at short notice or in the normal course of business (certainly within one year) such as trade creditors, rent, rates and similar commitments. Insufficient working capital may indicate over-trading and can result in the demise of the organisation. When profits and surplus cash have been turned into fixed assets in pursuit of expansion the result can be a lack of ready funds to meet immediate liabilities, technically a state of insolvency. The same conditions can arise by being too lenient with debtors or by over-stocking, and by incurring debts with suppliers or the bank which cannot be matched by incoming current revenue.

- The need to forecast the amount of working capital to be devoted to new projects is particularly important, and this should be provided for when cash budgets are being worked out. Failure to make adequate provision restricts the amount of research and development that can be financed and thus is detrimental to the continued success of the enterprise. Very often the development of a new product requires the design and development of special tools, jigs and ancillary equipment and the necessary expenditure on these aspects of a new project must be accepted as a charge on working capital rather than as a charge against capital expenditure. There are two reasons for this. The first is that the control of revenue expenditure is more easily delegated to a department than capital expenditure and second, that development costs usually arise piecemeal as their need becomes apparent, and repeated applications for capital sums is an inconvenience administratively.

- Any estimates and budgets for working capital must take into account two important factors: the current and probable future rates of interest and the probable trends in inflation. Both of these factors are beyond the control of the finance function, but must be included in the calculations of future working capital needs. Inflation erodes the buying value of working capital and this reduction in purchasing power must be countered as far as possible by an adequate product pricing policy, the establishment of cost-reducing practices throughout the organisation, a strict control on credit and the wise investment of surplus funds. Borrowing, also, must be strictly regulated, especially in times of high interest rates.

22.4   Cost and profit centres

(a)   Cost centres
While the finance function has overall responsibility for the financial

activities of an organisation, it can reinforce its control of expenditure by placing the responsibility for controlling costs right where it belongs; that is, where the costs are actually incurred.

- This is the basis of the concept of cost centres. In practice this means that appropriate activities are designated as cost centres and the managers and supervisors responsible for operating these activities are made directly accountable for the costs incurred in these operations. The centres must be large enough to justify the administrative costs involved and small enough to be effectively manageable. Thus in the factory a cost centre may consist of one operation such as paint spraying or a series of operations such as cutting, drilling and grinding. Similarly, the purchasing function may be considered as one cost centre, but in the marketing function each sales area may be designated separately.

- Some costs such as materials and labour specifically applied to the work of the centres are direct costs, whereas others such as supervision, repairs, maintenance and administration are regarded as overheads and must therefore be spread over the cost centres on some equitable basis. This may be by floor area, number of employees or any other appropriate basis per centre. It is important that these allocations be ascertained on a patently fair basis and agreed with the cost centres if this method of control is to be effective.

(b) Profit centres

These view the financial aspect of operations from the opposite point of view from cost centres, in other words from the viewpoint of income and profit and not expenditure and cost.

- Within the enterprise sections are designated as profit centres and these operate as nearly independently as possible. Agreed targets are established for each profit centre and it is the responsibility of the executive or manager appointed to each centre to endeavour to ensure that the targets are achieved. Profit centres tend to be much larger than cost centres, often complete divisions, and are free to operate independently within the framework of the policy laid down for them by top management. Decision-making and managerial responsibility are squarely on the shoulders of the profit centres' executives and managers, their objective being to produce the target profit agreed. In fact profit orientation is a very necessary attribute of a profit centre management team.

- In the setting up of profit centres it is essential to establish adequate accounting procedures that will reflect as accurately as possible, not only the financial aspects of a centre's operations, but also fair charges for the use of fixed assets such as buildings and equitable proportions of general overheads such as the use of a central computer. The difficult problem of transfer prices also has to be agreeably solved. Transfer prices are those prices charged for goods or services provided by one centre to another. There is much discussion about the basis on which such charges should be made; for example, actual cost, actual cost plus a minimal profit, market price and so on, but further examination of this problem is beyond the scope of this work.

(c) Control and accountability

The establishment of cost centres and profit centres is looked upon as a means of control of financial activity and also a means of assigning direct accountability for various aspects of it to specific managers. In this way remedial action can be taken precisely at the point where it is obviously needed. These centres are also a means of assessing managerial performance; the success or failure of a manager or management team in achieving agreed targets. However, the supposition that a cost or profit centre manager is entirely in control of the centre's activities can be questioned. Many of the aspects of the operations are not within the manager's own discretion. Some examples are the existence of corporate plans within which it is necessary to work, restrictions on the scope of products and services as inputs to costs or output for revenue, the span of the market within which a profit centre may be allowed to work, and the effect of other cost and profit centres upon any particular one; for example, the obligation to take the output of an associated centre rather than to be able to go into the open market for supplies.

(d) Investment centres

Before leaving this topic of centres for financial control, a mention must be made of investment centres. These are essentially the same as profit centres but with a particular difference. The performance of a profit centre is gauged by its achievement of a target of profit and this target will be different for each profit centre. Investment centres, however, have return on capital employed (ROCE, see **22.5** below) as a measure of performance and this will normally be the same, as a percentage, for all investment centres.

22.5   Return on capital employed (ROCE)

The return on capital employed is an accepted measurement of the performance of an organisation. The term 'capital' is open to a number of different interpretations, i.e. proprietors' capital, which means the actual investment of the owners or shareholders; total capital, which means the whole of the resources of the concern including bank overdraft, monies owing to trade creditors and other very short-term liabilities; and net capital employed, which comprises owners' capital (share capital), reserves, debentures, and other long-term borrowings. Unfortunately there is no absolute agreement on the items to be included in net capital employed, an example being bank overdraft, which some accountants include and some do not. However, for all practical purposes the items as given are adequate provided there is consistency in the inclusions when comparisons are being made.

- The return on capital employed is expressed as a percentage on the net capital employed and is frequently referred to as 'ROCE'. It measures the performance of an organisation by the return earned on capital resources employed and in so doing affords comparisons with other organisations carrying on the same types of operations and also affords comparisons with other types of investment.
- This latter measurement is important where a company is contemplating going to the market for capital: investors will take ROCE very much into consideration when deciding where to place their funds. Consequently if a share issue is contemplated the ROCE will be one of the factors that will determine the price at which they can be offered. In general the ruling rates of interest will have a marked effect on share prices because investors will not put up risk capital for a return much less than they can obtain from safe interest-bearing investments. If the ROCE is low share prices must also be low, so that the actual earnings per share reflect a percentage somewhere in keeping with the prevailing interest rates in the market.
- Risk is also a factor in ROCE expectancy, though difficult to quantify. Where the risk to capital is high it will be expected that the return on capital employed will also be high to justify the heavy risk. Where the risk is low the ROCE may be expected also to be low.
- It is important, therefore, that the finance function should establish controls over the use of finance in the organisation to safeguard it and to ensure a reasonable rate of return on capital employed, bearing in mind that short-term objectives in this direction may be very different from long-term objectives. In other words a less than satisfactory ROCE may be tolerated in the very short term if this is the preliminary to highly satisfactory returns in the long run.

22.6 Financial ratios

Much of the monitoring of the financial performance of an enterprise is done by means of ratios. These ratios are important in that they quantify financial and operational strengths and weaknesses so that appropriate action can be taken promptly where necessary. The variety of these ratios is large and a detailed study of all of them belongs in a specifically accounting text. However, mention must be made of the most important.

(a) **Return on capital employed ratio**

   ROCE has already been explained in **22.5** above. The formula employed to show the result as a percentage is

$$\frac{\text{Profits}}{\text{Capital employed}} \times 100 = \text{ROCE}\%$$

(b)   Working capital ratio

The importance of working capital has been dealt with in **22.3** above. The ratio employed here is how many times current liabilities are covered by current assets, expressed as follows:

$$\frac{\text{Current assets}}{\text{Current liabilities}} = \text{Working capital ratio}$$

The very minimum ratio is accepted as 1:1, in other words the current liabilities can just be paid out of current assets. As some assets, such as stock or work in progress may take longer to convert into cash than the creditors will allow, a ratio of 2:1 or more is considered to be desirable, with 2:1 as normal.

(c)   Acid test ratio

Also termed the 'liquidity ratio', this measures the vulnerability of an organisation to pressure by creditors and others for immediate payment of liabilities. This is very significant in labour intensive operations where a high proportion of outgoings are in cash for wages. The ratio takes into account only current assets that can be turned into cash immediately (sometimes referred to as 'quick assets') and so ignores stock and work in progress, which may take time to realise. The formula is:

$$\frac{\text{Cash} + \text{Debtors} + \text{Readily realisable securities}}{\text{Current liabilities}}$$

or

$$\frac{\text{Current assets} - (\text{Stock} + \text{Work in progress})}{\text{Current liabilities}}$$

$$= \text{Acid test ratio}$$

Ideally the minimum ratio should be 1:1. This means that all liabilities can be met in full immediately. Although in many spheres of activity less than this can be considered acceptable, nevertheless in the event of failure of some debtors, for example, the organisation would be extremely vulnerable in the case of pressure by creditors. Conversely, if the ratio is much more than 1:1 the wisdom of holding what amounts to surplus funds could be questioned, as these could possibly be profitably used outside the organisation.

(d)   Earnings per share

This is particularly important to an organisation contemplating seeking additional outside capital. It expresses the earnings made on each share in monetary terms, the formula being:

$$\frac{\text{Total earnings after tax (£)}}{\text{Number of shares}} = \text{Earnings per share (£)}$$

Intending investors can compare this figure with the market price of the shares and obtain the price/earnings (P/E) ratio. This provides a coefficient of return that can be compared with other investments.

(e) **Price/earnings ratio**

While an existing shareholder can obtain a personal P/E ratio, the normal use for this ratio is against current market prices for shares, to enable investors to make comparisons between different investments. The formula is:

$$\frac{\text{Market price of share}}{\text{Current year's earnings per share}} = \text{P/E ratio}$$

It will be seen that this ratio actually states how many years at present earnings will be required to retrieve the capital outlay required to purchase a share at a particular price. There is no accepted norm for the P/E ratio, but it is assumed that the higher the ratio the greater the potential of the enterprise and thus the more attractive the investment for those looking to the future. Where this expectation fails a share becomes expensive.

The ratios already presented indicate primarily the financial health of the organisation and its potential in the market for new capital. Other ratios are also used to measure performance, the most common of which are:

(f) **Gross profit to sales (GP)**

Ths provides a measure of gross profit expressed as a percentage of sales, as follows:

$$\frac{\text{Gross profit}}{\text{Net sales}} \times 100 = \text{GP\%}$$

This makes period-by-period comparisons easy and provides a simple monitor of trading performance before the application of administration costs.

(g) **Net profit to sales (NP)**

Again this is a useful measure of performance and a period-to-period monitor of net profit; that is, gross profit *less* costs of administration. The ratio is expressed as a percentage of net sales, as follows:

$$\frac{\text{Net profit}}{\text{Net sales}} \times 100 = \text{NP\%}$$

Comparison of GP% to NP% also indicates how much of the trading profit is being absorbed by the costs of administration.

(h) **Administration expenses to sales (AE)**

This provides an indicator by percentage of how much sales revenue is absorbed by administration, and shows whether administration is too costly. It also gives a period-by-period comparison of the proportion of revenue so absorbed, thus providing a picture of the trend in this direction. The formula is:

$$\frac{\text{Administration expenses}}{\text{Net sales}} \times 100 = AE\%$$

(i)   **Selling expenses to sales (SE)**
Finally, this ratio gives information about the percentage of sales revenue absorbed by the costs of actual selling, an important element in profitability. The formula is as simple as the previous three:

$$\frac{\text{Selling expenses}}{\text{Net sales}} \times 100 = SE\%$$

There are many other ratios used by the finance function to measure and assess performance, those given here being illustrative of the most important and most used. A full exposition of all the ratios employed can be obtained from specialist works on finance and accounting.

22.7   Management accounting

Management accounting is a branch of the finance function dealing with internal resource management and is a professional activity in its own right. Its purpose is to assist management in the formulation of policies and objectives and in the operation of the enterprise by presenting accounting information in a fashion easily usable by management.

- Management accounting grew out of cost accounting, which provided detailed information in regard to costs of manufacture, administration and other activities. The attitudes that costing engendered, that of inquiry and analysis, became harnessed to the need by management for accounting information beyond that provided by the purely financial records, and presented in a manner more in tune with management needs than that adopted by the financial accountant. It could be said that the emphasis of conventional accounting is on financial records, prevention of fraud, concern for financial statements of revenues and the like, while management accounting concerns itself with costs, the interpretation of accounting records, the isolation of variables and controls.
- The range of activities of the management accountant is very wide and overlaps some of the areas of financial accounting. Briefly, the principal areas of management accounting are:

(a)   **Budgetary control**
This is fully discussed in Chapter 12.

(b) Standard costing

This is a method of control of manufacturing costs in which the production of a unit has a standard cost worked out for it based on previous experience or estimates. Actual costs during production are ascertained and these are compared with the standard costs. Variances are examined to establish the causes for discrepancies. This exercise is termed 'variance analysis' and is not unlike budgetary control procedures.

(c) Absorption costing

This method of costing is designed to ensure that all costs are allocated to and absorbed by the final product. Direct charges such as labour and materials present no problems, but it is also necessary to apportion all indirect costs such as factory rent, machine maintenances, administration costs and so on so that all are absorbed. This must be done on an equitable basis, often in relation to machine time, floor area or other measure as explained in **22.4(a)** above.

(d) Marginal costing

This method recognises that there is a fixed cost for a manufactured unit which must be met before variable costs and profits can be satisfied. It follows, therefore, that the cost to manufacture one extra item after the fixed costs have been met is the amount of variable cost entailed in its production. This additional variable cost is the marginal cost. Marginal costing is a complete system of cost accounting which is commonly used; it includes the concept known as 'contribution', which is simply the amount by which sales revenue exceeds variable costs and thus contributes to fixed costs and profits.

22.8   The finance function in the public sector

The problems of financial management in the public sector are not dissimilar to those arising in the private sector in regard to the control of expenditure, though social considerations will figure highly in this area. However, there is less flexibility in the ability to raise funds for capital expenditure or for increasing revenue.

- The publicly owned industries, those undertakings that trade and thus come within the category of profit-making, are usually required to finance capital expenditure through raising selling prices to the consumer. Where insufficient funds can be raised in this way, particularly where the undertaking is actually suffering losses, government subsidies are usually called for, as with British Rail.
- In the public service sector income is relatively fixed, for instance the income from local taxes and government grants for local authorities, and other avenues for raising funds are severely limited. Projects such as leisure centres, municipal theatres and so on seem rarely to be profitable, and in truth are not usually embarked upon with this in mind.

Consequently, particularly in the service sector, the finance function is more concerned with the management of expenditure and costs and minimising the number of defaulting debtors than in the raising of revenue as such. The management of the finance function in the public sector is, in fact, a specialised study.

Questions

1 Define the term 'working capital'. What are the major considerations that an organisation should bear in mind when calculating the amount of working capital needed to finance an additional product? **(IAM)**

2 Outline the implications for working capital management of periods of high inflation.   **(IAM)**

3 Discuss the merits and demerits of using the profit centre and the cost centre: **(a)** as ways of measuring managerial performance, and **(b)** as aids to planning and control at all levels. You should relate your answer to an organisational situation of which you have some knowledge.   **(CIMA)**

4 In a certain industrial company 'return on capital employed' (ROCE) is used. The company is organised into three distinct operating divisions treated as separate investment centres and assessed on the basis of ROCE. There has been criticism expressed by the divisional management teams about this measure of performance and, in particular, about what they feel is the rigidity in long-term plans of specifying this particular objective precisely and with the implication that each division should attempt to meet the same target.

   Express your views about the use of ROCE as the key financial objective in these circumstances and in this manner.   **(CIMA)**

5 Write a brief explanatory note in relation to any **three** of the following financial terms:

   Absorption costing   Contribution
   Marginal costing   Break-even analysis   **(CIM)**

6 Explain the purposes and application of any **six** of the commonly used financial ratios relating to the operation of a business.   **(CIM)**

7 'Ratio analysis is a much used tool for appraising financial performance.' Discuss why ratio analysis is so commonly used, supporting your answer with reference to actual ratios.   **(IAM)**

8 In what ways may extra financial resources be made available to an existing company without resorting to a share issue?

(23) **The personnel function**

The personnel function ranks high in importance among those activities that have developed from the staff side of organisation. Among small undertakings matters appertaining to personnel are usually handled by a senior line manager with the assistance of one or two clerical workers who deal with day-to-day detail such as keeping personnel records and the like. In the larger organisations, however, there is normally a separate personnel department, headed by a personnel manager, which is responsible for all aspects of the work necessary in dealing with problems concerning employees, their conditions of work and their welfare. In the majority of cases the personnel department acts in an advisory capacity only, but so complicated and specialist have the duties of the personnel function become that in many large undertakings the personnel manager, often a director and always a senior executive, is endowed with the authority to negotiate with unions and employees' representatives, and to enter into binding agreements on behalf of management. The personnel manager will be responsible to and report to the chief executive and will be required to give advice on and be intimately concerned with the development of and implementation of the organisation's personnel policy.

The scope of the personnel function is vast and varied and a complete exposition would require a long and extensive study. Within this chapter, therefore, only the important aspects of the function can be touched upon in order to acquaint those interested in general management studies with the work of the personnel function.

23.1 Recruitment

- Except under very special circumstances all recruitment of staff at all levels below that of senior executive is normally done through the personnel department. The reasons for this are that this department will have considerable experience of the labour market and sources of supply of labour, of comparative rates of pay and conditions of employment offered by competitors, and of the organisation's personnel policy. In almost all cases all the procedures up to preparing short lists of possible employees will be carried out in the personnel department but the final list of interviewees and the ultimate selection of the final candidate will be a joint decision between the personnel officer and the line manager requiring the recruit. At operating level, for shop-floor workers and similar staff, often only the initiation of the recruiting procedure will be the responsibility of the personnel section, interviewing and selection being dealt with by the line manager or supervisor.

- The exceptions to the rule that the personnel department should actively recruit staff include the recruitment of senior officials such as heads of departments or divisions, and staff who will evolve a close personal relationship with a senior manager or executive, such as a personal assistant or private secretary. The first is normally a matter for the board of directors or other governing body. Selection of the latter involves the need for careful matching of personalities and so such recruitment is considered best left to the executive concerned. Nevertheless, the initial stages of recruitment are still normally the responsibility of the personnel department.
- The sources of recruitment to which the personnel department will address itself include:

(a) Present staff, particularly where the vacancy is at supervisory or middle-management level and there is a policy of internal promotion.
(b) Local schools, where beginners are needed.
(c) Universities and colleges of higher and further education, where potential management material and special aptitudes are required.
(d) Local employment agencies, both government (now known as 'job centres') and private. Many private employment bureaux are specialist agencies dealing with one or two types of profession or skill only, such as those for accountants, heavy vehicle drivers and so on.
(e) The professional bodies, many of whom maintain registers of members and student members for this purpose.
(f) Advertisements in the press both at national and at local level. Such advertisements will include particulars of the vacancy generally as set out in the job specification shown in **23.2** below.
(g) Advertisements in specialist journals, particularly trade journals and the journals of the professional bodies.

- Some organisations have a policy of internal staff promotion to the exclusion of external recruitment for positions above certain supervisory or management levels. The main objective of this is to encourage staff loyalty through a clearly defined career structure and to maintain the organisation's overall and operational philosophies. In such cases new staff will be recruited only at the lower end of the scale, and great care will be taken in the selection of newcomers. The main weaknesses of such a policy are that it may deprive the undertaking of new ideas brought in from outside and of fresh thoughts on the organisation's effectiveness. Its great virtue is that it usually attracts recruits who want to make the organisation their career and who are likely to stay with it, rather than those who want a career in a specific function and may use the organisation only to gain experience before moving on elsewhere. Recruitment is an expensive business and can be disruptive at certain levels. Where training is given to newcomers their leaving can mean considerable wasted expense.

23.2 Selection

- The key to a happy and efficient staff lies in proper selection, which in turn relies on a full understanding of what a job requires, usually embodied in a job specification. This job specification sets out the personal qualities required for the vacancy in question and will include the following, sometimes known as the 'Five-Point Plan':

(a) **Physical requirements**
   These include such attributes as age, minimum height, eyesight, manual dexterity and so on.

(b) **Intelligence**
   This includes mental attributes such as thinking critically, an analytical attitude, discrimination and an inquiring mind.

(c) **Aptitudes**
   Everyone has natural leanings towards certain activities. Some jobs call for mechanical or manual aptitudes, while others require more academic aptitudes, perhaps towards mathematics or art.

(d) **Attainments**
   These can be divided into educational and training achievements, evidenced by technical or professional qualifications, and practical achievements obtained through experience.

(e) **Personality and temperament**
   These are easy to specify but difficult to judge in an applicant. Some jobs call for a bright and enthusing personality (some sales jobs, for example) while others demand a more placid approach. Honesty, resourcefulness, tenacity, enthusiasm and the qualities for potential leadership all come under this heading.

- The personnel profession has now devised what is known as the 'Seven-Point Plan' which is, in effect, an extension of the 'Five-Point Plan':

(a) **Physical attributes**
   Is the applicant agreeable in his bearing, in speech and in appearance? Does he appear to suffer from any defects in health or physique that might make him unsuitable for the position?

(b) **Attainments**
   Where was the applicant educated? Did he acquire any educational qualifications? If so, what were they and at what level? What relevant training and experience has he had?

(c) **General intelligence**
   What standard of general intelligence does the applicant display? To

what extent does his career to date give evidence of his general intelligence?

(d) Special aptitudes

What special talents does the applicant have? Has he, for instance, an aptitude for the use of words, for mathematics? Does he possess any special manual dexterity?

(e) Interests

What sort of non-professional interests does the applicant have? Are these activities practical, socially biased or intellectual?

(f) Disposition

Does the applicant give the impression of being self-reliant and self-disciplined? Does he appear to be dependable? Would he mix well with other people? Is he argumentative?

(g) Circumstances

What are the applicant's family and domestic circumstances? If appointed, would he find the journey to the company's premises easy and reliable? Would the vacancy for which he has applied be advantageous for his future career and personal development? Would his appointment to this particular position be of benefit to the company?

- It is usual to require applicants for posts to complete application forms, designed as far as possible to elicit information relative to the job specification. From a comparison of the completed forms received a list of possible candidates can be selected and this is usually done initially by the personnel officer. Following this, a short list of about six candidates is prepared in consultation with the manager of the department where the successful applicant will be employed. Final selection is then made by inviting all those on the short list to be interviewed, where they can be judged on a person-to-person basis.

- Interviewing, as shown in **15.13–15.16** above, is a skilled task and may be carried out by one interviewer, who will usually be the head of the department concerned, or by a panel (particularly for a supervisory or management post), one member of which will certainly be the personnel manager. The purpose of the interview is to gain personal knowledge of the candidates and so to assess which one is the most suitable for the appointment. Basic information has been gathered from the application forms, and this information is a starting-point from which the various aspects of each applicant's knowledge, skills, personality and so on can be further assessed. The interview also provides the opportunity to give the applicants detailed information about the vacancy in question and about the organisation generally.

- The amount of time and effort spent on the selection procedure will depend very largely upon the type of post involved. Where recruitment is for unskilled or semi-skilled workers it will often consist simply of a brief interview with the foreman or supervisor in whose team recruitment is necessary. Where a skilled worker is required a longer interview will be given and a senior foreman, supervisor or manager may be involved. Within the administration, selection will be more formal. Detailed application forms will have to be completed and searching interviews will be conducted with the candidates on the short list, and the more important the post the greater the care that will be taken in selection.

23.3 Induction

- It is important for a new employee to be acquainted with the organisa-tion, its policies, practices and general objectives as well as where the new entrant's job fits into the organisation and its importance to the department concerned and the undertaking as a whole. This aspect of induction is calculated to generate a personal interest in the organisa-tion, an enthusiasm for the job and a general sense of loyalty: in other words it seeks to promote morale.
- A second aspect of induction concerns the more personal and specific aspects of a newcomer's employment, such as names and status of the senior members of the organisation, who the recruit's immediate supervisors and managers are and what authority they enjoy. Such matters as working procedures, the terms of the contract of employ-ment, remuneration and promotion policy, welfare and recreational facilities will probably have been discussed at the interview and will almost certainly appear in the staff handbook. However, these matters should be reiterated in the induction programme.
- Where employees are recruited several at a time – for example, at school-leaving time – it is possible to arrange induction on a group basis. This facilitates the presentation of films on the organisation, its history and future, and also enables senior members of staff to give lectures or talks on more domestic matters such as safety regulations, personnel policy, security and so on. Where one recruit at a time is engaged a senior or semi-senior member of staff should be assigned to the newcomer to provide guidance and information about the undertaking. The more general aspects of the concern which are best presented by films and lectures or talks can then be dealt with at intervals when sufficient new staff have been engaged.

23.4 Training

(a) The need for training

The personnel function will be very much concerned with the setting up of training programmes, which will be formulated in collaboration with the various operating and administrative functions. In the larger organisations training will be the responsibility of a special training officer usually under the authority of the personnel manager.

- A properly trained work-force at all levels, from shop floor to management, is important to the organisation for its continued success and survival, so that it can meet the challenge of business and technological change. It is equally important to the individual worker from the point of view of job satisfaction and earning power. However, training programmes must be developed and instituted according to a properly-thought-out plan, on the following lines:
  1 Identify the areas of training need.
  2 Plan training programmes based on forecasts of present and future needs.
  3 Implement training programmes in the most appropriate manner.
  4 Review and evaluate the success of the training programmes and methods of training.
  5 Modify the training programmes in the light of the reports emanating from **4**.
- Some concerns make the acceptance of a post conditional upon agreement to enter a training programme (for instance, an accounts clerk may be offered a post on condition that he or she undertakes to study for a professional qualification), but it is generally accepted that the ambitions of different recruits vary and an excellent potential worker may have no ambition to become a manager or a supervisor. Training should therefore be voluntary unless a specific skill is vital to the proper performance of a job.

(b) Types of training

There are several methods of training, and the type selected will depend very much upon the employee's actual job and the degree of skill required. Types of training can be broadly categorised as follows:

1 Craft training

This entails entering into an apprenticeship which results in ultimate entry into a recognised skilled trade or craft. Certain skilled jobs are the exclusive preserve of workers who have qualified by apprenticeship and others wishing to carry out this work are either prevented from doing so by the established workers or have to work at lower rates of pay. Apprenticeships have to be provided by the employer, and both employer and employee are bound by the apprenticeship indentures.

2 Operative training

This is for less skilled workers and for those trades where no formal apprenticeship schemes exist. Instruction is given on the shop floor, often supplemented by the worker's attendance at a technical college. Where the latter occurs the worker is normally given a day off each week to attend college on what is termed a 'day-release course'. Many office jobs fall under this category including shorthand-typing, typewriting, word-processing and office practice, especially where recruitment is straight from school. Many employers, however, do expect some skill to be present in other recruits and attendance at college is encouraged for the improvement of these skills.

3 **Professional training**

This covers both technical and commercial training and normally involves ultimately qualifying by professional or national examination. Some of the areas involved are mechanical engineering, accountancy, statistics, computer science, production engineering and so on. The new universities and colleges of higher education provide most of the training and education for such areas, either on the basis of day-release or on a 'sandwich course' basis where the worker spends a period, say a term, in college followed by a period with the employer, again followed by another period in university or college. In the latter case many of the qualifications are, in Britain, degrees rather than qualifications from professional bodies, such degrees being awarded by the universities or colleges under the auspices of the Council for National Academic Awards (CNAA). Such degrees rank equally in status with those awarded by the older universities. Indeed, in Britain under recent legislation polytechnics have been elevated to university status, though their courses remain in the main, vocational rather than academic as is the tradition of the older universities.

4 **University degrees**

Many of the older universities now award degrees in disciplines attractive to industry and commerce, such as degrees in accountancy, business administration, the various branches of engineering, marketing and others. Normally, however, people taking such degrees obtain them before seeking employment.

- The importance of proper training is exemplified by the fact that British governments have seen fit to encourage employers to train their employees, both by various acts of parliament and by exhortation. Various statutes are enacted from time to time and reference should be made to the latest legislation when necessary.

23.5 Manpower planning

An intelligent and ultimately effective training programme depends upon effective manpower planning. Without such planning the real training needs for the future cannot be calculated. The development of manpower estimates, in turn, depends upon corporate plans and strategies.

- The first step in manpower planning must be an investigation into the existing work-force at all levels from shop floor to senior management, to ascertain where manpower is deployed, the efficiency in the way it is being used (for example, is there over-manning or under-manning) and the degree of skill attained and needed by the various employment areas.

- From this data a realistic assessment can be made of the numbers of people that may be needed over the ensuing years divided into categories of jobs and skills required. Account will be taken of probable natural wastage by retirement and by voluntary leaving, the latter estimate being based on rates and types of labour and staff turnover for preceding years. Consideration must also be given to corporate plans and how they will affect staffing requirements, and also to the likely effects on staffing that may be brought about by foreseeable changes in technology.

- While this review is going on it may also be advisable to examine the criteria laid down for various categories of jobs and perhaps to reassess them in the light of changing conditions. For instance, the qualifications as existing for a production foreman may not be adequate for future recruits to such a post in view of changing technology.

- Thus manpower planning will forecast detailed staffing needs in both the short term and the long term, and this will facilitate the introduction of effective recruitment and training procedures to ensure the employment of the right numbers of people of the right qualifications and experience in the right jobs.

- Those responsible for manpower planning must be alert not only to the needs and changing demands of the organisation itself, but also to the external factors that influence the supply of labour of all types. This may come about by changes in social behaviour, such as a reduction in certain classes of school-leavers because of the larger number entering university or college, or by legislation such as the various statutes on sex equality. Calculation must, therefore, be constantly modified to ensure the fulfilment of the organisation's manning requirement at all times.

23.6　Remuneration

The question of remuneration can be a thorny one. In many areas of work basic pay is subject to negotiation between the employer and one or more trade unions, and at present the main criterion is not the worth of the job to the employer but a mixture of the cost of living and what is being paid elsewhere. In situations, therefore, where the work-force has strong union backing pay is not so much open to free market forces as to the influence of the threat of union sanctions. Where trade union influence is weak, or where there is no union influence at all, such coercion is much less evident.

A patently fair and just pay scale is essential to ensure a satisfied work-force, and the ability to earn extra money beyond basic pay is an incentive to greater productivity. Consequently most organisations operate bonus schemes which add to a worker's earnings through greater output than the standard laid down for basic pay. Unfortunately such incentive schemes are frequently a source of mistrust and unrest through disputes about standards of performance and rates for the job.

Clerical and managerial workers are less susceptible to union influence but even in these areas there is growing union involvement, particularly among local-authority workers and civil servants.

23.7 Job evaluation

Because of the discrepancies in pay rates both within an organisation and between different organisations (a major cause of industrial wage disputes) the process of job evaluation has been evolved.

- The first step in this procedure is job analysis, the technique of obtaining detailed facts about each job and the tasks it involves. Two assessments can then be drawn from these facts, the job specification which has already been described in **23.2** above, and the job description which states what the job entails, such as the tasks to be performed, the level of skill required, the responsibility and authority to be assumed, the type of working conditions and any particular features such as special hazards or unsocial features.
- The second step, following job analysis, is to determine the relative values of all jobs one with another. From this analysis the jobs can be evaluated and listed in order of value to the organisation, and pay scales established accordingly. The typical methods of job evaluation are:

(a) **The ranking system**
   In this system, from the job analyses jobs are ranked according to the degree of difficulty and responsibility involved, all jobs of similar status being ranked equally throughout the undertaking, thus providing a basis for comparable pay scales. From the rankings job grades are established.

(b) **Job grading**
   This is similar to ranking, but grades are established prior to ranking by reference to specific criteria of difficulty and responsibility within jobs, shown by the job analysis. A standard grade is thus selected and jobs are all given gradings by reference to this.

(c) **Factor points rating**
   This is a method that looks at separate factors in a job and evaluates each by giving points, rather than looking at the job as a whole as is done in methods (a) and (b). Each factor, such as skill, responsibility, job conditions and mental and physical demands, is allocated a number of points according to an assessment of its difficulty or value and all the points are then added. According to the total number of points awarded each job is graded. This is considered to be a more equitable method than those in (a) and (b).

However the grading is carried out, it is essential to recognise that it is the job itself that is evaluated and not the person filling the job.

23.8   Merit rating

In whatever way jobs are graded it is inevitable that some workers will perform better than others and deserve more pay. In order to reward the more efficient workers many organisations use a system of merit-rating.

- Thus each job grade will have attached to it a band of ratings for merit; that is, an evaluation of the way the job is performed from the point of view of quality, quantity and reliability. A regular appraisal, usually annually, of job performance by each worker will be carried out objectively, preferably by the worker's immediate superior or by means of appraisal reports filled in by the supervisor or manager, and these will be held by the personnel office. The various aspects of performance will be assessed and a merit-rating applied. According to this rating within the job grade, salary enhancement and promotion prospects will be established.
- Merit rating is mostly used for office workers, and the Institute of Administrative Management has devised a job grading and merit-rating scheme for this purpose which has found wide acceptance. However, merit-rating can be applied to any type of work that lends itself to individual appraisal. It will be obvious that merit-rating, unlike job grading, is concerned with people and the way they perform.
- Performance appraisal is also used to assess other aspects of a worker's performance. It assists in ascertaining a worker's potentiality for promotion, for transfer to other more demanding work and for suitability for further training. It is also used in the review of salaries and in considering the transfer from one salary scale to another. In such cases appraisal interviews are usually conducted by the head of the worker's department, often with the worker's immediate supervisor in attendance.

23.9   Health and safety

The responsibility for the health, safety and welfare of all workers falls under the auspices of the personnel function although it is usual in large concerns to appoint an officer specifically to look after health and safety. Industrial accidents account for considerable loss of labour hours in addition to personal suffering and it is therefore economically sensible as well as humane to ensure that working conditions are as safe and as healthy as it is possible to make them. There is much legislation laid down in Britain in this area, including the Factories Act 1961, the Offices, Shops and Railway Premises Act 1963 and the Health and Safety at Work Act 1974, and new statutory regulations are being added all the time.

All but the smallest organisations also usually provide their workers with eating and refreshment facilities (often subsidised) and recreational facilities. Medical attention of one sort or another, such as a resident nurse, is also normally provided. Where such a provision would be too expensive for a small concern a group of such enterprises will frequently contract together to provide a communal service, especially where they are all located fairly close together on a trading estate or within a neighbourhood.

23.10 Staff promotion

Without doubt the possibility of promotion is one of the most effective ways to encourage positive motivation and incentive in staff. There are, of course, workers who are reluctant to accept the added responsibilities that promotion brings but many do look forward to eventual promotion with the accompanying increased earnings and higher status. It is, therefore, important that an organisation has a fair and sensible promotion policy and that it is known to all relevant staff. Besides encouraging good morale it also assists the enterprise in planning the best use of its human resources. In addition, valuable members of staff who have benefited from training programmes provided by the organisation and who have built up valuable experience are less likely to be tempted to take their expertise to a rival organisation.

- Strictly speaking the term 'promotion' should be used for promotion within the organisation, but under this heading reference must be made to recruitment from outside usually for the more senior posts.
- A policy of internal promotion is, generally speaking, usually accepted as the most sensible one. It encourages a sense of security in existing workers, produces continuity of staffing, and avoids breaks in the personal relationships within the enterprise which are so helpful in ensuring that procedures run smoothly. This last point is particularly important where there are relationships with external contacts such as customers and suppliers.
- Recruitment for the more senior posts from outside the organisation, while bringing in new blood and possibly new ideas, may cause resentment in existing staff, may damage morale and may lead to the most able workers who are looking for promotion to seek employment elsewhere. Thus valuable staff may be lost.

  Two points must be made about internal promotion:

  1 **Promotion is based on past performance.** While it may be expected that like performance will continue after the promotion this may not occur. The person's attitude may change with increased authority and he may not have the temperament or personality to cope with it: or the person concerned may have been promoted beyond his level of competence. This latter occurrence is known as the 'Peter Principle' and was defined by Laurence J. Peter in his book *The Peter Principle* (Souvenir Press, 1969).

  2 **Problems of authority.** Sometimes it is difficult for staff to accept the authority of someone who has been a colleague on equal terms for

some time and, equally, a promoted worker may find it difficult or embarrassing to exercise authority over these same people. It is possibly prudent to promote employees at lower levels of management into different departments or to work with different groups.

Finally, it is important that a promotion policy be seen by all to be fair and equitable so as to avoid resentment in its implementation.

23.11   Staff turnover

This comprises staff leaving voluntarily or being asked to do so because of some failing in their work or behaviour. A high staff turnover is costly in terms of efficiency and because of the expense of recruiting and training new staff. Nevertheless some staff turnover is healthy for an organisation because it prevents stagnation of ideas which fresh staff can introduce. However, the rate of turnover must not be excessive.

Among the reasons for staff severances can be:

1 Inadequate supervision.
2 Supervision seen by staff to be unreasonable.
3 Poor promotion prospects.
4 Poor working conditions or inequitable pay.
5 Inadequate training which leads to lack of confidence.
6 Poor selection on recruitment.
7 Unsafe working conditions.
8 Inequitable distribution of work.
9 Boredom through lack of variety in job content or insufficent volume of work.
10 Business fluctuations.

The formula commonly used to measure labour turnover (LTO) is:

$$\frac{\text{Replacements } \textit{less} \text{ unavoidable severances} \times 100}{\text{Average work-force}} = \text{LTO\%}$$

or

$$\frac{100(R - U)}{W}$$

If labour turnover appears to be excessive it is important for the reasons to be investigated, as it suggests low staff morale. This is usually done by conducting attitude surveys, particularly of staff leaving.

23.12   Staff discipline

To ensure that an organisation runs smoothly there must be staff discipline though nowadays when an autocratic management style is not acceptable this is a difficult task: no longer will workers tolerate fines or similar pecuniary penalties for what the organisation sees as departure from acceptable behaviour.

However, there must be rules of behaviour for staff which must be accepted by workers, particularly in the areas of punctuality and absence. It follows, therefore, that a code of discipline must be drawn up and agreed with the workers and written into their service contracts. New recruits must be made aware of the code and the requirement for them to comply.

The surest way to achieve and maintain good staff discipline is to ensure a high morale, which is, after all, one of the marks of good management.

23.13 Staff dismissal

Dismissal occurs where an employer terminates the services of an employee because of some breach or alleged lack of discipline.

There are five categories falling under this heading:

1 Termination by notice.
2 Summary or instant dismissal.
3 Constructive dismissal.
4 Unfair dismissal.
5 Statutory Bar.

- Where dismissal is made by **notice**, the length of notice must conform to the rules set out in the contract of employment. Where no express length of time is given what is usual in the trade or profession will prevail. In Britain most cases are governed by legislation which sets out a minimum period of time. In cases where the length of notice required is one month or more it is often preferable to make payment in lieu of notice so that the employee leaves at once. This avoids the embarrassment of the continued presence of the person concerned and it also gives the employee free time for job hunting.
- **Summary** dismissal, that is instant dismissal, occurs where the employee is discharged on the spot, without notice or pay in lieu, and is valid only in special circumstances, usually some form of misconduct or wilful breach of discipline.

  Among the activities justifying the summary dismissal of an employee are:
  1 Wilful misconduct at work.
  2 Proven dishonesty or criminal acts.
  3 Gross negligence in carrying out duties.
  4 Absolute incompetence in doing the job.
  5 Disreputable acts in private life which may reflect badly on the organisation's reputation or prevent the worker carrying out his normal duties. These activities include drunkenness, immoral behaviour and drug abuse. Whether such behaviour can be considered

to be detrimental to the organisation will depend upon the status and kind of position the offender occupies within the organisation.

6 Failing to carry out orders consistent with the employee's terms of employment, or acts of insubordination.

7 Threats of or actual violence to fellow workers.

8 Unauthorised disclosure of business secrets to third parties.

9 Persistent unauthorised absence from work or persistent lateness without good cause.

The acts described in **1**, **2** and **8** apart, an employer would normally give a warning rather than discharge the offender for a first offence.

It must be said that an employer must have sound and irrefutable evidence of misconduct before dismissing a worker, otherwise legal action for wrongful dismissal may result.

- **Constructive** dismissal occurs where an employer invites a worker to resign instead of being discharged, or where the employer makes the employee's continued employment untenable, for instance by requiring him to carry out tasks which he finds objectionable, or changing his work pattern to his significant disadvantage. Constructive dismissal may be construed as unfair dismissal.

- **Unfair** dismissal occurs where the employer discharges a worker in circumstances which contravene the law, which contravene the employee's terms of service or which result in discrimination. In Britain there are the Employment Acts of 1980, 1982, 1988 and 1990, the Equal Pay Act 1970, the Sex Discrimination Act 1975 and the Race Relations Act 1976, contravention of the provisions of any of which could lead to a claim for unfair dismissal and subsequent compensation or an order for re-employment.

- An employee must be able to carry on his duties without breaking the law. If he cannot he may be fairly or legally dismissed. This is termed **'statutory bar'** and an example would be that of a lorry driver who has lost his driving licence through some contravention of the motoring laws. He could not continue in his normal employment without breaking the law and so could be justifiably dismissed.

Legitimate dismissal must always be fair and, most important, be seen to be fair, otherwise it can have an adverse effect on the morale of the staff.

23.14 Redundancy

Redundancy occurs where a dismissed worker's services are no longer required because the need for the particular work he performed has ceased to exist, because of technological changes, reduction in the volume of business or complete cessation of trading by his employer. It also covers the circumstances where an employee, instead of being made redundant, is transferred to another sector of the organisation and displaces another employee who is dismissed in consequence. This second employee is considered to have been made redundant.

In Britain, by virtue of the provision of the Employment Protection (Consolidation) Act 1978 a worker made redundant is entitled to compensation, known as redundancy pay, the minimum scales of which are laid down in this Act.

23.15 Grievances

As with all human activity the operation of a business or other organisation is bound to produce grievances from time to time. These may be small and minor and easily settled on a personal level, or may be major resulting in strike action or threat of such action. Consequently, it is prudent for there to be some formal grievance procedure to settle these matters.

- Major disputes involving all or most of the work-force are normally dealt with at a senior level and may involve a trade union and, in Britain, the services of the Advisory, Conciliation and Arbitration Service, known as ACAS, a body set up by Government to advise and mediate in major management/staff industrial relations difficulties, especially when the problem appears to be intractable. Industrial relations at this level are discussed in **23.17** below.
- Grievances involving one or a small number of workers are best dealt with internally and a formal procedure to deal with these should be established as it enables employers to deal with complaints quickly and fairly. An equitable grievance procedure well-known and accepted by the work-force demonstrates the employer's commitment to fair play and helps to ensure that similar problems are all dealt with on the same basis and that decisions will be consistent in like cases. It is recognised that grievances ignored or badly handled can lead to discontent which may spread beyond the staff involved.
- The exact procedures to be adopted will vary according to the size of the concern. In a small firm access by the complainant may be direct to a senior member of the company, whereas in a larger organisation there may be more than one level of management to go through if satisfaction is not forthcoming at the first level. In all cases, however, it is usual for the grievance to be taken up initially with the worker's immediate superior. Where there is a recognised union presence in an organisation it is very usual for the first step to be to the worker's shop steward. At all times the employer must be seen to be trying to be fair.
- Regrettably some complaints lead to litigation and the absence of a formal grievances procedure, or the failure to adopt its provisions, may prejudice the employer's case, whereas the existence of such a procedure will demonstrate the employer's desire to be fair.

23.16 The employment life-cycle

This is the complete record of an employee from recruitment to cessation of employment. These records show the employment history of each worker and include details of training, pay and pay increases, promotions, absences and their causes, job grading and any merit ratings, performance appraisals, reprimands, attitudes and motivation. In this way a picture can be built up of the worker concerned. Hence, a record of his or her career progress and potential are provided so giving a guide to possible future training or educational programmes, which would benefit both the worker and his or her value to the organisation.

The final entry in an employment life cycle record, will of course, be the date of leaving. This entry should also include the reason for the severance, e.g. retirement, voluntary leaving, dismissal and why, and any other relevant factors. This complete record should be retained for some time against the possibility of requests being made by third parties, such as other employers, for information about the worker. A usual demand is for a reference, and in this regard it should be noted that an employee or ex-employee has no right to demand a reference though it is usual for such a request to be met. Where a reference is given it must be true and accurate in the opinion of the past employer, without any suggestion of prejudice or malice.

23.17 Industrial relations

Industrial relations is a very wide topic sometimes seen as separate from personnel management, but nevertheless within the broad compass of the personnel function.

- Essentially industrial relations is concerned with the relations between management and production workers and concentrates very largely upon the conditions of service, the working environment and wages.
- In the 1960s and 1970s the power of the trade unions grew considerably and the influence of organised labour, as it is called, was evident in all issues concerning worker–management relations; often it seemed to be greater than that of the employers. Various legislation was passed, some to strengthen and some to mitigate the strength of union power which, while it might be beneficial to workers generally, was seen to be damaging to the economy as a whole. The power held by a handful of skilled workers, for instance, to disrupt a whole manufacturing under-taking or local authority service, or to close down a whole industry, was a matter for great anxiety among employers and Government. In addition, because the trade union movement is historically directly linked in Britain with the Labour Party there has been inevitably concern about the amount of influence and interference in Government that might occur. In the 1980s, however, the power of the trade unions

in Britain was significantly curtailed by Government legislation, with the result that there is now less anxiety on the part of employers and Government over the strike threat.

- Industrial relations were historically the concern exclusively of the trade unions and the employers' organisations. As a general rule national level negotiations were carried out which set the pattern for pay and conditions throughout a particular industry. This formed the basis for separate negotiations between individual employers and union representatives, and the results of these negotiations were further modified by agreements at local plant levels. Two circumstances caused modifications to this general pattern. The first was greater direct intervention of Government into industrial negotiations through imposed pay policies and consequent legislation, and the second was the growth of the demand among trade unionists for comparable pay and conditions throughout the different plants of an organisation or throughout an industry. The Government itself is also now a large employer of direct labour which forces it to be a party to industrial relations negotiations.

- In order to reduce disruption through industrial disputes it was historically the practice to resort to joint consultation. Nationally this was, in very many industries, dealt with through joint industrial councils (JICs), supported by the Government, consisting of equal numbers of members from employers' associations and relevant trade unions. JICs dealt with a wide range of matters including conditions of work, welfare and training. In many cases there was an undertaking by the industry that matters of dispute had to be submitted to the joint industrial council before any strike action was taken. A further device to endeavour to solve industrial disputes, set up under the auspices of the British government, is the Advisory, Conciliation and Arbitration Service, known as ACAS. This attempts to mediate between the parties in dispute and is generally very successful.

- At local level disputes and grievances are often dealt with by joint consultative committees composed of representatives from management and workers. All manner of topics may be raised with such committees from safety to discipline, from welfare to training. Such committees do not have executive powers but are able to report and recommend. To ensure that they are trusted by the workers, which is a major requirement for their success, they should be composed of members from both sides who are knowledgeable and competent, whose integrity is unquestioned and whose judgement is dependable. It is also essential that the reports and recommendations made by these joint consultative committees are seen to be given due weight by management.

- It will be noted that no mention of pay has been made in the range of matters subject to joint consultation. This is because it was historically the custom in Britain for problems relating to wages to be dealt with through collective bargaining. This is a wide-ranging and difficult subject requiring a study of its own. The parties to collective bargaining are the trade unions on the employees' side and the employers' trade associations on the other, although there can be variations. Essentially, however, the basic pattern of procedure is similar to joint consultation.

23.18   Worker participation

The subject of worker participation in the organisation, particularly in the sphere of decision-making, was considered in Chapter 3; in **3.5** the question of actual worker directors was discussed as was joint consultation in **23.17** above. Both involve workers in the actual process of decision-making, though the latter in an advisory capacity only.

However, neither method involves workers financially, but a third proposition does, that of co-ownership. In its purest form it proposes that workers become actual shareholders in their companies, thus participating in the distribution of profits and having the power to vote at annual general meetings. The actual acquisition of shares by the workers poses a problem, especially as they can, if they work for a public company, purchase them through the stock market if they really desire to become co-owners.

- Two solutions have been successfully applied in practice. The first is to offer shares to workers at attractive prices and the second to award shares as bonus payments. The opportunity to share in the profits of their company is considered to encourage loyalty and a co-operative attitude in the workers and to provide a positive incentive for greater productivity.

- Although it is assumed that shares will have voting rights, some managements may view this with apprehension and in some cases shares issued to employees have no voting rights so that control remains firmly in the hands of the existing shareholders and management. In such cases it is considered that the fact of profit-sharing is sufficient participation and incentive. Perhaps such managements have learnt a lesson from the experience of an American company which lost control to its work-force through the issue of shares with voting rights as bonuses, where the numbers of shares subsequently held by workers exceeded those held by the original owners.

23.19   Trade unions

Membership of trade unions is no longer confined to workers in production, but extends to cover office workers, computer staff and even supervisors and managers. This is especially the case in local and central government and in the publicly owned industries. Such unionisation brings some benefits and some disadvantages to the organisation.

- **Advantages**
  - (a)   Time is saved in pay negotiations when dealing with a union as compared to dealing with individuals. This is particularly relevant

in respect of supervisors and managers where it helps to promote equitable schemes of remuneration and to avoid inequalities and possible consequent resentment.

  (b) Where there is mutual respect – that is, where morale is good – employees can more easily be given a picture of the organisation's problems and thus obtain a better understanding of them through meetings with shop stewards and local union officials. Improved industrial relations should thus result.

  (c) Workers feel the strength of association and thus are able to have, through union representatives, constructive discussions on procedures relating to working practices, disciplinary measures and the like. Where relations are good, worker dissidents are often contained by the majority of workers.

  (d) Co-operation with trade unions may help an organisation to meet more easily the obligations placed on employers by government regulations and statutes.

  (e) Changes in working practices and necessary redeployment of workers can be more easily effected if implemented with union co-operation. Where redundancies are inevitable union co-operation can be particularly helpful in obtaining fair compensation for those affected.

  (f) Joint consultation is made easier.

- **Disadvantages**
  - (a) Managerial decisions may be delayed because of the lengthy discussions necessary at plant and local union level for these decisions to be implemented. Effective joint consultation can help minimise this.
  - (b) A powerful union, particularly where there is a closed shop (where all workers are required to be union members), can perpetuate and intensify restrictive practices unnecessarily. An example would be the insistence on a qualified electrician to change the plug on a simple machine such as an electric typewriter. This puts up costs and causes delays which create further costs.
  - (c) Where more than one union operates on a site delays and disruptions may be caused by inter-union disputes.
  - (d) Unreasonable demands may be made on management if a union is powerful, to the ultimate detriment of the organisation and even the industry.

There is no doubt that trade unions can contribute positively in all areas where they operate, provided their power is used reasonably and with discretion.

— **Questions** —

1 The chief management accountant of a firm is due to retire and a replacement has to be found.
  You are required to
  (a) explain the methods which may be used to recruit a replacement;
  (b) explain the means you would use to select the applicant most suitable for the post.   **(CIMA)**

2 Discuss the policy issues which organisations should consider prior to recruiting personnel.   **(IAM)**

3 You are required to explain the purpose and to describe the process of induction in respect of
  (a) a new employee joining the company;
  (b) a current employee transferred to a well-integrated group within the organisation.   **(CIMA)**

4 What benefits might be expected to be obtained by a firm which makes a continuing investment in staff training? What forms might such training take?   **(IComA)**

5 Discuss the application of manpower planning as a means of providing for managerial succession.   **(ICSA)**

6 Describe the objectives of performance appraisal. How would you carry out the performance appraisal of a subordinate?   **(ICSA)**

7 Describe a system of job evaluation. What are its advantages and disadvantages?   **(ICSA)**

8 **(a)** Distinguish and, in each case, provide an example of:
       (i) summary dismissal
       (ii) unfair dismissal
       (iii) constructive dismissal.
  (b) Describe the procedure through which employees who consider they have been unjustly dismissed may seek to obtain redress.   **(IAM)**

9 **(a)** Define 'Redundancy' as you understand it.
  (b) What are the main reasons why the dismissal of an employee may be 'unfair'?   **(IAM)**

10 Outline and comment upon some of the grounds by which a contract of employment may reasonably or legitimately be terminated, or an employee dismissed.   **(ACCA)**

24 Management support services

Most large organisations include a management services department which is staffed by specialists in various fields to assist management in many aspects of its activities. Such specialists act in an advisory capacity only and have no executive powers. Usually they are grouped together in one unit whose head reports to the chief executive or to a senior executive, who in turn is responsible to the chief executive for the activities of the management services staff. In some organisations, on the other hand, the different specialisms remain separate with their own leaders but responsible as before.

It is important that managers at all levels be aware of what services are available and how they can assist them. It is quite unnecessary for managers to be practitioners in these skills. The following notes are, therefore designed to describe but not instruct in the various service facilities.

24.1 Organisation and methods and work study

(a) Organisation and methods (O and M)

Commonly termed simply 'O and M', this is a group of techniques that seek to simplify office work and so to cut costs in this area. It has been said to be the application of common sense to reduce waste and, indeed, most of its operations are concerned with just that, the application of common sense to solve clerical problems. It can deal with the installation of complete new systems and procedures or with what is often called 'work simplification', the making of a particular task or series of tasks simpler or easier.

● O and M assignments are carried out by investigating what is currently done and questioning why, and though the organisation of the clerical procedures under review is of concern, the methods employed bear the greatest burden of investigation. By careful study the clerical workload is made lighter by reducing paperwork, eliminating redundant activities such as unnecessary manual copying from one document to another, reducing the movement of people and documents by improving office layout and generally cutting down wasteful clerical activities. The widespread use of such office equipment as dictating machines and photocopiers owes a great deal to practitioners in O and M, who have realised the amount of wasted effort involved in writing shorthand and in manual copying.

- Much O and M now involves clerical work study – that is the practice of detailed analysis and timing of tasks and subsequently setting standards of performance. Initially those concerned with office work claimed that it did not lend itself to work study techniques because most procedures were not repetitive enough. However, a very large proportion of the work done by office personnel has, in fact, been found to be suitable for work study techniques.

(b)   Work study

Originating in the factory ninety years ago, work study seeks to investigate and examine all aspects of work so as to improve efficiency and reduce waste of effort, thereby improving productivity.

Work study has two parts, motion study and work measurement.

- Motion study examines in minute detail each aspect of a task with a view to avoiding unnecessary movement and reducing it where it cannot be eliminated. Economy of motion is the aim. This is sometimes achieved by reducing, for example, the extent to which an operator's arm must travel to move a control or manipulate material. In other cases the simultaneous use of both hands to accomplish part of a task instead of the use of one while the other is idle will effect an improvement in the economy of movement. How materials to be used are stacked and where is also a fruitful area for motion study, as is layout generally.
- The second part, work measurement, is self-explanatory. It is the practice of measuring how long the various elements making up a task take, and when these time measurements are added together they form a total time for the complete operation. The purpose is to establish how long a specified job should take a qualified worker to carry out at a given level of performance. There are two categories of work measurement: direct time study, which involves actually timing the job as it is performed, usually by means of a stop watch; and indirect timing. Techniques of indirect time study include synthetic timing, predetermined motion time study (PMTS) and analytical estimating, and they use elements of previous direct time studies and analytical estimates. These techniques are highly sophisticated and can be employed successfully only by experienced work study practitioners. Indirect methods can be used to provide reliable standards for jobs that are proposed but are not actually in operation.

(c)   Implementing O and M and work study

O and M and work study are both put into practice in a similar fashion, which can be set down in seven main steps:

1 Select the job to be investigated.
2 Investigate and record the existing methods.

3 Examine critically the methods in use from the observations and records made.
4 Define and develop improved methods.
5 Establish performance standards for the new methods.
6 Install the new methods.
7 Maintain the new methods, making modifications as found to be necessary.

24.2 Operational research (OR)

Operational research (operations research in the USA), is the use of mathematics and mathematical models to assist management in arriving at management decisions.

- It is important to remember that OR cannot subsitute for management, neither can it be a reason for management to abdicate the need for judgement in coming to decisions. What it can do is to present management with alternative solutions to problems and so allow judgement to take place on sound scientific and mathematical grounds rather than on the basis of experience and intuition. OR is useful only where all the elements of a problem can be quantified and expressed mathematically. It has no place in problem-solving involving sociological or psychological elements, and is only as accurate as the data it uses.
- The areas where OR has proved to be of most use are those concerning resource allocation (for example, machine-loading and transport-routeing), stock-control, production planning and scheduling, capital investment decisions and similar problems. It solves these problems through a number of mathematical techniques, among the most used being:

(a) **Linear programming** where comparisons can be made and evaluations formulated between different operations which have a straight line (linear) relationship between the variables within them. For example, lorry *A* may consume one gallon of fuel per mile transporting one ton and lorry *B* may consume two gallons of fuel carrying three tons over the same distance, fuel consumption being directly proportional in both cases to the load carried and the distance travelled. Where there exists such a relationship between methods then this is an area for linear programming.

(b) **Probability theory**, which is concerned with events where chance is, or appears to be, the determining factor in results. In fact in almost all cases the outcome is caused by a combination of a large number of circumstances which make a specific result probable but not absolutely predictable. Probability theory forms the basis of queueing theory, which is important in many areas of operations.

(c) **Queueing theory**, which is a technique applied to solving problems concerning the intervals and frequency of groupings of people or activities requiring attention. Examples are passengers calling at ticket offices, workers attending the stores for materials or tools, aircraft landing at airports and lorries wanting to load at loading bays. Queueing theory can offer solutions in regard to best intervals, costs, provision of facilities and other related problems.

(d) **Network analysis** (or the critical path network) is a technique of determining the critical elements in a sequence of operations so that the total programme can be completed in the least possible time. The method is to analyse the project into a network of activities (hence the term 'network analysis') which are plotted on a diagram. Those steps that are vital to the progress of the project, when connected together, form the critical path and cannot be delayed without detriment to the whole programme. Times for each step are indicated on the network and these, added together through the critical path, indicate the minimum time required for total completion. Other activities shown on the network diagram have less influence. Most networks are lengthy and complicated and are usually run on a computer.

Applications include long-term projects such as construction and civil engineering works, computer installations (from initial concept) and similar operations.

Critical path analysis (CPA) and programme evaluation and review technique (PERT) are the most widely used terms in network analysis. The main distinction between them is that CPA assumes reasonably accurate predictions of activity times whereas PERT accepts that such predictions are unlikely to be accurate and allows for this by taking into account three estimates: the shortest possible timings, normal timings and the worst timings likely to occur. Figure 24.1 shows a simple critical path network.

24.3 Management information systems

A management information system (MIS) can be defined as a formal system to provide all levels of management with all the relevant information they need with which to make appropriate decisions for the total control of an organisation.

- From this definition it will be observed that how the system should operate is not considered; only the fact that it should be formal is important. In other words the primary considerations for the installation of a management information system are: who needs the information, what form it should take and what it should contain, whom the information is to go to and what purposes it is to serve. It is irrelevant how the necessary data is to be processed, but in fact so voluminous is the information flow in a modern organisation that the use of a

—— Activity ——

A gang of six men have to complete a project on site 4. They have finishing-up jobs to do on various sites before this as shown below. What is the earliest time all the men can arrive on site 4?

Activity	days
A 1 man works in the yard for	1
B 3 men have to complete work on site 1	3
C They then go and work on site 3	4
D 2 have to complete work on site 2	2
E They then go and work on site 3	3
F Work on site 3 for the 5 men takes	4

The critical path shown by the network in Figure 24.1 is 11 days, the earliest time that all the men can arrive on site 4.

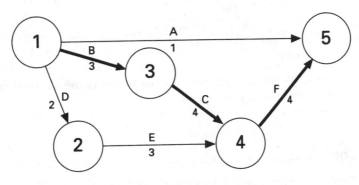

Key: Letters on lines = Activities
Numbers on lines = Times in days
Numbers in circles (nodes) = identification for use by computer only

Fig. 24.1   A simple critical path network

computer for processing is essential. The establishment of a data base in a computer system is of considerable advantage in connection with a management information system because it provides fast access to all the data and information within an organisation on all aspects of its operations.

- Management information is made available by means of various kinds of reports including statistical reports such as sales analyses, and control information such as budget variance reports. Ideally such information should be processed from data already in the system, but data must be acquired from external sources when necessary, for instance in cases involving market trends, general economic outlook and other external factors which may influence management decisions.

- To be properly effective a management information system should produce reports that are clear and accurate. Some consideration must be given, however, to the degree of accuracy because in many cases absolute accuracy may be unnecessary, too costly or its attainment may cause unacceptable delay. Reports should be produced promptly (a late report is often a useless report) and should be as up to date as possible. Other considerations to be taken into account are the frequency with which each report should be produced, its format and how much detail it should contain and its precise circulation list. Finally, the cost of operating the system is important and this must be commensurate with the benefits that accrue from it. Some of these benefits can be quantified directly and others evaluated only inasmuch as actions arising from the output give rise to benefits. Among the benefits to be obtained from an efficient management information system are:

(a) An increase in the efficiency of the organisation.
(b) Better management decisions.
(c) More effective utilisation of resources.
(d) Better and less costly administration.
(e) Increased profits.

- One or more of these benefits must accrue to justify the maintenance of any management information system.

24.4   Consultants

The problems that an organisation encounters from day to day are usually adequately dealt with by executives, managers and staff in the normal course of their duties. After all, this is why they are employed. However, there are occasions when a problem seems to be intractable, is in an area unfamiliar to the organisation, or where previously applied solutions are no longer effective. It is then that an outside consultant may be engaged.

- Most consultants specialise in a particular area, or in at most one or two, and their special value apart from their considerable experience over many assignments lies in their detachment from the problem. As an outside party a consultant is able to look at a problem objectively and is not influenced by existing practices, prejudices or personalities. In addition, an independent consultant owes no allegiance to any particular section or group in the organisation.
- A consultant must be appointed and supported throughout the assignment by the governing body and the chief executive. Only in this way will the consultant have the necessary authority to go anywhere in the organisation and question any member of it. However, the consultant must not identify himself with top management or any member of the management team. To do this is to prejudice his opportunities to

persuade management and staff to talk freely. The utmost confidence must be built up between the parties so that there is a completely free interchange of total information. It is sometimes said that consultants can speak more freely than internal managers and staff, and that they suffer no inhibitions in this respect. This is certainly true, but their true value lies in their expert knowledge and experience. It is for these qualities as well as for their disinterested attitudes that they should be engaged.

- Consultants are most frequently called in for the following reasons:

(a) To advise on ventures such as the installation of new plant, penetrating new markets or introducing new manufacturing methods.

(b) To restructure the organisation or management pattern, especially in times of rapid growth.

(c) To raise new capital.

(d) To advise on relocation.

(e) To sort out difficulties being experienced in functional areas where internal solutions have not been effective: these include stores control, marketing, profitability, O and M and so on.

(f) To endeavour to save a totally ailing concern. This is usually an act of desperation by the management and often the call comes too late for effective remedies.

- Competent consultants provide a valuable service but are expensive. Their recommendations are based on very careful investigation and analysis of the problem areas and should be implemented to the full. They should report direct to the chief executive, with whose authority they speak. Finally, their activities must not be restricted in any way if they are to be able to diagnose and recommend fully on the problems submitted to them.

Questions

1 How important is it that members of a Management Services Division should work closely with people from functional departments? How may such collaboration be achieved?   **(ICSA)**

2 Explain what is meant by the term 'operational research' and describe a typical problem which might be solved, using this approach.   **(CIM)**

3 (i) What do you understand by the term 'Management Information System'?

(ii) Which characteristics should be embodied in effective Management Information Systems?   **(AIM)**

4 Describe what you understand by the phrase 'management information system'. In particular you should explain how the effective provision of information can assist management decision-making.   **(ICSA)**

5 (a) Examine the purpose of:
   (i) a Gantt Chart
   and
   (ii) a Network Analysis Chart (Critical Path/Programme Evaluation and Review technique as used in operational planning).
   (b) Describe the circumstances that would be most appropriate to the use of each type of chart.   **(IAM)**

6 'The great advantage of using consultants is that they are able to say things which the internal management could not say.' How far does this justify the use of consultants in business?   **(ACCA)**

The manager and change

We live in an age of fast recurring change. This places a burden on the manager to be aware of the need to meet the challenges presented by changing circumstances and to overcome the problems which arise.

Change can be divided into two categories, the first being internal changes brought about by organisational requirements including advances in technology, and the second by external changes brought about by economic and political factors. In the first the manager is playing very much on his own home ground and he is very largely in control of the process: in the second most factors are outside the manager's control and need an objective and flexible approach.

25.1 Internal change

- Internal changes embrace organisational changes such as changing from a centralised to a decentralised system in one or more functions, to changes brought about by the rise in new technology such as the computerisation of a production process. The problems for the manager to deal with are fundamentally the same, and can be set out in nine stages:
  1 Determine the objectives of the change.
  2 Define the actions required and set targets to be achieved.
  3 Set up plans to achieve these objectives.
  4 Examine and finalise the plan.
  5 Provide the necessary resources.
  6 Devise and set up necessary controls and budgets.
  7 Implement the plan.
  8 Review implementation and carry out an appraisal.
  9 Put in place necessary alterations following the review.
- It will be seen that careful and effective planning is necessary to bring about change smoothly and efficiently. However, something more than mere planning is required to deal with the human side of change, and this is particularly so where significant changes in work practices, work groupings, and relocation of staff are concerned.
- Resistance to change is inherent in all human beings, particularly where alterations to well or long established habits or routines are concerned, and it could be argued that the most difficult aspect of introducing change is to carry staff along with the change.
- Adverse general attitudes to change, apart from the instinctive resistance just mentioned, arise because of a resultant feeling of insecurity,

unfortunate previous experiences of changes, inherent mental inertia against making changes in work practices, the way the change is made known, the manner of implementation and, possibly, a non-co-operative attitude fostered by the working group. More specific adverse attitudes can be attributed on a personal basis to the fear of monetary loss, personal inconvenience, decreased job satisfaction and, possibly, reduction in social estimation.

- Counter measures to minimise resistance to change, and perhaps engender positive acceptance or even enthusiasm include:
  1 Explaining exactly what is to be accomplished and why.
  2 Pointing out the benefits of the change to the organisation and the adverse results if changes are not made.
  3 Stressing how the change will specifically be of benefit, monetarily and socially in the workplace, to the worker himself.
  4 Seeking the reactions of staff to the proposals before they are implemented and discussing modifications to take account of serious objections.
  5 Showing understanding of the concerns of staff and seeking to allay their fears.
- No proposals for change will be wholly accepted by all members of staff: the objective must be to reduce to the very minimum the number of work-people who are either suspicious or actually hostile.
- Among the positive proposals to accompany change must be the provision of adequate training for staff whose roles are changed and who are suitable for retraining, the guarantee of removal expenses for staff agreeing to relocate to another workplace where this is required, and the redeployment of staff whose jobs are no longer required but who are not suitable for retraining. Where redeployment is not possible generous financial provision should be made available, over and above the minimum requirements of statute in regard to redundancy pay. Where there are large numbers of redundant workers it is not unusual for employers to set up facilities to find other employment in suitable cases.

25.2　Internal change and outside contacts

In very many cases internal change will have an effect on customers and/or suppliers. For example a reorganisation of the sales ledger system may reduce the credit period for customers, or a change in production methods may alter a long established order and delivery routine with a supplier. The first, it may be said, would be more difficult to establish than the second.

In these cases it is prudent to establish contact with the outside parties well in advance of the implementation of the change, explaining the reasons for the change and seeking their co-operation. It must be said that even tightening up credit control, where this has been slack, will meet with customer resistance and the utmost diplomacy is required to persuade customers to change their paying habits even to bring them in line with existing terms.

25.3 External change

External change is that imposed on an organisation because of external influences such as market changes, changes in consumer habits, environmental and political eventualities, supply difficulties or statute, and, for companies in Europe, the EC.

- Few changes outside of the control of the organisation can be predicted with any certainty and some not at all. However the adage 'if little can be planned then what can be must be' should guide the manager in this area.
- Changes in the market directly affecting the enterprise, such as trends in prices, can be foreseen to some extent by market research and observation. Similarly, changes in consumer habits can also be forecast through market research and by internal examination of order book and customer inquiry records. The slowing down of demand for certain items should also prompt enquiries into why, so that any changes can be taken account of in all aspects of the supply position.
- Equally, possible problems in the supply position of materials or goods may be indicated by increasing difficulties in procurement, the offering by suppliers of substitutes and increasing prices. Indications of impending difficulties can also often be brought to the manager's notice by reports in trade papers or the news media of possible shortages. An example here is the increasing difficulties of producing peat supplies in Britain, where substitutes such as pulverised bark are increasingly offered and where there have been many news items of the problems in the peat cutting industry.
- Changes likely to be brought about by circumstances not directly in the control of an organisation are those involving concerns for the environment, political decisions often by directive, and changes in the law. It is not usually possible to predict what these changes will be and it is not, therefore, possible to devise specific plans to accommodate these changes. Some, such as environmental issues, are first brought to light by one pressure group or another and the general public response should be monitored and if vehement enough should be acted upon. In such cases tentative plans can be devised early in the protests so that action for change in working practices, effluent disposal, or whatever, can be worked out and put in place when necessary.
- In regard to political or statutory changes, there is usually some forewarning of their imposition, especially those demanded by statute, since there is some time lag between the proposal to legislate and the passing of the law. In these cases it is important to obtain as much information of the requirements as early as possible so that plans can be

put in place in good time to examine thoroughly the organisation's response to the required changes and to be in a position to implement them immediately they become law. In most cases the opinions of legal and other specialist experts will be needed, if only for the interpretation of the law.

- In Britain and Europe constant changes are, and will be in the future, required by the EC authorities. It would be advantageous if it were possible to predict what changes will be required but experience shows that this is very often impossible. Further, some of the decisions coming out of Europe are subject to resistance by those affected. In these cases contingency plans should be worked out while the arguments go on so that the organisation is ready for the change if it proves necessary.
- Major decisions, like the proposal for a common currency, take years to be implemented so there is time for all aspects of the possible change to be studied and provided for.

25.4   Relocation

A major change affecting the organisation, its staff and outside contacts is the need to relocate, that is to remove one or more parts of the enterprise to new premises, for whatever reason. This can be a managerial headache and requires careful planning to ensure the continuity of the operations of the organisation.

- The decision to relocate having been made, the first task is to appoint a senior member of staff to be responsible for and oversee the operation. This person could be the Facilities Manager where such a post exists, probably assisted by a senior member of the operations staff. The physical aspects of the move, such as providing utilities services at the new site, physically moving equipment and machinery and ensuring that the new premises are ready for the move, as well as ensuring the continuity of the business operations, must be assured. The next important consideration is staffing. Existing staff should have been consulted before the final decision to move and where members of staff do not find the move acceptable for any reason then replacement staff must be recruited: where supervisory and other senior staff do not wish to move this may provide the opportunity for promotion for some staff. In the event of redundancies consideration for those work-people must be given, as set out in **25.1** above.
- Well in advance of the move a carefully worked out plan must be produced for the actual removal: the minimum dislocation of work must be caused. Continuity of communication with outside contacts such as suppliers and customers must be maintained and information as to date of move, new address, telephone and fax numbers must be given well in advance.
- Some departments can be moved piecemeal, particularly where there is

little external contact: the accounts department is a case in point. Where external communication is heavy, for example the sales department, it is advantageous to move the whole department at once. Redirection of mail should be arranged with the Post Office and automatic redirection of telephone calls from the old number must also be arranged.

- If the relocation project is likely to be a particularly difficult one it might be advantageous to employ the services of an outside consultant, who will be able to look at the proposal objectively, and who will be able to bring to bear on the project a vast amount of experience in this area. In the event of engaging an outside consultant it will still be necessary to appoint a senior officer of the organisation to liaise with the consultant so that there is a specfic point of contact.

25.5   Facilities management

This is a term that has recently entered the language of management and is the subject of a special examination paper by the Institute of Administrative Management. The role of Facilities Manager encompasses a very wide field and is essentially practical, covering knowledge, experience and responsibility for:

- Buildings, their construction, maintenance and the law appertaining to them.
- Equipment, its provision and maintenance.
- Building and equipment layout.
- Law and practice of landlord and tenant.
- Environmental and engineering services, including plumbing, heating, lighting and air conditioning, cost control of these services and energy management.
- Project management and control.

25.6   Creative thinking

The management of change gives rise to the need for creative thinking though few managers would see it this way. A great deal of resistance to change is the result of not thinking imaginatively and creatively.

- We tend to see creative thinking as being the province of the great inventors, artists, writers or musicians. However, each one of us has the ability to think creatively, and as this is so important to the performance of a manager the process should be examined. It should be remembered that every time we use an article for a purpose other than that for which it was designed we have thought creatively: a brick used as a doorstop is an example.
- The barrier to creative thinking in any but simple terms is the fact that

we normally look at things in the conventional way: to think creatively we have to see not the conventional item, but its basic structure.

- A simple example will illustrate this. How many uses can be found for the ordinary domestic spring clothes peg? As a clothes peg it can, of course, be used for its intended purpose, and also as a paper clip, a book mark and any other use requiring a clip of that size. However, the peg is, in fact, two wedges held together by a spring. So the peg can also be put to use dismantled wedging up a wobbly table, stopping a window rattling, opening a split ring keyring, as a distance marker for sowing seeds, a stirrer for stirring small pots of paint, mixing up certain adhesives, and so on. Most of these uses are, of course, 'inspirational'.

- Creative thinking can be divided into four stages: analysis, mulling over, inspiration and solution. In a simple problem as that of the clothes pegs these 4 stages are probably instantaneous. More complex problems need time.

  1 In analysing a complex problem we investigate data about it, question the accepted assumptions, and examine its constituent parts.

  2 We can then mull over this information, turning it over in our mind for a solution. At this point it is useful to remember that the unconscious mind will continue to work on a problem even when one has left the conscious state. To 'sleep on it' is, in fact, sound advice. We could call this the period of gestation.

  3 The inspiration comes when we suddenly see a solution, though in truth it is not sudden and not inspiration but a realisation of a possible idea brought about by 'mulling the problem over'.

  4 The final stage, the solution, comes from examining the idea born out of the period of gestation and working out the practical issues involved (see Figure 25.1).

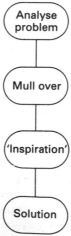

Fig. 25.1   Stages in creative thinking

- However, the solution is often only the beginning of the creative process as it tells us 'what' should or could be done, but not 'how'. The practical issues now to be faced may be able to be worked out by conventional means but, on the other hand, may need to go through the whole four stages again. A very simple example will illustrate this. A hotel is worried about the cost of the new plumbing required for its *en suite* bathrooms. Thinking creatively produces the solution that pipework could be cut down by using the same supply pipes for the bath and the basin. This is the initial solution. Further thinking round this solution is needed to make this idea practical. Going through the four creative thinking processes again produces the practical solution of using a flexible shower connection so that the basin can be provided with water by this means as well as the shower bath, thus saving the need to have separate supply pipes and taps to the basin.

- Another example of this creative thinking process is that of a major cornflakes company trying to expand its market. The public generally has always thought of cornflakes and associated cereals as a breakfast food. This places their consumption firmly at the beginning of the day. However, thought of just as a food, which they fundamentally are, they can be eaten at any time of the day. Currently it is being suggested that cornflakes make a satisfactory supper dish. This is a creative approach to the eating of cornflakes.
- Of course, it is very rarely the case that the four stages in the creative thinking process are consciously gone through, or if they are they are not recognised as creative thinking.

25.7 Change in the work environment

The last few years have brought significant changes in the overall work environment owing not only to technology advances but also through economic changes, political factors and the decline of manufacturing industry in Britain and the older established Western industrial countries. Particularly the rise in the manufacture of many of the goods traditionally made in Europe and the USA by developing countries such as Taiwan, South Korea and now China has changed the outlook for industry in the West. Cheap labour, an eagerness to develop their economies and a willingness by their work-people, either voluntarily or by compulsion, to work long hours has made these Far Eastern countries a significant threat to Western manufacturers because of their much lower costs. Further, the quality of their goods is improving all the time. The older industrial countries are therefore having to re-think their strategies, relying more and more on robots instead of human workers, and in consequence reducing the prospects of employment for very many of the labour force. A greater reliance is also being made on the service industries such as banking and insurance.

25.8   Change in the social environment

Socially there has been a change in values and expectations.

- No longer does a worker think in terms of a life-time career in the organisation and most either voluntarily or through force of circumstances make one or more changes during their working lives. Often this means a change of career entirely and probably learning new skills. Loyalty to one employer is now becoming rare. The increase in the number of women workers, particularly in part-time employment, has resulted in changes in work patterns and often the provision of special amenities such as flexible working hours to accommodate the particular needs of women with families.
- There has also been a change brought about by the fall in the birth rate in Western countries. This has resulted in a reduction in the number of young people coming forward for employment which, in times of economic growth will mean fewer work-people and pressure on salary and wage rates.
- Finally, the increased employment of women and members of ethnic minorities has led to legislation penalising any discrimination on the grounds of sex, race or religion, which means that the manager has to exercise special care in all forms of personal relations, particularly in the fields of recruitment, promotion, pay and dismissal.
- A change that the manager must face is an increasing emphasis on quality both in manufacture and in services. This has given rise to two approaches to the problem of the establishment and maintenance of high quality, quality circles and quality assurance.

(a)   **Quality circles**

This is a concept that had its origins in Japanese quality control practices and its introduction into British organisations has the support of the Department of Trade and Industry.

1 In its brochure entitled *Quality Circles* the Department defines a quality circle as 'a team of four to twelve people usually coming from the same work area who voluntarily meet on a regular basis to identify, investigate, analyse and solve their work-related problems. The team presents its solutions to management and is then involved in implementing and monitoring the effectiveness of the solutions'. Besides matters affecting quality these groups also have as their concern matters of safety and productivity.

2 The usual quality circle comprises a number of workers from the shop floor led by a foreman or supervisor, who is elected by the group to be leader. In some cases a quality control officer or inspector will be a member of a circle to introduce some formal quality control expertise.

3 The purpose of quality circles is to seek to improve quality and reliability by identifying problems and working out solutions and

then to implement these solutions. As with value analysis, discussed at **21.7** above, quality circles are a tool to improve quality and productivity while cutting out waste. The significant difference between the traditional methods of quality control and quality circles is that in the latter there is direct involvement and participation by shop-floor workers in this important aspect of production management, and with management's agreement the workers themselves implement the improvements they have worked out.

4 The advantages of quality circles are said to be that employees at shop-floor level become more aware of production problems, which motivates them towards personal involvement, and this leads to higher morale and to increased quality and productivity.

(b) Quality assurance

In Britain, where sometimes quality has taken second place to productivity, companies who wish to improve their management of quality issues can undertake to be assessed by an independent external organisation to British Standard 5750, the national standard for quality management systems.

The standard (which is known internationally as ISO 9000 and at a European level as EN 29000) provides a model management system that companies can use to help them install their own specific system. Once the management team are happy that their system meets all the requirements of the standard, they can then apply to be assessed by an outside body. When this certification body has inspected them and found that the system complies with the standard, the company can be issued with a certificate and can be entered on a special register held by the Department of Trade and Industry.

There are three major certification bodies, the Quality Assurance of the British Standards Institution (BSI), Lloyds Register and SGS Yarsley. There are also some certification schemes run specifically for certain industries, such as water or ceramics, so it is worth checking with the Department of Trade and Industry first, especially as they have a system of grants that can help companies cover the costs of registration. Consultancies can be used during the installation of the management system, but this role cannot be fulfilled by the certification bodies.

Quality assurance is a determined effort on the part of the British Government to improve and maintain quality in British manufacturing and service industries. It is no small matter achieving registration as Figure 25.2, reproduced here by courtesy of BSI, shows.

Another change is the interest the British Government now displays in all aspects of management in British industry. With a view to improving the performance of British industry the Department of Trade and Industry has launched its Enterprise Initiative. Under this scheme the Department provides information and assistance on all aspects of general and functional

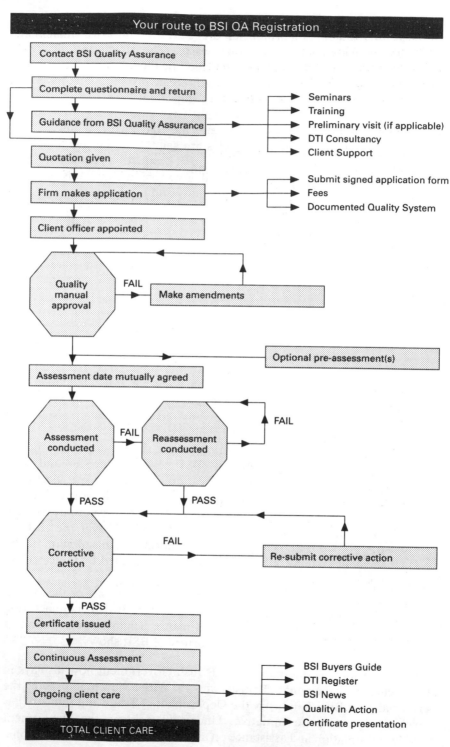

Fig. 25.2   Quality assurance   *Source*: BSI Quality Assurance.

management, and to this end sponsors seminars, provides consultancy services and produces publications on every aspect of running a business.

Change is taking place at an ever-increasing rate in the technical field and in management thinking and practices. For the modern manager this means keeping a flexible outlook, keeping abreast of developments and above all keeping an open mind to fresh ideas.

Questions

1 Consider whether major organisational changes need careful planning. How would you set about preparing to plan and implement a major change in an organisation? **(ICSA)**

2 Discuss the impact of changing technology on an organisation and its employees. **(ICSA)**

3 'The successful exploitation of new technology requires attention to the human resource.' Discuss. **(ICSA)**

4 Assume that you are the Facility Manager of a large national company occupying headquarters in a city centre. The company is reviewing its policy towards headquarters and related functions as part of a restructuring. The company is seeking reductions in corporate overheads which they feel are adversely affecting the company's competitiveness. [Among other things] the company decide to consider options to relocate. Identify the main options for the relocation. Suggest alternative ways of managing the project and propose the methods you will use to evaluate them. **(IAM)**

5 Why has 'facilities management' become more important in recent years? **(IAM)**

6 How many uses can you find for an ordinary plain paper clip? Name not less than **fourteen**.

7 By the use of appropriate examples, illustrate how social change is affecting management. **(CIMA)**

8 Explain what is meant by the following terms. In each case give **two** brief examples:
   (i) Changing work environments.
   (ii) Changing expectations and values in society. **(IAM)**

9 You are required to describe and assess the usefulness of
   (a) quality assurance;
   (b) quality circles. **(CIMA)**

Selected reading list

Mastering Basic Management is designed to be an introduction to the wide-ranging subject of management. For those who wish to further their studies the following short reading list will be of assistance. It is by no means exhaustive and most works will give guidance on further appropriate reading. In all cases the latest editions should be consulted, consequently no dates are given. Books already mentioned elsewhere are also omitted from the list.

General management

Adair, J. *The Action-Centred Leader* (London: Financial Society)

Adair, John, *Training for Leadership* (Farnborough: Gower Press)

Ansoff, H. I., *Corporate Strategy* (London: Penguin Books)

Brech, E. F. L., *Principles and Practice of Management* (Harlow: Longman)

Drucker, P., *The Practice of Management* (Harlow: Longman)

Dutfield, M. and Eling, C. *The Communicating Manager* (Durant: Element Bush)

Eyre, E. C., *Office Administration*, Professional Masters Series (Basingstoke: Macmillan)

Handy, G. C., *Understanding Organizations* (Harmondsworth: Penguin)

Humble, John W., *Management by Objectives* (Farnborough: Gower Press)

Kempner, T. (ed.), *A Handbook of Management* (London: Penguin Books)

Oldcorn, Roger, *Management*, Professional Masters Series (Basingstoke: Macmillan)

Pedler, M., *A Manager's Guide to Self Development* (Maidenhead, McGraw-Hill)

Peters, T. and Waterman R., *In Search of Excellence* (New York: Harper & Row)

Stewart, R., *Managers and their Jobs* (Basingstoke: Macmillan)

Vroom, V. H., *Work and Motivation* (Chichester: Wiley)

Woodward, Joan, *Industrial Organisation: Theory and Practice* (Oxford: University Press)

Functional management

Attwood, Margaret, *Personnel Management*, Professional Masters Series (Basingstoke: Macmillan)

Bailey, P. and Farmer, D., *Purchasing Principles and Techniques* (London: Pitman)

Baker, M. J., *Marketing* (London: Macmillan)

Foster, Douglas, *Mastering Marketing* (London: Macmillan)

Knott, Geoffrey, *Financial Management*, Professional Masters Series (Basingstoke: Macmillan)

Radford, J. D. and Richardson, D. B., *The Management of Production* (Basingstoke: Macmillan)

Thomason, George F., *A Textbook of Human Resource Management* (London: Institute of Personnel Management)

Management support services

Lucey, T., *Management Information Systems* (London: D.P. Publications)

Lucey, T., *Quantitative Techniques* (London: D.P. Publications)

Index